# Stand Out or Sit Down

## Stories and Lessons for Teens and Young Adults to Find a Job They Love

### TENAZ PURDY

To all my students past and present who have openly and generously shared their stories and experiences with me.

# Contents

Introduction ......................................................................................................1

Lesson 1    It's More Than a Job ..........................................................14

Lesson 2    Successful Job Hunting Starts with You, Not the Job .....................31

Lesson 3    Parental Involvement: Window  Washing or Scaffolding?.............43

Lesson 4    The Right Job for You.....................................................63

Lesson 5    Search for Job Openings ........................................................74

Lesson 6    Let the Technology You Love Work for You, Not Against You .....85

Lesson 7    Create Your Resume and Cover Letter.................................95

Lesson 8    The Walk-In Inquiry.................................................................116

Lesson 9    Application Preparation ....................................................126

Lesson 10   Complete the Job Application.............................................135

Lesson 11   Application Follow Up and the 30-Second Commercial................154

Lesson 12   Interview Expectations ........................................................161

Lesson 13   Present Your Best Self in the Interview .............................172

Lesson 14   Interview Preparation .........................................................184

Lesson 15   Nailing the Interview ...........................................................191

Lesson 16   Interview Follow-up...............................................................211

Lesson 17   You Got the Job? Time to Quit and Tie Up Loose Ends.................220

Afterword ..........................................................................................227

Acknowledgements .........................................................................228

Appendices.........................................................................................229

Bibliography.......................................................................................243

About the Author ............................................................................248

# Introduction

I couldn't understand how an adult with years of life experience failed to see the benefits of having a job at a young age. The incident puzzled me but confirmed the importance of what I was teaching my students.

As the newly hired coordinator of the high school's work study program, I was handing out my program material during Curriculum Night for incoming freshmen and their parents when a father with his son in tow walked slowly past me while scanning the pamphlets on my table. Without stopping, he looked up at me and asked, "Why would I want my kid to work while he's in school? He'll be working for the next 40 years." He didn't wait for a reply.

The year was 2002 and I didn't know it then but learned soon enough that this parent was not alone in his views about his son, school, and a part-time job. In fact, over the next few years, I began hearing similar sentiments from more and more parents, "She needs to focus on her studies," or, "He's too busy with school and his activities."

As it turned out, these were not isolated attitudes but a national trend as

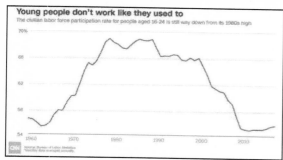

**Figure 1 Age 16-24 Labor Force Participation Rate**

*Figure 1* depicts, where the percentage of 16 to 24-year-olds participating in the workforce — either working or actively looking for work — declined steadily since the 1980's, then sharply since 2000. From 2000 to 2017, the percentage of 16 to 19-year-olds in the workforce fell from 52.0% to 35.2%, a staggering 32% decline. In the same period of time, the percentage of 20 to 24-year-olds in the workforce fell from 77.8% to 71.3%, a decrease of 8.4%. What is happening?

**High school and college students are foregoing working for studying.**

1

With encouragement from parents and pressure from college admissions counselors, high school students are choosing to pursue a more rigorous academic course load, including higher level math courses, more AP and honors courses, and extracurricular activities to beef up their college applications. Even seasonal employment has declined drastically, as teens are taking more summer classes, not to make up for those they failed but to enrich their academic resumes. Summer workforce participation rates for teens have gone from a high rate of 78.1% when I got my first summer job in 1978, to 43.2% in 2016, a 30% decline. To further exacerbate this trend, some states have mandated extending the length of their school year resulting in more time dedicated to academics and less time for a summer or part-time job.

The intense focus on academics doesn't end with a high school diploma. College students are opting to pursue multiple majors and minors and going directly from earning their undergraduate to graduate degrees at the expense of gaining work experiences in between. Many are even waiting until after graduation to do internships. Why? Because with more students than ever attending college, an undergraduate college degree alone is no longer viewed as an advantage but a basic requirement. I hear all the time that a college degree today is what a high school diploma was 30 years ago, and that more education is what will differentiate graduates when it's time to land that high paying "dream job" after college.

The overall results were not anticipated.

### College grads are not prepared for the workforce.

While school should be a student's highest priority, the trend to exclude work experiences is problematic because over the last 20 years, businesses have reported that college graduates are not adequately prepared to enter the workforce. The generation of workers they are referring to are the millennials, born from 1981 to 1996, who have just recently fully matriculated into the full-time workforce. Their attitudes and beliefs are dramatically different from older generations of workers, namely the Baby Boomers (born 1946 to 1964) and Generation Xers (born 1965 to 1980) and have earned them a distinctive reputation.

First, employers say that millennials change jobs more than three times the rate as older generations, at a cost to the U.S. economy of approximately $30 billion annually. This behavior is called job-hopping and it has given millennials the label of being *disloyal*.

Employers also report that millennials fresh out of college are unwilling or unhappy to do mundane tasks that they consider beneath their ability level or worth. Conversely, established business culture dictates that as the "low men on the pole," those new to the workforce should *pay their dues* by working their way up to increased responsibilities and pay, just as older workers did. For this attitude, millennials are labeled as being *entitled*.

A third problem involves career readiness skills where 47% of managers say recent college grads do not have adequate workplace skills, with professionalism and work ethic as the highest area of concern. For example, they point to a lack of independence and self-sufficiency as a growing concern, evidenced by parents who fill out job applications for their 20-some-year-old children, call them out of work when they're sick, and even fight with employers over pay raises and job promotions. Compare this with the 87% of college graduates who believe they are well prepared for the workplace. What is causing this gap in perception?

## There is a disconnect in expectations.

Millennials are credited for being the smartest and most educated group in history. They've been told since high school that prioritizing education above all else will result in a well-paying job where their skills and talents will be appreciated and well compensated. Yet many report frustration and disillusionment in discovering that the workplace is not what they expected regarding work hours, work duties, work ethic, and loyalty to their company. So they go into their first full-time jobs with great confidence in their career preparation, but they were never told about the common norms and expectations of the workplace. This results in a disconnect in perceptions of the level of career readiness between graduating college seniors and their employers. For example,

- Seventy-seven percent of students feel their professionalism and work ethic is proficient, compared to 43% of employers.
- Sixty-one percent of students feel their communication skills are proficient, compared to 42% of employers.
- Fifty-three percent of students feel their career management skills are proficient, compared to 18% of employers.

Why are these expectations so out of line with each other? Because too many

3

college graduates do not have realistic expectations of the workplace — expectations that can only come from actually experiencing the workplace. Waiting until they are seeking their first full-time career job is too late.

### Employers look for the best candidates, not necessarily the best educated candidates.

While a six-week college internship or a summer job in high school are better than nothing, employers are looking for a resume with robust and diverse work experiences over long periods of time. That you've had jobs through high school and college tells an employer that you know what to expect when you take a job. When they see that you've been working since you were a teenager, what they really recognize is a hard-working, motivated individual. When they see that you stayed at your part-time jobs for longer than six months, or up to a year, or maybe even longer, they see loyalty, maturity and your ability to work with others. When your resume shows a repeated pattern of balancing your commitments to school, a job, your extra-curricular activities, and your personal life, they see a well-rounded individual with good organization, time management, and problem-solving skills. These are the soft skills that every employer is looking for.

To build a robust work history by the time you begin a career, you must do something very important right now.

### Step outside your comfort zone.

For those parents who still believe their child can learn about workplace expectations--like responsibility and accountability — at home and school, let me be more specific. A job will help you develop those skills *outside your comfort zone*. That means you'll get experience dealing with a more diverse population than you're used to, not just culturally but generationally, where Generation Zers (born 1997-present) meet Baby Boomers and all the others in between. Working and cooperating with people of different backgrounds, experiences, and expectations exposes you not just to a world that's new for you, but a world you will step into in a relatively short period of time.

> As a coach of the varsity girl's tennis team, I think I can speak for most high-school and collegiate level coaches when I say that we

need to hear from our players directly, not from a parent, when they need permission to be late, leave early, or miss a practice or match. Unfortunately, we get phone calls and emails from parents, "My daughter will need to miss practice on...." As a school activity, there's not much of a recourse other than gentle reminders that may or may not work. But if we were employers instead of coaches, two things would happen. First, the reminders wouldn't be so gentle, "I need to hear from her. She's my employee not you." If the employee doesn't show up for work without permission, that would constitute a *no show.* After two *no shows,* most businesses would end their employment.

This is responsibility and accountability to those outside your comfort zone, where a note or phone call from mom or dad won't work.

### When you're still a student, make work a priority.

It's so important for young people like you to view a job not as a distraction to your education but a vital part of it. It gives you independence, an opportunity to explore your potential future career, and experience managing the money you earn. It will also provide you with an early start to getting employer references for future job searches, and to build your *network* of professional contacts.

If, however, your job is not a high priority, you may get dissatisfied when the job gets hard or interferes with the other aspects of your life. Many employers report that while they're able to hire young workers, they have a much tougher time keeping them because they are not making themselves available for the number of hours and days that businesses need them. Attendance issues like being habitually late, calling out too often, or being a no-show often arise, causing them to quit or be fired. As a result, employers hire endlessly; the *Now Hiring* sign never comes off the store window, or the job ad stays on the online job posting board indefinitely. Employers invest a lot of time, energy, and money into hiring new employees, training them, and getting them up to speed on even the simplest entry-level jobs. So if they see job-hopping behavior in your work history, it'll take about ten seconds for your resume or application to hit the trash can.

As a rule-of-thumb, you should remain at your part-time, entry-level job for at least six months. But if you don't enjoy your job, six months can feel like a life sentence. That's why you have to take the time right now to learn how to find a job you'll love, and not just the first job that comes along.

### Learn from others your age.

I've helped students like you for the past 20 years, not just through high school, but through college and beyond, to find and succeed in the jobs that are right for them. I ran a work study program called Cooperative Education (a.k.a. Co-op) where high school juniors and seniors worked at part-time jobs which gave them a paycheck, school credits, and a grade from their supervisor. In one or two short years, they learned what the workplace expected of them as well as what they can expect from the workplace.

In this book, I'll share their experiences with you through the entire job searching process, because just as important as knowing what you *should* do in certain situations is knowing what you *shouldn't* do. Reading the actual accounts of what they went through and understanding the resulting rewards or consequences of their actions will help you make good decisions of your own.

### Find a job that's right for you, not just any job.

If you don't, there *is* a chance that you'll land a job that you like and will succeed in. However, there's a greater chance that you won't. I have a student right now who's working as a busser in a restaurant and hates it because they *make* him work on Friday nights. Another one hated her job as a camp counselor because little kids get on her nerves. The problem here isn't the job; these are great placements for young workers just starting out. The real problem is that the student and the job aren't a good fit.

From the time you walk into a business to pick up an application to the end of the job interview process and every step in between, getting the job is all about selling yourself — your skills, accomplishments, attitudes, and work ethic. In order to sell yourself, you have to know yourself. Who are you? What do you enjoy doing in your spare time? What are your favorite classes in school? If you can incorporate the things you enjoy doing into your job, wouldn't you also enjoy doing your job?

### Lack of work experience is not a barrier.

6

In a recent exchange on Facebook, the mother of one of my students lamented that no one is hiring her daughter because she has no work experience. I'm always amazed when I hear that, because businesses that depend on young workers know that many have never had a paid job. If that stopped them from hiring a teenager or young adult, no one would find a job...ever. Work experience has to start somewhere, but it seldom starts at a paid job.

Volunteering at a nursing home or animal shelter is experience.

Lawn mowing, babysitting, or taking care of your three younger siblings is experience.

Being an officer of your college fraternity or sorority is experience.

Organizing a school or community fundraiser is experience.

I'll teach you how to take the skills you acquired from these types of activities and demonstrate their relevance to the job you're applying for.

### Who will hire me?

So that you don't feel compelled to take the first job that comes along, you need to familiarize yourself with the job market for young workers. If you're under the age of 18, state and federal labor laws will limit the hours you can legally work or the types of jobs that are safe for you to perform. However, certain types of businesses like restaurants, grocery stores, and retailers who offer mainly entry-level jobs depend heavily on teen labor. Also, teen hiring goes up significantly during the summer months, especially for 14 and 15-year-olds, when seasonal employers like amusement parks and ice cream shops are in full swing. These are great jobs to start out with, but you don't have to limit yourself to them. If you love animals, why not work as a Kennel Assistant? If you think you might want to become a teacher as a career, work as a Teacher's Aide. If math is your favorite subject in school, work as an Accounting Clerk or a Land Survey Assistant. Businesses don't normally go looking for teens to fill these types of positions; you have to seek them out yourself. I'll teach you how to find a job that not only matches your interests and abilities but will give you a glimpse into a possible future career.

### Things are about to change at home.

The adults around you can be great resources to help you find a job. But if

7

their advice begins with the words, "When I was your age…," you might tend to tune them out. Unless they understand how to effectively use technology and social media to connect with the contacts in their professional network, they may not be aware how communicating and information gathering during a job search has evolved. But I urge you to hear them out, because while technology has changed, employers' expectations of applicants during the job search process have not.

However, parents can go too far.

One of the greatest benefits of having a job is that it helps you learn how to be responsible and self-sufficient. Adding a part-time job to your already busy schedule will require you to negotiate with your parents or guardians about schedules and household chores. Even if you're away at college, if your parents are used to doing things for you that you should be doing for yourself, now is the time to encourage them to take a step back. By taking on the additional responsibility of a job, you're telling them that you're ready to have some independence; I'll help you and them understand why it's important that they give it to you.

**Applying, accepting a job offer, and everything in between.**

Matching who you are to the type of job that's right for you is only the beginning. While it's obviously important that you make a good impression in an interview, you have to impress potential employers at every point of contact, from the minute you email a resume or pick up an application at their place of business, to the moment you accept the job offer. As the saying goes, you only get one chance at making a good first impression and I'll help you do that. I'll walk you through filling out an application, whether online or paper, section-by-section and alert you to the traps that could end your prospects before they even begin. I'll teach you how to create a solid resume that highlights your best qualifications and communicates why you're the right person for the job, even if you have no paid job experience whatsoever. All of this work is for the purpose of getting you invited to an interview, a skill I'll help you master in a very short period of time.

While you need to get these key steps right, there's something else that's even more important—something that will distinguish you the most from other candidates.

8

## Excellent communication skills will make you stand out.

Poor communication skills isn't a problem isolated to the young — employers report that it's a growing issue among all age groups. So while a hiring manager may give you some slack because of your inexperience, imagine how impressed they'll be when you demonstrated not only that you're qualified for the job, but that you can also communicate effectively.

Don't underestimate the importance of verbal skills, like how you speak or make eye contact; listening skills where you actually process what's being said instead of thinking about the next thing you're going to say; written skills like good spelling and grammar, and proper formatting of professional correspondences like business letters and emails; and finally, non-verbal skills like your facial expressions and posture.

Demonstrating good communication skills during the job search process is critical, because employers will associate the way you present yourself to them with the way you'll present yourself to their customers.

## You'll use this information for the rest of your life.

People change entire careers an average of three to five times during their lifetime, and they'll have an average of 29 different jobs within those careers. While it's uncertain what the job situation for young workers like you will be 20 or 30 years from now, what *is* certain is that changes in the workplace caused by rapid advances in technology will require us to continuously adapt to our surroundings. Knowing how to re-evaluate your values, goals, interests, and skills to find a new job or even a new career will be critical.

It became critical for me when my career in business came to a sudden end.

I was the Director of Product Strategy for a software development company in Boston. I lived in Pennsylvania with my husband and two toddlers, and the travel requirements of my job put a significant strain on our family. But in the end, the sacrifice would be worth it, because part of my compensation package for taking this job was 35,000 shares of the company's stock. When they go public, I would be a millionaire. At least that was the plan. But in 2001, when the technology sector of our economy crashed, putting us into a recession, I was one of the hundreds of thousands of technology professionals who found themselves out of a job. The company went from 135

9

employees to 25 almost overnight and needless to say, they never went public. My career, along with my hopes and dreams for that million dollars, unraveled in a matter of days.

That was the bad news. The good news? I had been considering a career change for some time.

The question was, what do I do next? You may think that such a life-altering decision took a lot of time, lengthy discussions with my family, and intense soul-searching. It didn't. Several things I knew about myself helped to make my decision to become a teacher a very easy one.

First, and very simply, I had always wanted to be a teacher. But back when I was in school, teachers were very poorly compensated, so being a teacher meant just scraping by financially. In my mind, it meant wearing worn clothes, driving an old car, packing my lunch, and working a second job through the summers just to pay the bills. Money was too important to me at the time and working in technology gave me lots of it. Therefore, teaching was not for me.

Then, call it fate, call it a sign from above, or call it just plain dumb luck that a close family friend who had recently left her own career in Social Services to become a teacher asked if I would come and read to her first-grade class. I was a Programmer/Analyst at my first job out of college, and I was working 12 to 14-hour days to meet a project deadline. I was eating breakfast, lunch, and dinner at my desk. I had no personal life, just work. Nevertheless, I went during my lunch break, I read to her kids, and I was hooked. She sent me a picture that she took of me while reading, and that picture immediately went on my refrigerator along with the rest of my dreams. I didn't know how or when or where, but I knew someday I would be a teacher.

While the thought of teaching was firmly planted in the back of my mind for the next decade, what most compelled me to pursue it as a new career was the simple realization that I would be good at it. While I learned many things from my career in business, the most profound and life-altering revelation I had — and the talent I discovered within myself — is that I was good at developing the skills and talents of others. I came to realize that my life's calling was not to help make the shareholders of Saks Fifth Avenue richer by selling more tweed pants and designer handbags, but to pass along what I knew to others. While I held numerous technical and managerial positions in my career, my main area of competency was as a Business Analyst, and since it wasn't easy to hire highly technical individual who also understood business, I hired the best technical candidates I could find and taught them the business. And I was good at it.

So at age 38, I had to reevaluate the things that I thought I knew about myself. The things I valued in my life had changed because my time with my family became far more important than the size of my paycheck. I also discovered that my interests had changed—I never thought I'd love reading to those first graders as much as I did. And over the years, I had cultivated a skill that became my primary focus as a manager—developing the skills and talents of others.

So becoming a teacher was a foregone conclusion at this point, and within a year of leaving my business career, I returned to school, began substitute teaching, earned dual teaching certificates in Business Education and Cooperative Education, and ultimately received my master's degree in Curriculum and Instruction. In other words, I reinvented myself not just with a new career but with a whole new way of defining who I was. As an educator and job coach, I'm happy to report that I, in fact, do not wear worn clothing to work, and I drive a 3-year-old car that I love. I do however pack my lunch because I have 26 minutes to eat it. And this is the first time in 20 years that I am working over the summer; it's so I can write this book.

Changing jobs or entire careers isn't just likely, it's inevitable. I was able to change the course of my life towards a more rewarding career by reassessing who I was and then matching it to the career that was right for me. It's a technique that'll help you find not just the first job that you'll love, but every job thereafter.

### I know what employers expect. I was one of them.

People who believe the old cliché, "those who can't do, teach," have never taught. The job searching and employment skills I teach didn't come from a book; they came from years of managing, hiring, and sometimes even firing the employees that worked for me. The truth is that many of us have actually done—in the real world—the things we are teaching, and we have done it successfully. In my own school, a colleague who teaches Investing and Wealth Management was previously a Certified Financial Planner for Merrill-Lynch. My daughter's 10th grade Biology teacher has a master's degree in Marine Sciences and worked as a Biochemist for 10 years before going into teaching. A robotics teacher was a Systems Engineer for IBM. And so on. While researching a career in teaching, I was told by a Human Resources associate in a school district, "We don't care what you've done before. All we care about is that you have a valid Pennsylvania teaching license." This turned out to be far from true, because do you know who cares? My students care. Their parents care. Their employers care. And that's all that matters. I could be delivering a lesson about what not to wear to an interview, and as soon as I say the words, "I remember at Saks when an applicant came in wearing a...," something magical happens. They stop what they're doing, they pick up their heads, and they listen.

**I am an experienced job coach and business teacher.**

Employers loved participating in the Co-op program not just because they got student workers who were educated on how to succeed on the job, but because they had me as a resource to consult with when issues arose. Year after year, I maintained a close working relationship with many of the same employers, so when a student didn't get the job or was having a problem at work, I could call the employer and find out what was really going on. My position allowed me to help my students and their employers develop and maintain successful professional relationships that often lasted for years after the students graduated from high school.

But as I soon found out, the only constant in life is change.

The Great Recession of 2008 resulted from the housing market crash, where homes all over the country went into foreclosure and revenues from property taxes took a nosedive for public schools nationwide. My school district was no exception. Teachers were laid off and programs were cut, among which was the Co-op program. In 2009, I became a full-time classroom teacher of courses in business and entrepreneurship, financial literacy, investing, economics, business communications, and computer programming. With a highly competitive job market, these skills became more important to learn than ever before.

But in the back of my mind, with the lack of vocational programs like Co-op, there was still something missing. There existed a clear gap between businesses in the community with job openings and the students who were looking for those jobs. Very often the secretary in the main office would send

12

an email to the entire faculty stating, "So-and-so called, and they are looking for a high school student to do such-and-such, from 3 p.m. to whenever. If anyone knows of a student who is interested, have them call yada-yada." It was the same message again and again, with a different company name. I know for a fact that the majority of those emails went unanswered. So in 2014, I closed this gap by creating a student job placement program, with an online job posting board. Hundreds of companies in the local area have posted their open positions on the board, and hundreds of students have found jobs through these postings. To help students learn how to get these jobs, I created a job-hunting club where they come for my help to complete job applications, write resumes, and rehearse scripts of what they will say to a prospective employer. Not only is the job placement program helping our students find jobs, but I am told that job seekers all over the community, adults and teens alike, are referring to it. I run this program in addition to my full-time teaching job, but I'm not paid for it. I do it voluntarily because that's how strongly I feel that young people need to be taught these valuable skills. Unfortunately, I still see and hear about the mistakes our students make—mistakes that are avoidable with some basic, yet focused instruction as they take their first steps into a competitive workforce.

### It's why I wrote this book.

As you can imagine there are plenty of books about finding a job and even more books that focus on writing a resume and interviewing. But a vast majority of these books are targeted towards mature professionals looking to further their careers. They don't address the unique issues faced by teenagers and young adults who are just starting out in the job market by supplementing their high school or college academic education with a part-time job. Other books also include material that will not apply to young jobseekers like you, who may have very few job skills and little-to-no work experience. I've taken a lot of that material that's irrelevant to you out of the way so that you can focus on the steps you need to take based on your experiences, abilities, and interests.

In other words, I wrote this book specifically for you, to help you enter the workforce now, so that later you can begin your career with confidence in your workplace skills and common expectations that can only come with experience.

13

# Lesson 1

# It's More Than a Job

Remember my student who worked as a busser at a restaurant and hated it because they *made* him work on Friday nights? Unfortunately as I predicted, he didn't last there for more than a few months because, as he put it, "It just wasn't worth it."

These are the words I hear again and again from young people after quitting their job after only a few months. The "it" they're referring to are the sacrifices that we make when we commit ourselves to having a job. While working earns us money, it also has a cost. It's not a monetary cost but an *opportunity cost*, meaning that the time we spend at our job could be time spent doing other things that are important to us.

Going to work while watching your family go out to dinner is a sacrifice.

Knowing your friends are hanging out at the mall on a Friday evening while you have to work is a sacrifice.

So what will make these sacrifices worth it? It's something that goes far beyond just a paycheck. It's the understanding that a part-time job is a vital part of your education, not a distraction from it. As I discussed in the introduction, working while you're in high school or college teaches you how to deal with people and situations outside your comfort zone. It gives you authentic learning experiences that you can't get from home or a classroom to prepare you to enter the workplace when you start your career. Working addresses the current situation that college graduates and their employers are facing:

- Employers believe that college graduates are not fully prepared for the workforce, especially in areas of professionalism, work ethic, communication, and career management.
- College graduates are frustrated because the workplace is not what they expected regarding work hours, work duties, work ethic, and loyalty to their company.
- Employers want to see a robust history of work experiences through

14

high school and college to know that college grads have realistic expectations of the workplace.

- Employers looking to hire college grads are not necessarily looking for the best educated candidates, but the best candidates who have demonstrated their ability to successfully balance school, work, home, and a personal life over time.

Adding a job to your education now will not only help you successfully transition into your career but has several important immediate benefits. First, a job will enable you to learn new skills—not just job skills but those all-important soft skills. It will also help you learn how to juggle your responsibilities at work, school, and home. Then, by going through the job searching process as I outline in this book, you could have a job that gives you a preview to your potential future career. While making money is important to you right now, what's even more important is learning how to manage that money. Some of my students, however, work for one very bad reason. You don't want to make that mistake and I'll tell you why later in the chapter.

First, let's understand what motivates us to work so that there's not a question in your mind that working right now needs to be a high priority.

## WHAT MOTIVATES US TO WORK?

To answer this question, let's examine a theory called *Maslow's Hierarchy of Needs*. Dr. Abraham Maslow, a famous psychologist, believed that individuals have five basic needs that motivate our behavior. A lower-level need must be met before the next level need becomes important. Let's look at the individual needs as *Figure 2* shows and relate them to our motivation to work.

Survival needs are the most basic; we need food, clothing, shelter, and medical care. These are the needs that initially motivate us to find a job and make money. Once our survival needs are met, we have safety needs—protection from physical harm. We work to give us job security and peace-of-mind that we are able to avoid the unexpected.

**Figure 2 Maslow's Hierarchy of Needs**

15

Everyone works to meet their survival and safety needs.

**Everyone works for the money.**

If your survival and safety needs are met because you're living in someone else's home or supported by the adults in your life, it's your *material* needs for survival and safety are most likely being met. And if your primary reason for working is for the money, it's likely you're looking to satisfy not just your *needs,* but also your *wants.* If your motivation to work is to buy video games, save for college spending money, or hit Starbucks on a regular basis, you're not just working to fulfill your needs, but also your wants. And that's perfectly okay to do. What's more, here's a little secret most people don't know... employers like it when you're working for the money. It keeps you motivated to come to work and do a good job.

While working for the money will satisfy your needs — as well as your material wants---money isn't the only good reason to work. If it were, people who have lots of it would stop working, wouldn't they?

Tom Brady is worth over $180 million and just added a sixth super bowl ring to his collection. As the oldest NFL quarterback in history currently, Brady is in his 40's but has committed to playing at least another five years.

Oprah Winfrey has a net worth of $2.8 billion. She continues working as a media executive, actress, talk show host and television producer.

Warren Buffet, business magnate, investor, speaker, and philanthropist, has a net worth over $87 billion. He's in his nineties and continues to serve as CEO and Chairman of his company, Berkshire Hathaway.

Why are these individuals and others like them still working? Let's continue upward on Maslow's hierarchy to find out.

**Working satisfies our social needs.**

Social needs like companionship, the feeling of belonging, and being accepted by the people you respect, are next on the hierarchy. If I asked you what you liked best about going to school, your answer would most likely be "seeing my friends." Being with the people at work can be just as satisfying. Not only will you do a little socializing during work hours, but probably after work as well. And the relationships you make at your job can last for years after you've left. Of the three best friends I have in the world, one was my college roommate, one was a co-worker, and one was a former boss.

After our social needs are met, we look to fulfill our need for esteem — the worth or value we see in ourselves and that which we get from others. This is called self-esteem, and it's a need that's met at work when you see yourself doing a good job and when you're recognized for your accomplishments by your managers, co-workers, and even your customers.

**Job satisfaction primarily comes from the fulfillment of our esteem needs.**

It's why succeeding at your job is so important — not just for the money, not just for your boss, but to make you feel good about yourself.

The highest level of need according to Maslow is self-actualization, where you're living up to your full potential and all the meaningful goals in your life have been achieved. It's a lofty goal that can take a lifetime to achieve, and very few people actually reach this level. For those who do, over 90% report that the source of satisfying their need for self-actualization is their successful career. Tom Brady, Oprah Winfrey, and Warren Buffet may be among the few who fall into this category based on their life accomplishments.

When you hear people saying that they get satisfaction from their jobs or that they're passionate about their jobs, they're not referring to the size of their paychecks. They're referring to the satisfaction of those higher-level social, esteem and self-actualization needs in the upper half of Maslow's hierarchy. Success on your job will lead to success in your career, a key factor in helping you achieve your goals in life. Think about how amazing it is that you're starting on this journey at such a young age.

Let's now discuss the immediate benefits of working.

## LEARNING ON THE JOB

Whether you're 14 or 40, success on the job starts with learning on the job. Employers hire workers like you to perform the duties of a job like cashiering, cooking, stocking shelves, changing the oil in a car, and so on. Whether you have prior experience with these duties or not, your employer will train you so you can get up to speed as quickly as possible. After all, it's in their best interest that you succeed at your job.

Employers report that while it's easy to train their employees on job skills, it's much more difficult to train them on soft skills like getting along with supervisors and co-workers, having efficient work habits, accepting constructive criticism, communicating effectively, adapting to changes, and problem solving, just to name a few. And then there's the most important skill that young people learn on the job, sometimes the hard way: good attendance. Being habitually late, calling out too often, and being a *no-show* are the most common reasons why young employees are fired.

While required job skills can differ based on the type of job you have, soft skills transfer from job to job. So the more you work, the more you'll refine and master those skills that you'll need for the rest of your life. By the time you're ready to start your career, you'll know what to expect in the workplace.

Here's an added bonus for you. Because you're still young and inexperienced, employers will tend to be more patient with you than someone with more experience because they know you're still learning the basics. Many employers even enjoy hiring young workers for this reason. Some will even be *mentors* who take a special interest in teaching, supporting, and guiding their employees at work and sometimes even throughout their career. In every job you take, finding and building a relationship with someone to mentor you should be a priority.

## LEARNING HOW TO JUGGLE

You can't be successful if taking on a job causes you to neglect all the other aspects of your life. Think about your part-time job as a second job, because your first and most important job is to be the best student you can be. It's your number one priority.

**School comes first. Everything else is a negotiation.**

Your education through high school and beyond establishes the foundation for the rest of your life. You'll need to apply all the things you learn in school — knowledge from your academic subjects as well as soft skills like responsibility, organization, and time management — to your job.

However as a teacher and a mother, I believe very strongly that students should be engaged in extracurricular activities that expand their minds, bodies, and spirits. It's important for you to explore the world around you, whether that's through sports, music, art, technology, entrepreneurship, or any of the plethora of opportunities available to you today. Trying something new and seeing yourself being good at it will build your self-esteem which in turn will help you be more successful in school and at work.

> I have two daughters who were very involved through school and in the community. They both played an instrument for school and for the county youth orchestra, and they were both involved in numerous sports. They volunteered their time to the local library and a nursing home. And starting in their sophomore year of high school, they both had part-time jobs. Needless to say, they were busy, but participating in the activities they love helped them become well-rounded individuals.

If you're about to add a part-time job to an already busy schedule, it's inevitable that there will be times when school, your job and your extracurricular activities may conflict with one another. While school comes first, you'll be expected to be organized, keep a calendar, and plan ahead so that you don't disappoint the people you've made commitments to.

I'd love to say that stories like the one I'm about to tell you are few and far between. Unfortunately, I get requests like these pretty often from students, and sometimes even from parents.

> It was a Monday morning and waiting in my inbox was the following email from a parent addressed to all four of his son's teachers:
>
> Dear Teachers:
>     Please excuse Vijay from any homework assignments that were due today. He was in Altoona, Pennsylvania all weekend representing his school in a robotics competition. Unfortunately, we did not get home until late last night. Thank you for your understanding.

When I read this email from Vijay's father, I asked myself, "Was there an emergency over the weekend that caused him to not do his homework? Or was the trip to Altoona planned?" Our community has certainly seen its share of natural disasters, including two 50-year floods occurring two years

19

in a row, and hurricane Sandy that left hundreds of families without homes and electricity for months. Some students also face serious personal issues dealing with their health, family relationships, or financial issues. We teachers understand emergencies and make concessions for the unexpected. But Vijay's situation wasn't an emergency because the trip to Altoona was scheduled well in advance, which gave him the opportunity to prepare for Monday's assignments before the weekend. The fact that the trip was a school-sponsored activity is irrelevant. Try to put yourself in a teacher's position; if we give extensions for every student who had a game, match, concert, or competition the night before, can you imagine the chaos it would create in the classroom?

For my class, Vijay had a study packet due on that Monday for a unit of study in AP Macroeconomics. The unit lasted 12 days and the study packet was assigned on the first day of the unit. That means he had 12 days to complete the assignment because he knew 12 days in advance when it was due. Barring a real emergency, I expected the study packet to be turned in on time. So on Monday after receiving his father's note, I understood that he needed an extra day to complete the packet and Vijay understood why I had to reduce its grade by 10% when he turned it in late, on Tuesday.

So how do you successfully fit a job into your schedule so that you can avoid situations like this?

**Be more resourceful with your time.**

Studies have shown that working less than 20 hours a week while going to school actually improves the grades of working students. Why? Because adding a job to your schedule forces you to structure your time more efficiently. Let's say it currently takes you 3-4 hours a night to do your homework and now you're wondering, *how will I get all my homework done if I have to go to work right after school*? But in those 3-4 hours, were you really focused on doing your homework, or were you taking lots of breaks to text your friends or to spend time on social media? Did you start right away, or did you procrastinate until the last minute to get it done, or worse, not do it at all. Having less time to get your school work done may actually help you get it done faster and more efficiently. Getting rid of all the distractions—actually put your phone away, not next to you where you'll hear or see notifications—is a good start.

## Your job should be a close second priority.

When you agree to work for a business, you're committing yourself to be the best employee you can be.

Another reason why employers loved participating in the Co-op program was that students had to work a minimum of 15 hours a week. You should be able to work between 15 and 20 hours a week. If you can't work the minimum number of hours a job requires, don't take the job.

That means working hard and fast to learn not only the duties of the job, but those soft skills that are so important—especially showing up when you're scheduled and arriving on time. When conflicts arise with your busy schedule, you have to negotiate a solution.

> As a Co-op student, Nick left school at 12:30 pm everyday and started work at Acme Markets at 1:00 pm, Monday through Friday. One day, he walked into my office to punch out on the time clock, and turned to me and announced, "I'm going to call out of work today. I have to help my father move."

This is why Co-op students have to get my permission to call out of work, so that I can counsel them out of making mistakes like this one. Nick's boss was expecting him at work in half an hour, which was not enough notice to find a replacement. While helping his dad move was important to Nick, it wasn't an emergency. Emergency reasons to call out with little notice are things like, "I just found out I have strep throat and I'm contagious." Nick's excuse was a planned event, which means he had time to work out a solution that would have satisfied his employer as well as his dad.

## Negotiating begins with communicating and ends with compromising.

Nick should have done one of two things. First, if the date of his father's moving was not flexible, he should have spoken to his boss and requested the day off *before* he was put on the schedule. Second, if he learned about the move after he was put on the schedule, he should have spoken to his boss right away, and possibly even found someone to cover his shift himself.

Being responsible means keeping organized about your schedule, prioritizing your activities, communicating with the people who depend on you, and coming up with a compromise that everyone involved can live with. And how will you stay organized with your schedule?

## The technology to keep you organized is literally at your fingertips.

That smart phone you have can be a distraction, but it can also be your most valuable tool. Use your calendar to keep track of your work schedule, appointments, and important events. This way you don't have to rely on your memory, and you can see potential conflicts before they occur.

In case you're wondering what happened with Nick, I explained to him how his actions would affect his employer's business and what he could have done differently. And I did not give him permission to call out under these circumstances. He went to work, finished his shift, and helped his dad after work. It was a good compromise.

## Don't neglect your responsibilities at home.

Now that you're working, depending on how much you helped around the house before you found a job, you may need a lighter workload at home. I can't tell you what that workload should look like; that has to be negotiated between you and the people at home who depend on you.

> Before my daughters started working, they had responsibilities around the house like most teenagers. They did their own laundry, helped make lunches for school, and took care of our dog, Jack. But that routine changed drastically when my husband and I realized that they had become busier than we were. We agreed to pick up most of their chores as long as they tried to keep their rooms in decent shape and helped around the house when they could. It didn't always work out; there were times when schedules and workloads at school and work changed, and so we did our best to modify the routine. In other words, we negotiated. And from time to time, we renegotiated.

Finally, there's even a fourth priority that often gets pushed aside when kids enter high school.

## Make time for your hobbies, interests and a social life.

There's an old proverb, *all work and no play makes Jack a dull boy*. All work and no play also contributes to the high degree of stress that teens face, which can lead to anxiety and depression. When I started teaching 20 years ago, I would encounter a handful of students every year that showed signs of anxiety or depression. Today, it's a regular occurrence, especially for students who load up their schedules with honors and Advanced Placement courses.

> Cory was almost a model student in my AP Macroeconomics class until the day he cut my class. When I questioned him about it, I expected him to do what most students would do: look me in the eye and lie by telling me that a parent signed them out at the office. Cory on the other hand fessed up right away: "I was in the library." Well that was a first for me. I sat him down in front of me, and asked him to explain. "I wasn't ready to take the test." He went on to explain that he's currently carrying an academic load of three Advanced Placement classes. He has an afterschool job tutoring math. And as I already knew, Cory was a talented swimmer who had already missed quite a few days of school as he advanced to the district and state tournaments. Being his junior year of high school, he was also busy taking the SATs and ACTs, and visiting colleges. He looked down at his hands that were folded in his lap, and as he spoke they began to shake. Between the pressures at school, the after school job, the daily practices in the pool, and the looming decisions about college, Cory was overcommitted to the point that the stress he was feeling was causing physical symptoms.

**Don't overcommit.**

If you have no time for yourself or your friends or the things that bring you joy in your life, you've stretched yourself too thin. And since school is your number one priority, you may need to give up something else, like the job or the sport or the volunteer work, or whatever is consuming too much of your time. With all the things that are vying for your attention, it's important not to neglect *you*.

## EXPLORE YOUR POTENTIAL FUTURE CAREER

While a part-time job can add to your stress right now, it can also help you alleviate a different stress — the one you have about the uncertainty surrounding your future career. Would you buy a car without test driving it? If the answer is "no," then why would you invest your money, time, and effort pursuing a career without testing it out first?

Approximately half of the students who ask me for a letter of recommendation at the beginning of their senior year in high school are still uncertain about their college major. Having the work experience now that's related to a potential career field can help you make that decision and alleviate the fear of the unknown. If you're a college student, it's even more important for you to figure it out. A part-time job or an internship will help you do just that.

The difference between a job and a career is that a *job* is work performed for pay for a particular company. A *career* is a series of related jobs based on common interests, knowledge, training and education, and experience. Jobs within a career should help you advance through that career in terms of salary and position. I began my career as a programmer and business analyst, and after working at four different computer-related *jobs* at four different companies, I ended my *career* as a Director of Product Strategy.

Experiencing a variety of industries, job duties, and authentic work environments allows you to *try* your career options before you commit to one. That's why when I helped to place my students in their Co-op jobs, an important goal was to try to find a job that in some way related to their intended college major or their potential career goal.

---

Andie enrolled in the Co-op program with a job she already had as a lifeguard. But because she expressed an interest in working with animals as a career, I helped her find a job with a veterinary hospital. Unfortunately, the job didn't work out for reasons I'll explain later. And because she loved working with animals, I thought she might also enjoy working with children, and I helped her find a job as a Teacher's Aid at a pre-school. Andie loved this job, and about a year after she graduated, I received this email from her.

I just wanted to thank you for helping me get a job at the Goodall School. I was just promoted to a full-time Assistant Teacher, working with 1 and 2-year-olds, and I love it! I decided

---

to major in Elementary Education at Philadelphia Biblical University and just finished up my first year. If it weren't for you I'd probably still be lifeguarding or working with dogs, but somehow you knew that I would be good with kids and love doing it. I've learned a lot in the year I have worked here and it is giving me a great head start in what I am learning now in college. Thank you so much for helping me find this job and continuing to push me past the limit I probably wouldn't have pushed towards. I have found that I learn the best when I am outside of my comfort zone.

Andie A.

There's one important line in that note from Andie that I want to emphasize: "I've learned a lot in the year I have worked here and it is giving me a great head start in what I am learning now in college." The job at the pre-school offered Andie a glimpse at a career field she may never have otherwise considered.

While it's helpful to have a job now that's related to your potential career choice, it doesn't have to be in exactly the same industry or involve exactly the same type of work. How can working at Chuck E. Cheese's help you figure out your future career? Let's say you get a job as a Cast Member and you discover that you like working with young children. Your future may not involve working at Chuck E. Cheese's or in the restaurant industry at all, but you may start to think that if you like working with children, you may want to work with them as a career, like teaching, coaching or counseling.

Here's another interesting phenomenon. Let's say you think you want to be a teacher, so you get a job at a summer camp. As it turns out, you dislike this job and you discover that being around children all day just isn't for you. Do you still want to be a teacher?

**Knowing you disliked a job is just as valuable as if you had loved it.**

Can you imagine making teaching your career goal, majoring in Education in college, and then realizing in your junior year that teaching is not for you?

Knowing the career that's right for you before you expend valuable resources to pursue it is more important now than ever before. At the risk of sounding pessimistic, the 10-year job outlook for high school and college graduates looking for their first full-time job is not much better now than it was in 2009, during the Great Recession. Although the Great Recession officially ended in 2010, almost ten years later, the unemployment rate for 16 to 24-year-olds is more than twice that of the national average. These are young people who are willing and able to work and are actively looking for a job. To compound this problem, graduates are leaving college with overwhelming debt and realizing that they are less than enthusiastic about their career choice. Working now to test out your potential future career will help you avoid making a poor career choice in the future.

## LEARN MONEY MANAGEMENT SKILLS

Having a job doesn't just give you money, it gives you financial independence. That means you won't have to go to mom or dad for money every time you want something. And your parents will be happy to take a big step back from monitoring your spending since it's not their money. But because your parents won't be managing your money, you need to manage it yourself.

For almost every class I teach, whether it's business and entrepreneurship, investing, or even computer applications, teaching money management is a priority. The hardest part about this lesson is the motivation for it — why is this an important skill to learn? To many of them, managing their money means spending it on the things they want and need, and then leaving the rest in the bank. Here's how I convince them that this method isn't called money management, it's called *not knowing where my money went*.

---

Teaching money management begins with my Dunkin Donuts lesson. I start by spotting that student with a Dunkin Donuts coffee, Starbucks venti cappuccino, or a Red Bull on their desk. I point to the kid and ask, "How much did you spend on that?" Let's say the answer is $2.50. I'll then show them on the white board how the coffee cost them $2.50 *today*. If you drink one of these every school day, that's $12.50 per week, $55 a month, and $450 per year. On coffee. The average 15 to 17-year-old teen makes about $4,900 a year gross pay, which after taxes is

---

about $4,000. That means that roughly 11% of their paycheck would go to drinking one Dunkin Donuts coffee a day. And that doesn't even include weekends and summers. If you include those, that's $912.50 a year, or about 22% of your annual pay.

Now, if you know that you're spending almost a quarter of your earnings on coffee and you're okay with that, great. The problem is that unless you do the math, you won't realize how quickly a $2.50 cup of coffee every day is consuming your paycheck. You'll wonder, as many of my students do, where all your money went. For this reason, before you get your first paycheck, you need to have a plan for it. You need a budget, or a spending plan, where you decide up front how much of your earnings you're willing to spend, and what you'll spend it on. In 2016, teens made approximately $91 billion a year in income. The average annual income from their part-time jobs for 12 to 14-year-olds was $2,767, and for 15 to 17-year-olds was $4,923. The income for 18 to 24-year-olds is much higher at around $33,000 per year, but that includes full-time workers. If you're in college working up to 20 hours a week, you can assume you'll make roughly the same income as a 17-year-old.

So what will you spend your money on? If you're among the 55% of teens who say they are working primarily for spending money, you may spend some of yours on food and clothing, which combined make up about 40% of teen spending. *Figure 3* provides a breakdown.

Next, how much of your money will you save to meet your future financial goals? Will you be among the 57% of teens who say they are saving to buy clothes, 51% who are saving for college expenses, or 36% who are saving for a car? Will you keep your savings in the bank? Or will you invest it so that your money can make even more money?

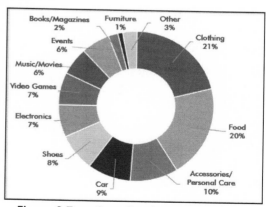

Figure 3 Teen Spending by Category

Once you have an idea of what your income, expenses, and savings/ investments are, you have everything you need to create a budget. Approximately 40% of 16 to 24-year-olds working part-time have one. It's one of the most important tools you'll use to meet all your financial goals in life.

But having and maintaining a budget is only the beginning. If you don't already have a bank account, you'll need one now; you'll most likely have your paycheck deposited directly into that account from your employer. When you get your first paycheck, how will you know it's correct? You'll need to know how to calculate your pay and read your paystub so that you know what was taken out for taxes and other deductions. And every year you'll have to file your local, state, and federal tax returns. And while getting a credit card can be scary because of the debt you can accumulate on it, it can also be a great opportunity to build a good credit history.

Learning good money management skills now will help you have a healthy relationship with your money for the rest of your life.

## BOOST YOUR COLLEGE APPLICATION

I told you earlier that if you're still in high school, there's one very bad reason to have a job. This is it and here's why.

Having a part-time job while doing well at school shows college admissions counselors and potential employers that you're responsible and can manage your time well. This is a great reason for working as a teen, but it can also be the worst reason to work if that's your only reason. If a job is not among your top three priorities, and your commitments to school and other activities leaves little time for anything else, then you're not making a job a high enough priority. Remember that working while going to school is an important part of your education.

As in Cory's case above, junior year of high school is the worst as far as stress is concerned. You may have to add SAT or ACT prep classes, state standardized testing for graduation requirements, and college visits to your already busy schedule. If you've had a job prior to this year, you may very well be good at juggling by now and be able to keep that job. But adding a job now just to impress colleges is a bad idea.

The problem is that while working a few hours a week is okay with you, it's usually not okay for the employer. As I said before, employers like it when money motivates you so that you want to work. They've made an investment in you by hiring you, training you, and putting you on the schedule, and they want you to be available to work a reasonable number of hours per week—approximately 15 to 20 hours a week. If you get the job by committing to work a certain number of hours and a certain number of days a week, and then later change your availability to suit your busy schedule, chances are that you won't be employed there for long.

If this happens and you quit or get fired due to lack of availability, you should not include this job on your college application.

If you lie on your college application about being *currently* employed or saying that you were at a job longer than you were, it's very possible that you'll get caught in the lie. College admissions counselors are trained to look for inconsistencies on applications, like when school, extracurricular activities and a job all seem to add up to more than 24 hours in a day. If they suspect that you're lying, they may call your employer, coach, or club advisor to verify your claims.

**Colleges check up on approximately 10% of applications because of suspected inconsistencies.**

If you get caught lying, you might as well cross this school off your list. Colleges don't just want students who are good academically; they want students who are honest and have good character.

### Next up...

Which of Maslow's needs do you think Curriculum Night Dad was working to fulfill? Like too many Americans, he probably worked for the paycheck, which satisfied his survival and safety needs. But as you now know, success at your job can be the source of many good things in your life that results from the fulfillment of your social, esteem and self-actualization needs. And to succeed at your job, it sure helps if you're happy at your job. That's why it's so important right now to learn how to find the job that you love. Let's get started on that.

## CHAPTER SUMMARY QUIZ

The following quiz summarizes the chapter.

1.  Seeing yourself do well in your job primarily fulfills which of Maslow's five needs?
    a.  Survival
    b.  Social
    c.  Esteem
    d.  Self-actualization

2.  Which of the following commitments should be your number one priority?
    a.  Your job
    b.  Hanging out with friends
    c.  School
    d.  Community Service

3.  Avoid schedule conflicts by doing which of the following?
    a.  Maintaining a calendar with your commitments
    b.  Planning ahead
    c.  Negotiating and compromising
    d.  All of the above

4.  Having a part-time job as a teen or young adult helps you do all of the following *except*:
    a.  Determine your future career
    b.  Earn money
    c.  Learn to manage your time and be more responsible
    d.  Have more free time

5.  Approximately what percent of college applications will colleges check up on?
    a.  5%
    b.  10%
    c.  25%
    d.  75%

Answers: 1d, 2c, 3d, 4d, 5b

# Lesson 2

# Successful Job Hunting Starts with You, Not the Job

I know people who've spent more time researching their next vacation spot than what career they want to pursue. They're among the approximately 50% of Americans who choose a career path without doing any career planning whatsoever. They simply *fall* into a career, either by accident because an opportunity happened to present itself, or by social pressure.

> I was interviewing my student, Matt, for the Co-op program, and asked him if he had an idea about what he wanted to do as a career. Without hesitating he responded, "I want to work for the Army Corps of Engineers." The answer came back so fast and with so much specificity that it physically took me aback. I asked him why. He shrugged and explained, "I don't know. It's what my uncle does, and he seems to like it, so...."

This is a good example of how someone falls into a career for all the wrong reasons. If you do this, there's a chance that it'll be a great career for you. There's a greater chance that it won't, and that you'll be unhappy in a job that may not go beyond fulfilling your survival and safety needs.

Your happiness in your career is influenced by three things. First, you must enjoy the work you do. Second, you must have the skills to do your job. And third, you must like the environment in which you work. That's why choosing the right career has to start with *you* – your values, goals, interests, skills, and preferred work environment.

If choosing the right career starts with you, shouldn't starting your first job start the same way? This is called self-assessment and doing it right could take weeks or even months. My Co-op students had to find a job within the first two weeks of the school year, and so they didn't have weeks or months to learn about themselves. I had to help them fast track the process and, in this chapter, I'll help you fast track it too.

31

## SELLING YOURSELF STARTS WITH KNOWING YOURSELF

Discovering the right type of job for you is just the beginning. You then have to convince employers that you are *the* person for the job. In other words, you have to sell yourself.

If you were selling a product, you'd have to know all about the product and how it works, as well as what your potential customer is looking for. You'd then have to convince the customer that your product will satisfy their needs. Selling yourself is no different. There's a reason for the term *job market*. It's where the buying and selling of your knowledge, skills, and labor takes place. You are the seller and the business is the buyer. And just like the market for products, in order to sell yourself, you have to know yourself.

Once you know who you are, you can compare these attributes with the requirements of the job and determine if you and the job are a good fit. For example, if you enjoy helping and working with people, you probably won't like working as a Filing Clerk in a medical records office. If, however, you're analytical, you like things organized in a specific order, and you like it when numbers add up, you may like being a File Clerk very much. Or an Accounting Clerk. Or an Inventory Clerk.

And here's a bonus. Presenting yourself to a potential employer after determining that you and the job are a good fit will not only convince you that the job is right for you but will help convince the employer that you are right for the job.

## DREAM ON

Whenever you talk to others about your future, whether it's the career you want, or the places you want to travel or the car you'll buy, don't ever let them tell you to stop dreaming. Dreaming is an important part of determining your future goals.

**Dreaming helps you visualize the life you want.**

When you daydream, do you dream about helping others by pulling someone out of a burning building or rescuing a person who's drowning? Are you traveling or living a life filled with adventure? Are you financially comfortable and living a lavish lifestyle? Whatever the dream, it's an important first step in determining the kind of work you'd like to do. Dreaming is like a GPS; you first have to know where you want to go before you determine how to get there.

> Cassie was a Co-op student who had dreamed of being a famous model someday. She was beautiful and intelligent, but unfortunately, she was five foot nothing and so her chances of making it as a model were slim. But she was determined to have a glamorous lifestyle, and so for her Co-op job I helped her get a position as a photographer's assistant at a Sears photography studio. If she couldn't be in front of the camera, maybe she'd enjoy being behind one? After she graduated from high school, I didn't hear from her at all, until the day I stepped onto the stage in our high school auditorium to have my picture taken for the yearbook. Behind the camera after so many years was Cassie. I was so happy to see that while taking yearbook pictures wasn't exactly the glamourous job she dreamed of, she loved her Co-op job enough to make a career out of it.

Dreaming as in Cassie's case would only become a problem if that's all she did to prepare for her future. She used her dreams as inspiration to develop her goal to become a photographer. She received on-the-job training at her Co-op job and was eventually promoted to a full-time photographer. She even took classes in photography at the community college. As in Cassie's case, the difference between a dream and a goal is an action plan with a timeline and milestone tasks to reach that goal. Dreams don't produce results; goals do.

## WHAT'S IMPORTANT TO YOU?

In other words, what do you value? It's an important question to ask yourself before you begin the job search because the personal values that are most important to you should be consistent with your job. For example, if you're a vegan, working at a produce market may be much more acceptable than a steakhouse. If living a healthy and fit life is most important to you, working at a fast food restaurant may be out of the question.

While you want to be as flexible as possible and keep your options open, it's critical that your job and your values don't conflict with each another.

Luke is a student in my Microsoft Applications class. One day, without even looking up from his computer screen he blurted out, "Mrs. Purdy, I work at Carlisle's Pizza and I hate it because they *make* me work on Friday nights!" He went on to explain that it's the one night of the week he gets to spend with his friends, going to a movie or hanging out at the mall. Unfortunately, Friday and Saturday nights are the busiest times of the week for restaurants, so that's when they need him the most. This job is not a good fit for Luke because the hours of the job conflict with his social life, a value that's clearly more important to him than the money he earns there.

Hearing Luke complain about his job every Friday morning for a month or so—"Mrs. Purdy, I don't wanna go to work tonight"—I predicted he wouldn't last there much longer. And unfortunately I was right. Luke was the student I referred to earlier who quit his job because "it just wasn't worth it."

Our values fall into the following major categories: fame, money, power, religion, humanitarianism, family, health, aesthetics, creativity, and social contact.

Each year I have my students complete the values activity and each year three values appear consistently as the number one choice for many of them. The first is money; no surprise there since all those needs and wants must be fulfilled. The second is social contact; also no surprise there since most of us prefer working with other people over working alone. The third may surprise you; it's humanitarian, the value of helping others. The survey is located in Appendix A. Even if you think you know the values that top your list, take the survey anyway. The results may surprise you.

## YOUR FAVORITE CLASSES

What's your favorite class? Did you do well in that class? Most people find that one usually goes with the other.

**You'll enjoy doing what you're good at, and you'll be good at what you enjoy doing.**

Adults don't ask young people about their favorite class for no reason. The school subjects you love, whether it's math or English or art or whatever, gives us a glimpse into who you are and what you can do. It can, and often does, become part of your identity: *he's a good artist* or *she's into programming*. Chances are if you like a particular subject and you're good at it, you'll like incorporating the subject matter into your job.

> As part of my job posting program, when a business called with an open position, there were two ways in which I could help. First, I could post the position on my online job posting board so anyone can see it and apply. Or better yet, I could match the requirements of the open position to a student who might have an interest in the position and related skills. And who could do a better job finding those students than their teachers?
>
> Need an Office Assistant for a busy law firm? No problem. I teach Microsoft Applications, and Keyboarding/Word Processing. A colleague teaches Business Law. If we can find an interested student who's taken at least two out of three of these, we're in business.
>
> A web designer to build the campaign website of a candidate running for State Representative in November? I'll ask my colleague who teaches Desktop Publishing/ Web Design.
>
> An assistant cook at a farm-to-table take-home restaurant? We have several culinary courses in our Family and Consumer Science department. Let me ask the department chairperson.

I could go on, but you get the point. The correlation between the classes you enjoy and have done well in and the type of job you'd enjoy is very strong.

Here's something else that's equally important to consider.

### Which school subjects do you dislike?

Whether you disliked a class because of the subject matter or because you didn't do well in it, you may want to avoid jobs that require similar knowledge or skills.

While we're talking about school subjects, I want to share a critical piece of advice with you.

### Use your elective courses to explore your potential career goals.

If you love math, take a class in Computer Science, Accounting, Finance or Robotics. If you love social studies, take a class in Economics or Psychology. If you love English, take a class in Journalism or Video Production. Your electives not only give you an opportunity to apply the things you're learning in your academic classes, they may help you identify a new career option. I can't tell you how many of my students end up majoring in Computer Science, Economics, or Finance, when prior to taking those courses they had no idea what those subjects really entailed.

## YOUR INTERESTS AND HOBBIES

*Interests and Hobbies* is a section often seen on a resume. People think they're the same thing, but they're not. Hobbies are activities you regularly participate in, usually for fun. Interests are topics or activities you'd like to do or know more about. For example, horseback riding is a hobby if you ride horses regularly. If you don't but would like to, then horseback riding is an interest. So think about what you currently do or would like to do in your down time. If you choose to do something that you're not required to do, it's because you enjoy doing it. If that activity is part of your job, wouldn't you enjoy doing your job?

My husband, Steve, manages a team of sales people. While he's happy with his job on most days, he has one key regret about his career: when choosing his career path, he didn't follow his passion. Steve is a very creative person with an interest in art and design. But as a kid, he received the bad advice that if he allowed his interests to become his job, he'd eventually grow to hate those interests. What he hates now is that because of the consuming nature of his fast-paced, high-pressure job, he has very little time to pursue a hobby in art or design or in anything else creative for that matter. He's done a few things over the years—a drawing here or a landscaping project there. In his heart, he knows he picked the wrong path. Don't let his regret be your regret too.

Before you list your current hobbies and examine your interests, here are a few words of caution. As a job placement coach, one of the things I do is to review students' job applications before they're submitted to a company.

And every now and then I see an application where the student has either left the "Interests and Hobbies" section blank or has written "Hanging out with friends."

### "Hanging out with friends" is not an interest or a hobby.

If this is all you can come up with, you're demonstrating that you have no interests, and you have no hobbies.

Now it's possible that it slipped your mind that you spent time as a kid doing puzzles or learning how to kickbox. The interest inventory in Appendix B may jog your memory. However, if you complete the interest inventory and you come up empty, you're telling employers something very important about yourself. They'll question your level of self-motivation, curiosity, and your willingness and ability to learn new things.

A second area of concern I have in this area is for those who spend a majority of their free time playing video games. Given the proliferation of devices like consoles, cell phones, and tablets, it's a growing past-time where 72% of teens and 70% of college students report playing regularly. While it may not surprise you that almost 85% of teen boys play video games, you may be surprised that the number is almost 60% for teen girls. What may surprise you even more? Of the college students who play regularly, only 40% are boys and 60% are girls.

So, is video gaming evil? Not at all. I loved playing *Defender, Gauntlet,* and *Donkey Kong* when I was your age, and still play *Bubble Shoot* at the end of the day to relax and get away from everybody. It wasn't too long ago that my entire family and I were playing Trivia Crack almost to the point of obsession. So while I don't think video gaming is evil, I do think it becomes a problem if that's *all* you're interested in doing, because the time you spend video gaming is time you're not doing other things, like exploring your interests and discovering who you are.

> I recently gave one of my business classes their final project assignment: to create a sports franchise that would serve as their business to own and operate. The room immediately buzzed with excitement and within minutes, the students had picked their favorite sport.
>
> Ben on the other hand, stared at his computer and after 10

minutes or so, I approached him. "So, what are we thinking?" Without looking up at me he whispered, "I don't know." I prompted him, "Anything you played as a kid...soccer, football, karate?" Nope, nope, and nope. "Any sports you like to watch on TV?" Nope.

Okay, so not a sports-related business. "How about a business related to art, or music, or something you're interested in?" Again no response.

"Well, what do you do in your spare time?" With a tiny spark in his voice he replied, "I like to play video games." Aha! I asked with optimism, "Any video games related to sports, or art or music?" Nope, nope and nope.

There's nothing wrong with playing video games. In fact, employers are beginning to acknowledge the part it plays in strengthening workplace skills like online collaboration and problem-solving.

## When video gaming becomes a problem.

The problem occurs when playing video games is your only interest, because there are no college majors or careers in just video game playing. If your response to what I just said is, "I can be a video game tester," as is the reaction I often get from my students, please do some research on that. This is not a job where you'll be playing video games for fun, but to find programming bugs. Game testers report that this can be a very tedious job with long hours and low pay.

There is, however, a demand for game *developers*, and not just in the gaming industry. For example, high tech companies are hiring highly skilled game developers to train robots to inspect hazardous areas using artificial intelligence and virtual reality technologies. So if you love playing video games, why not learn how to develop them? Start by taking a class in programming, and if you enjoy it, proceed to graphic design or even robotics. Join your high school's coding club and if one doesn't exist, start one.

Whether video game playing is your only hobby, or you have no interests or hobbies whatsoever, exploring different activities, joining an after school club, or taking elective courses at school in the manner I've discussed here could spark an interest or even a passion you didn't know you had. Following and developing your interests in this way may very well lead you to a job or career that you love.

Complete the Interest and Activities Inventory in Appendix B. You'll select your top three interest areas and incorporate them in your search for a job in Chapter 4.

## YOUR MARKETABLE SKILLS

Your interests and hobbies are the things you enjoy doing. Your skills on the other hand are the things that you know *how* to do. They could be the result of a natural talent or something you learned. The skills you have are *marketable* if they're of value to an employer. For example, if you can touch the tip of your nose with your tongue, that's great. That's a skill. Unfortunately, there's no job that would require you to have this skill and therefore, it's not a marketable skill.

When considering your marketable skills, you have to consider two types of skills that I've already discussed. There are technical job skills that are specific to a particular job, like changing a diaper or fixing a flat tire. Soft skills on the other hand demonstrate how well you perform those technical job skills and are transferable from job to job. They include things like how well you communicate, work with others, problem solve, and manage your time.

The skills you've acquired don't only have to have come from a prior job. They can come from a variety of sources like the classes you took in school, chores you do around the house, your extra-curricular activities like music, art, sports, and the volunteer work you've done for others.

Use the marketable skills inventory in Appendix C to assess your skills; it'll help you when you search for occupations and construct your resume. Unlike skills inventories you can find on the internet, it's geared towards young people like you who don't yet have years of work experience.

## YOUR WORKING ENVIRONMENT

Closely linked to your values and interests is the environment you'd like to work in. For example, if you value social contact, you'll want a job where you work with others, not alone.

Jasmine worked at a fast food restaurant that paid minimum wage, but because of mounting financial pressures at home, she asked me to help her find a job that paid more. So with the understanding that money was her number one priority coupled with the fact that she had taken an Accounting class the prior school year, I helped her find a position as an Accounts Receivable Clerk at an auto detailing business. About two weeks later I visited her and her employer to conduct a workplace observation as part of the program guidelines. What I found there was a perfectly respectable business, a supervisor who was very nice and very professional, and Jasmine, sitting at her desk in the back of a tiny room no larger than a walk-in closet. As I conducted my business with her boss, I could see Jasmine from the corner of my eye working through a stack of papers in front of her. She never looked up from her work even once, almost as if to avoid making eye contact with me. I ended my visit, but the next day I stopped Jasmine as she was clocking out to leave for work. "So are you enjoying your job?"

"It sucks, Mrs. Purdy." I of course knew this already. "All I do is sit at my desk and enter invoices into the computer. I don't see anyone. I don't talk to anyone. It sucks."

As it turns out, Jasmine loved her accounting class but hated her accounting job, not because of the duties but because of the environment where she had to work. She missed the social interaction that often comes with working, and it didn't take long before the $15 an hour she was making just wasn't worth it. Because she was so close to graduating, she stuck out the job for a few more months and gave her two weeks' notice just before she graduated.

The checklist in Appendix D will help you identify your preferred working environment. In Chapter 4, I'll remind you to check this list when you search for potential jobs.

## PUTTING IT ALL TOGETHER

Don't even think about looking for a job until you've learned all the things about yourself that I've outlined in this chapter. Your dreams, goals, and values are important to keep in mind as you explore all your job options. Having interests that are similar to the duties of the job is important but won't guarantee that you'll be good at the job—you also have to have the right skills for the job. If you can make all these factors work together, wonderful things can happen for you.

> Mike wanted to be an Architect, so I helped him get a Co-op job at a land surveying company. Land surveyors prepare construction sites by using instruments to measure distances and angles on the site, and by determining property boundaries. This was a good job for him because land surveying and architecture are related fields: both require good math skills, attention to detail, and some knowledge of the law. Their work environments are similar and they both require similar amounts of education. While Mike wasn't qualified to be Land Surveyor, he was hired as a Crew Member responsible for carrying and setting up equipment, recording measurements, entering data into the computer system, and producing reports. Mike loved the job and it convinced him that architecture was in fact a good career choice for him.

## GREAT RESOURCES FOR YOUR CAREER JOB

There are literally dozens of interest and skills assessments websites that you can use for your self-assessment. However, unlike the inventories I've given you here, they're really aimed at people with more experience and education who are looking for a career job. Also be careful about inventories and surveys that claim to be "free." While taking the assessments are free, some require you to pay to see the results.

When you're ready to find your first career job or if you're changing careers, there are two resources I recommend. They are CareerOneStop and O*Net Online, both of which are sponsored by the U.S. Department of Labor. While they are two separate sites, they work together to walk you through your self-assessment and develop a list of potential occupations. We'll use O*Net Online in Chapter 4-What Types of Jobs are Right for Me, to research your potential part-time jobs.

### Next up...

If you're getting a job while still living at home, life isn't just going to change for you; it may change drastically for your family. Even if you're away at college, depending on the relationship you have with those around you, important changes may need to be made. If they don't, it could not only blow up your chances of landing the job you want now but may impact your ability to adapt to the workplace of your future career jobs. The next chapter will explain what needs to happen and why.

## CHAPTER SUMMARY QUIZ

The following quiz summarizes the chapter.

1. Finding a job or exploring career options must start with what process?
    a. Searching for job openings
    b. Getting a work permit
    c. Self-assessment
    d. Fill out job applications

2. Dreaming is a problem when it's the only thing you do to determine your future career.
    a. True
    b. False

3. Playing video games is always a problem because it distracts you away from other obligations.
    a. True
    b. False

4. What does having no interests or hobbies tell a potential employer?
    a. You're not a well-rounded person
    b. You're a person who does not like to try new things
    c. While you might be a good worker, you won't be very interesting to talk to
    d. All of the above.

5. Which of the following should you explore to determine what you're good at doing?
    a. Your marketable skills
    b. Your preferred work environment
    c. Your dreams
    d. Your interests and hobbies

Answers: 1c, 2a, 3b, 4d, 5a

42

# Lesson 3

# Parental Involvement: Window Washing or Scaffolding?

How involved is too involved?

My husband and I raised two daughters who are now grown and out of the house. No one ever sat us down and told us what to do, so a lot of what we learned was by trial and error. We relied on common sense to guide us, and we tried to model ourselves after our own parents. But we soon discovered that common sense wasn't all that common, and so we certainly made our share of mistakes.

When our daughters began working, one at age 15 and the other at age 17, our entire family went through a transitional period, not just with household routines but with the amount of involvement we would have in their busy lives. By taking on a job, our daughters were saying that they were ready to start standing on their own two feet, and that it was time for us to take a step back and let them. When you get a job and living even part of the year at home, your family will need to go through a similar transitional period of their own.

While your parents may no longer have the day-to-day involvement in what you're doing in high school, college, or at work, they can certainly have a lot of influence on the decisions you make.

### Accept your parents' help as you transition into the working world.

They may have years of experience doing what you're about to do, and while things like technology have changed since they were teenagers, human nature has not. Employers are still looking for the best possible people to hire and you'll need to convince them that you're one of them. Talking to your parents as you navigate this process can be very helpful.

There's just one caveat.

A successful experience for you, whether at school or at work, requires that all parties who can influence your decisions share similar values, goals, and expectations.

**Your teachers, employers, parents or guardians, and
you must all be on the same page.**

Adding a job to your life will require compromising and negotiating on everyone's part. If the expectations of your parents are not in line with that of the school or work, you'll almost always follow in the direction of your parents because they are by far the most influential adults in your life.

In this chapter, I'll discuss the relationship employers expect to have with you as well as the level of involvement they expect your parents will have in that relationship. I'll share with you the experiences my employers and I have had with parents of varying degrees of involvement. Some are too involved. Some should be more involved. And some are involved at just the right level.

As you read these stories, understand that many of them are exceptions. Some of them are even outrageous. I tell you these stories to highlight the impact parents can have on their children's entry into the real world — both positive and negative. Each year, I encounter anywhere from 180 to 200 students in my classes, the vast majority of whom are terrific, hard-working, well-adjusted young adults. The parents I meet are mostly lovely, supportive, and engaged parents. Often when I meet a parent for the first time, I say to myself, no wonder that kid is great; he or she has great parents.

Before I continue, I need you to do two things. Here's the first one.

**You have to do your part.**

Depending on their level of involvement in your life, it may be difficult for them at first to give you the independence you'll need to succeed in your job, especially if you're still living at home. So for every piece of advice I give to parents that applies to your situation, ask yourself, "What can I do to help my parents be involved in my life at the appropriate level?" For example, I'll tell parents to never call you out of work as they do for school, because they're not the employee, you are. That means, however, that you have to make that call at the right time and in the right way. If your parents see you being responsible and making good decisions, they may feel more comfortable taking a step back and giving you the independence you need.

This chapter is important to read not just for you but also for your parents or guardians. That's why from this point forward, I'm going to address them directly. So my second request is that after you finish reading it, pass it along to them and encourage them to read it too. If you do, I promise it will help you. That's your one and only homework assignment I'll ever give you.

## BE THE SCAFFOLDING

Parents should allow their kids to be as self-sufficient as is appropriate for their age and ability. They should support their kids as they learn new skills, not do for them the things their kids should be doing on their own. They should encourage, not pressure. They should follow-up, not hover. With your support, your child should experience for themselves all the complexities and nuances associated with going out into the world and finding a job. In education, supporting a child's learning in this manner is called *scaffolding*, a technique within a broader concept called the *zone of proximal development* created by Soviet psychologist Lev Vygotsky in the early twentieth century. Scaffolding is a term used to describe the help that's given to a student by a person of knowledge and experience, to learn what would have been too difficult to learn on their own. In *Figure 4*, think of the "What I can do" circle as the student's comfort zone. Scaffolding is the help that's provided to move the student out of their

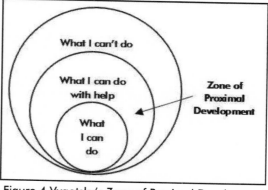

Figure 4 Vygotsky's Zone of Proximal Development

comfort zone and into the "What I can do with help" circle, or the zone of proximal development.

To understand this concept, just imagine a window washer on a skyscraper who needs the scaffolding to suspend them. The scaffolding supports them in reaching higher levels of the building and is there in case they lose their balance. In this scenario, the window washer is the child; the scaffolding is the parent.

Don't grab the squeegee and wash the windows for them. Be the scaffolding.

The study of human development tells us that when children reach their teenage years, it's only natural that they begin the process of separating from their parents. This sounds like trouble, but not only is it normal, it would be unhealthy if the separation process didn't occur. Teens sometimes find it difficult to communicate what they're feeling, and they may show it by acting out. If they're misbehaving or talking back, they may be trying to tell you that it's time for you to start taking some scaffolding down and give them some *structured* independence. Next time you hear "Leave me alone!" it may mean, "Let me try." When they say, "Stop nagging" they may be saying, "Stop worrying, I've got this."

### What does scaffolding look like?

In our own excitement of having a child that's working, giving help and advice can quickly turn to micro-managing. Resist that temptation because it can not only be overwhelming, it can sabotage a child's efforts to become self-sufficient. Here's what I mean by scaffolding in the context of working.

- Encourage your child to do as much of the hands-on work as possible, with your assistance. Do not do things for them like completing their job applications as they watch.
- Let them come to you for advice or help. This allows them to control issues they can resolve on their own versus the ones that require your assistance.
- Counsel them and even rehearse some dialogue with them about what and how to communicate with their supervisor or co-workers when difficult issues arise.
- Encourage them to do their job to the best of their abilities. Stress the importance of being a reliable employee by going to work on time, not calling out except for emergencies, and giving ample notice for requesting days off.
- Help them learn organization and time-management skills. These skills have never been as critical for them to have as they are right now as they juggle to meet all their commitments.

- Know when your child is asking for help and when they're venting. Just like you and I have bad days at work, so will they. Not every complaint is a request for your involvement.

Most importantly, be a good role model for your working child. I commonly find that parents who do well at work have children who do well at work.

## PARENTING OUT OF FEAR

It's hard to watch our kids make mistakes that we know how to avoid. As parents, we want our children to benefit from our wisdom and our experiences, both successes as well as our failures, so they can be independent, self-sufficient and resilient adults by the time they leave our home. In our eagerness to help them reach this goal, we sometimes go too far. There are things that we know they can and should be doing for themselves, yet we do it for them anyway. We tell ourselves that we're trying to make things easier and less stressful for them, when in reality, we do it to make things easier and less stressful on us.

### This is parenting out of fear.

The line between supporting and doing too much is getting thinner and thinner with the passing of each generation. When I was a teen, a parent who crossed that line was called *overprotective*. It starts with little things at home. For example, are you doing their laundry when they have more time on their hands than you do? Are you registering them for the SATs, or even doing their taxes for them? Do you really want their first experiences like these to be when you may not be around?

### Are you really helping?

I hear parents say all the time that they're just trying to help their child, but in fact, they're encouraging a condition called *learned helplessness*. Every time we grab the squeegee and do it ourselves, we rob our children of the opportunity to gain knowledge, master new skills, build confidence and self-esteem, and ultimately become self-sufficient. At its extreme, learned helplessness can be potentially debilitating and difficult to reverse, because the more we do for them, the more they allow us and need us to do for them, and the less they do for themselves. That's not helping them, that's crippling them.

### The helicopter parent.

The last twenty-five years or so has seen a parsing of the term, overprotective parent, into more specific and descriptive terms. The 1990's brought the emergence of the term, helicopter parents — moms and dads that hover over their kids anxiously to monitor every move they make for fear they'll make a mistake. They are those parents who micro-manage their child and interject themselves into issues that their child should be able to resolve on their own.

> Almost all my Co-op students will have found jobs by the end of the first week of school. But some just have a harder time than others. Anthony was a quiet student who tried his best but was not a good communicator. Since many of the job openings available to young people are in retail, and retail involved dealing with customers, he was having a tough time convincing an employer to hire him. I worked for days making phone call after phone call on his behalf, and I finally found a potential placement for him. A manager of a large electronics retail store was willing to give him a chance and hire him as a stock clerk. I sent Anthony the next day to apply for the position. I was delighted, until I got a call from the manager later that same afternoon. "I just can't do it," he said apologetically. And here's why. Like many companies, this one requires all applicants to take an employment test, and Anthony was asked to take it on a computer in the store. Not only did Anthony's mother come in with him, but she was the one who took the online test while Anthony watched.

Situations like this are more common than you think, especially since many online employment tests can be taken at home. We've all heard stories of parents who do their child's homework, build their middle school science projects, or even write their college essays, because these things can all be done in total privacy.

The twenty-first century brought a new, more intense type of parenting.

### The snowplow parent.

I first heard that term in 2013 while visiting colleges for my eldest daughter,

Marisa. "While helicopter parents hover *around* the child," explained one college admissions speaker, "snowplow parents go *ahead* of the child and clear the way of any obstructions to their success." That description sounded awfully familiar to me, and I had to ask myself, "Am I guilty of that?" I'm definitely not a helicopter parent; my husband and I generally allowed our girls the freedom to make their own, age-appropriate decisions. If they needed our help, they knew where to find us. But problems that were barriers to their overall success was another matter entirely.

It's hard not to want to get involved when you find your high school junior sobbing while curled up in a fetal position on her bed at 6 p.m. on a school night. The problem? Marisa's application for the National Honor Society was due in less than 24 hours, and she forgot all about it. If you've never seen one of these, it's not quite as lengthy as a college application, but it's close. In addition to requiring all the usual information—personal, academic, extracurricular, volunteering, and honors—it requires letters with signatures from sponsors as verification of their participation and service hours. Just as she reconciled herself to defeat, the project manager in me sprang into action. An action plan was formulated with tasks, responsibilities, and timelines. The application was due at 2:30 the next day; she busted her butt and got it in at 2:20.

Deadline met. Disaster averted. Her future secured.

Not snowplowing, you say? More like scaffolding? What if I told you that in order for her to get a few of those letters with signatures from her teachers and sponsors, this snowplow parent had to call in a few favors from some colleagues? Teachers are busy people, and they don't look kindly on students who burst into their classroom asking for a letter *today.* I hated asking for those favors, not just because I inconvenienced my colleagues, but because what I did deprived my daughter of learning a valuable lesson about responsibility. But I did it anyway because the potential consequences when college application time came around would be too great. It was a difficult decision to make but in the end, I did what I felt I had to do.

While things like this happen, the real problem occurs when it becomes a habit and a child becomes dependent on you. If it's happening for school, it's likely to happen when they start a job. Employers complain constantly that parents are picking up employment applications and dropping them off. And then, this.

An older woman, maybe in her 40's, came in one day and asked for an application. After I handed her one, she took it to one of the tables in the back of the restaurant and filled it out. About 20 minutes later, while I was helping a customer, she handed the completed application to one of my servers, Jen, behind the counter. I finished with my customer, looked over and saw all three of my servers gathered around the application and talking in whispers. 'Since we don't get too many applicants that age,' Jen explained as she handed it to me, 'I glanced at it." It was for a 17-year-old boy.

There is no way we'd bring this boy in for an interview because we first want to see who's applying. How interested do they seem in working? When a parent drops off the application, and even fills it out for them, we know it's the parent who wants them to work more than they want to work.

Michelle Landis
Franchise Owner, Salad Works

A parent who does this is not only depriving their child of a great opportunity to connect with a potential employer and make a good first impression, they're telling the employer that they're forcing their child to work, their child can't handle the responsibility of having a job, or both. If you drop off your child's application or fill it out for them, it'll likely be in the trash can before you make it back to your car.

Employers expect to deal strictly and exclusively with their employees, not their parents.

When students are unemployed, their job every day is to find a job, for a minimum of three business contacts a day. After five days and over a dozen contacts, I couldn't understand why my

> student Jalyn wasn't finding anything. So, I called two or three of the contacts where she applied and was told by all of them that Jalyn did in fact speak to them. Unfortunately, she was accompanied by her mother who injected herself into the conversation by asking and answering questions.

Would you hire Jalyn if you were an employer? Try to put yourself in the place of a manager and ask yourself, regardless of whether you sympathize with this mother or not, what is your impression of Jalyn? Is it that she's a mature young person who can handle herself professionally? Or is it that any time you may have to deal with Jalyn you'd also be dealing with her mother?

## Employers do not want to deal with parents.

Because of the cyclical nature of learned helplessness, parents can easily find themselves snowplowing their children well into their twenties and beyond. I know parents that are still making doctors' appointments, contacting college professors for performance updates, and filing tax returns for their grown children.

> Jillian, a recent college graduate, was scheduled for an interview for a high school teaching position but never showed up. Later that day, the assistant principal who was conducting the interview received a phone call, not from Jillian, but from her mother. She was very apologetic that Jillian missed the interview but stated that it wasn't her daughter's fault. She explained, "I was supposed to call her and wake her up in time, but I didn't. It was my fault, not hers." Oh, and could she schedule another time for her daughter to come in.
> Needless to say, no further interviews were needed.

Parents should avoid direct contact with the employer unless it's an emergency. Your input into common work-related issues is not only unnecessary, it can be irritating. And it won't just reflect badly on you but also on your child. Managers have a business to run and managing their employees is hard enough without parents getting involved.

Here are some basic guidelines.

- Don't force your child to get a job. Their lack of interest will be evident immediately.
- Don't accompany your child to look for a job. If you're their ride, stay in the car.
- Don't ask if you can sit in on an interview with your child.
- Don't write an excuse for your child to give to the supervisor if they were late or called out.
- Don't call out of work for your child. Employers want a phone call directly from the employee. It demonstrates accountability.
- Don't send in a note to the supervisor about the days off that your child needs from work. This is the employee's responsibility, and it's irrelevant that you've given your permission.
- Don't call the employer to discuss your child's job evaluation, pay, or benefits. While it may not be illegal to share that information with you if your child is a minor, it would be unprofessional.

If your child is used to you doing these types of things for them, your taking a step back will encourage them to take a step forward.

## THE UNDERINVOLVED PARENT

Although this is not a situation that I come across very often, it can have crippling results not only at school but also at work. Sometimes parents are uninvolved because they are consumed by their own problems; addiction and divorce are high on the list of causes. Others are intimidated by contacts with the school due to cultural differences or a language barrier. If you don't speak English, would you be comfortable getting on the phone with a teacher, participating in parent-teacher conferences, or attending Back-to-School night? And finally, sometimes parents of challenging children reach a stage where they have given up and thrown in the towel. This was the reason here:

> Brianna had worked for a health food store for over a year before she joined the Co-op program. She had already developed a good relationship with her boss, who had given her supervisory responsibilities like closing the store and taking the nightly deposit to the bank. But while work was going well, her

performance at school was not. Day after day she would saunter in 10...20...30 minutes late with a cup of coffee in her hands and slump down in her chair in front of me. Co-op had strict rules on attendance and punctuality and after three unexcused latenesses, their On-the-Job Training (OJT) grade is lowered. Because she missed so much of my class, that grade suffered as well. Talking to her didn't help; she was indifferent to all my attempts to get her to take the program rules seriously. But because she was doing well at work, I tolerated her latenesses, and she tolerated the lowered grade.

That is until one day her manager called in frustration to warn me that the next time Brianna was late, he was going to fire her. Apparently, he had an appointment the prior day and expected Brianna to be there on time to manage the store. She was late as usual, and he missed his appointment. As it turns out, I had wrongly assumed that Brianna was just not a morning person. There was no excuse for being late for a job that started at 1:00 pm and apparently, she was as habitually late for work as she was for school. Brianna was now in a high-risk situation, because being fired would result in her failing the marking period. I called home to rally the support she would need to break her lateness habit.

To my surprise, I barely completed the first few sentences about why I was calling when her mother interrupted, "You know what? I really can't help you. She's 18 years old and she can do whatever she wants. I'm sorry." She hung up before I could respond.

Are there parents who really think that when a child turns 18, a switch turns on and they become fully formed adults? Or is it that they've had a contentious relationship with a difficult child and now they've simply had enough? Knowing what Brianna was like, my sense was that it was the latter. I suddenly felt very sorry for my student, because regardless of how children get to this point, when a parent has no expectations of their child, what expectations will the child have of themselves? And it didn't matter that her employer and I *had* expectations of her.

**When the parent's expectations conflict with those of school or work, the parent will always win.**

When her mother threw in the towel, she essentially pulled all of the scaffolding out from under her and just like the window washer, Brianna went into a free-fall, figuratively speaking. Despite my efforts to get her to turn things around, by the end of that same week, she quit her job without my permission, and dropped out of the Co-op program. I had no choice but to give her a failing grade for the marking period. A child's home, school, and work lives are so closely entwined that a problem in one will no doubt spill into the others.

## PARENTS WHO ENABLE

As parents, teachers, employers and every other adult in our children's lives, we know that our kids will do as we do, and not as we say. We're not perfect. I've certainly been guilty of my own transgressions in front of my children. I've written my fair share of notes explaining their early morning "illness" to excuse a lateness following an all-nighter. I've also allowed them to take "mental health" days from time to time.

But there's a big difference between bending the rules from time to time and having a pattern of behavior that encourages children to do the wrong thing. People often throw the term *enable* around to describe a variety of parental behaviors that seem well-intentioned but have bad results for the child. Here is a more accurate definition that has evolved in reference to parenting.

**Enable: To offer help that perpetuates a problem rather than solves it.**

Enabling is when a child keeps forgetting their lunch at home and a parent habitually treks into school to deliver it to them. Where is the incentive to remember to take lunch?

Enabling is a father who, in the presence of his son, demands "proof" from teachers and administrators that the boy is misbehaving in the classroom. If a child knows that mom or dad will come to their rescue like this, what's their incentive to stop the bad behavior?

Enabling is a mother who, after learning that her son is copying answers to a take home quiz from an answer key posted by another student on Instagram, defends the practice by claiming that it's just "internet collaboration" and that "everybody does it."

Rewarding any type of behavior, good or bad, encourages the behavior to continue. Here's a story that I want you to remember because in the next chapter I'll tell you about the very real consequences that resulted from rewarding this behavior.

---

As a tennis mom, I would often watch my daughters take lessons and drills from the viewing area of the local tennis club. In one particular drill that my youngest daughter, Samantha, was in when she was in middle school, there was a boy who had earned the reputation for never doing a ball pickup. When the instructor's basket is empty, everyone must pick up balls off of the court before the drill can resume. While every other player in the drill picked up balls, he would sit on the bench drinking his Gatorade, or chat with the pro, or run to the bathroom. The other kids complained to him and about him constantly for not pulling his weight, but it fell on deaf ears. It annoyed me that this went on for months and I often wondered why the instructor wasn't correcting this child's behavior.

One day I was taking a drill of my own when I saw this boy on the adjacent court. I went to my own instructor, Sal, during a ball pickup and asked, "Do you see that kid over there? The one who's on his phone? Why is he allowed to sit on the bench on his cell phone while everyone else is picking up balls?"

For one very simple reason, he explained. You see Sal used to have this boy in one of his junior level drills. When the boy refused to pick up balls, Sal eventually went to his mother to solicit her help. Her response? The next week Sal began the drill only to discover that the mother had removed her son from his drill and put him with another instructor.

---

By removing this boy from the drill, mom certainly avoided a confrontation or hurt feelings; unfortunately, she also missed a great opportunity to teach him values like teamwork and cooperation. That's what enabling does. It robs a child of the opportunity to learn how to cope with adversity and solve life's common problems. While this isn't the worst example of enabling that

55

I've experienced, I have seen my fair share of parents who have crossed the line.

Let me preface my next story by explaining a very serious Co-op rule called No School-No Work. As the name implies, if a student is absent from school, they may not go to work. The same rule applies to other after-school activities like sports and clubs. If you're well enough to go to baseball practice, you're well enough to come to school. For Co-op students it's even more important, because their job may very well turn into a full-time career after high school. We don't want the promise of that job to encourage kids to stop coming to school, or to drop out entirely. That's why violating this rule is a serious offense and could result in a failure for their Co-op grade for the marking period. School comes first. Period.

Christina worked for her mother who had a jewelry kiosk in the middle of the mall. She was a sweet girl but had terrible attendance, which made me wonder if she was calling out of work on all these days like she was supposed to. My hunch was that she wasn't, because no employer would tolerate so many missed days, unless of course her employer was also her mother. During one of the days she was absent, I called her work as standard practice to alert her supervisor that she is not in school and therefore should be calling out. Her mother was there and confirmed that she was indeed very sick and is not expected at work. One of the unfortunate parts of my job is to verify in person that a student who shouldn't be at work is not at work. So I paid an unannounced visit to the mall and sure enough, I saw Christina helping a customer at the jewelry store. I confronted the mother by telling her that Christina is not allowed to be at work and that we would have to speak tomorrow about what to do about the situation.

Now you can imagine how apologetic this mother would be, right? I imagined that our discussion tomorrow would go something like this: 1) mom would apologize, 2) I would state the obvious that Christina can no longer work for mom, and 3) we would discuss options for a new job. What I didn't imagine was my coming in to work the next morning to this voice mail message that I have saved to this day:

56

Tuesday, December 20, 2005, 1:52 pm

"Hello Miss Purdy, Mrs. Purdy, I guess you can't take your calls because you're at the mall spying on my daughter. Let me explain something to you, ok? I do not lie, I did not lie to you, she does have a doctor's appointment and I was waiting for the woman that you seen at the counter to come pick her up because I only have one car and 3 children, and you know what, you are rude and you are ignorant. I want my child off the co-op program. I don't want her to have anything to do with you. You're going to give me shit? Listen lady, you can kiss my you know what."

And then this, a few minutes later:

Tuesday, December 20, 2005, 1:55 pm

"Hi this is Christina's mother again. Christina is not going to sell any more [fundraising] candy either. She'll give you what money she owes you, and then you're getting all of your candy back. You wanna be like this, you don't even wanna listen to people? And don't even dare try to fail her because if you do, I will take your ass to court. So she was at work, so what? Boo hoo."

For young people to truly experience the expectations placed on them in the workplace, they should never work for a parent. Just like a parent should never be their child's classroom teacher. When workplace issues arise, you must be an employer first and a parent second but being objective with your own child can be very difficult.

Needless to say, the follow-up meeting with Christina's mother never took place. So Christina had a choice to make—either continue to work for her mother or remain on the Co-op program; she couldn't do both. In the end, she made the right decision and stayed on the program, and in return I gave her a passing grade. I couldn't in good conscience fail her because the mistakes she made and the rules she broke were largely due to her mother's negative influence. Because Christina's career goal was to work with children, I helped her get a job at an excellent day care center where she'd have good role models who would teach her not only workplace skills, but the life skills like honesty and dependability she desperately needed to learn.

**Being in denial can have serious consequences.**

Before you can truly help your child solve a difficult problem, you first have to acknowledge that a problem exists. If your child is doing the wrong thing, it's easier to be in denial than to acknowledge their bad behavior. But if you don't acknowledge the problem, how can you help them fix it?

Students must go through an application process and interview before they are enrolled into the Co-op program. I usually interview them one-on-one, but if I believe the student will require a lot of support from home to succeed on the program, I ask a parent to be present. The latter was the case with Brian, who in his previous year in high school had a terrible attendance record of 32 absences, and a 1.6 GPA. His mother came to the interview, and I expressed my concerns about whether Brian can handle the strict rules of the program. To this his mother replied, "Brian was hanging around with the wrong crowd last year." I looked at Brian who remained expressionless, and asked him if he had any disciplinary issues, to which his mother responded, "He was suspended once, but it was for stealing food from the cafeteria, which was ridiculous because everybody does it." I see. Before speaking again, I physically swiveled my chair to square up with Brian, looked him straight in the eyes and asked, any other problems? Again from mom, "Brian does have some legal problems and he may be missing some school. But he didn't do anything. He was just at the wrong place at the wrong time."

I enrolled Brian into the program with great reservations. I helped him find a job in the shipping department of a manufacturing company earning $15/hour, and for the first week or so things seemed okay. Then the latenesses began, followed by absences, followed by calls from his supervisor that not only was he missing work due to school absences, but was calling out of work even on the days he was in school. Calling out of work on a school day without my permission is synonymous with cutting a class and constitutes a major infraction. The issues continued and while his employer and I tried very hard to straighten him out, I couldn't get mom to return a single phone call.

The final straw came one day when the supervisor called to tell me that Brian failed a drug test and had to be terminated.

But Brian had bigger problems than his status on the Co-op program. After he was fired, he just stopped coming to school and I never saw him again. I'd love to say that this was the end of my story, but things took a fast turn for the outrageous.

Remember the legal problems his mother eluded to, that "he was at the wrong place at the wrong time?" Apparently, the wrong place was in the middle of a parking lot, and the wrong time was in the middle of the night, when Brian and a group of boys assaulted another teenage boy. How do I know this? Because a few weeks later, his mother called and offered me this story in the sweetest voice, like she was sharing a secret with her very best friend.

"So listen, the court date is set for next Thursday and before he goes in front of the judge, his PO (parole officer) needs to hear that he's doing good in school and at work."

With growing incredulity, I continued to listen quietly.

"I need you to talk to his PO and tell him he's doing good." Wait. What?

I was so stunned that I didn't know what to say. Then, "Mrs. A., I know we haven't spoken in some time because you haven't returned my calls, but you must know by now that Brian was fired from his job because he failed a drug test."

Her response was almost as shocked as mine. "Well, yes. But the judge can't know that!" And again, those words, "He didn't do anything. He was just at the wrong place at the wrong time."

It took me a minute to gather my thoughts. "So, let me make sure I understand what you're asking. You want me to perjure myself to an officer of the court, and tell him that Brian is doing well in a job he was fired from?" Well that didn't go over well, because her tone went from sweet to indignant when she replied. "I guess I'm wasting my time. I thought maybe you'd want to help him, but I guess not."

I would have loved to tell this mom that she was not helping her son but hurting him by making excuses for him. But I knew in that moment that any more push back from me would have no impact on her and may inflame her temper further. I had to let it go. Years later I had Brian's cousin in my class who informed me that as a result of Brian's day in court, he was sent to a "wilderness camp" to rehabilitate and serve his sentence.

## CHILDREN NEED PARENTS, NOT ANOTHER FRIEND

A parent should never be friends with their children. I hear this from time to time: "My dad is my best friend," or "My daughter and I are best friends." Your son or daughter probably does not need another friend. What they absolutely do need is a parent, because only parents put the needs of their children before their own. Sometimes that involves giving them some tough love, like in the following example. They'll never get this from a friend.

It was my first year as a full-time classroom teacher, and I was having a tough time managing one of my computer applications classes. It was late in spring semester and by that time of year, the kids are antsy and ready to be done with school. Jonathan, a highly unmotivated sophomore, was more than just punchy; he was on a crusade to do as little work and as much socializing as possible. All my attempts to keep him on task failed, and his disruptive behavior deteriorated to the point where I had to call home. Mom listened quietly as I detailed her son's behavior and my attempts to correct it. Then, in a calm but tense whisper, "I apologize for my son's behavior. You will *not* have this problem starting tomorrow."

Now I've placed my fair share of these phone calls, but not one of them ever ended like that. I was very curious to see the outcome, and I didn't have to wait long. From the second he entered my room the next morning until the last day of school in June, this kid was a different person. He sat in his chair, barely spoke, and did his work. And as a result, the noise and activity level in the entire classroom subsided almost immediately.

I enjoyed the next few days in my peaceful classroom, but when my curiosity got the better of me, I called him over to my desk for a chat. "So, I take it mom spoke to you?" He nodded in response without looking at me. "What did she say?" I couldn't wait to hear what magic this mother had performed.

"She took my car away." Again, without looking at me.

Wow. As I looked at this boy slumped in his chair and refusing to make eye contact with me, I felt a wave of guilt wash over me. It seemed like a harsh punishment, but I could only assume that my phone call home wasn't the first of its kind.

"Well, I'm sorry if my phone call instigated that, but your mother must love you very much." And I'll never forget his response. He finally looked up at me, nodded in agreement, and said, "I know."

Two things I knew were clearly confirmed for me on that day. First, you don't reward bad behavior. Allowing a child to have a car, or a cell phone, or any type of privilege while misbehaving simply encourages the behavior to continue.

And second, teens won't just respond positively to your scaffolding, they may actually appreciate it. After my talk with him, Jonathan did something I never expected him to do—he came to visit me the following semester. I come across students like Jonathan often enough to know that they're just testing me to see how far they can go; it's just what some kids do. But what he did by coming to visit me is a pattern I've noticed through the years. Students who give me the hardest time with their behavior are usually the first ones to visit me the following year. It used to confuse me. I'd say to myself, here is a kid who I had to discipline. I changed his seat to separate him from his friends. I called home. Maybe I even wrote him up. Jonathan couldn't wait to leave my class in June last year, and here he is in front of me telling me how his summer went. That's when I realized that children *want* structure and boundaries, even if they don't realize it in the moment. I give *mother of the year award* to his mother who got involved at the right time and at the right level. She and I wouldn't have gotten the outcome we did if we hadn't been consistent in our expectations.

### Next up...

Eighteen years seems like a long time to have with our children. But in relation to all the years beyond, it's not that long. It is, however, all the time we have before the scaffolding has to start coming down. Once they leave to begin their next stage in life, whether that's college or beyond, our ability to influence their decisions diminishes significantly. Be the scaffolding *now* as they enter the world of work. By taking a step back and supporting them at the right level, it won't be long before you see them ascending higher and higher as they achieve their goals. In the end, when parents, the school, and the employer work together to establish common expectations and provide consistent support, how can a child not succeed?

## CHAPTER SUMMARY QUIZ

The following quiz summarizes the chapter.

1. It is dangerous for teenagers to begin to separate from their parents:
   a. True
   b. False

2. A parenting technique to help teens begin to stand on their own two feet is called what?
   a. Ladder
   b. Squeegee
   c. Scaffolding
   d. Trampoline

3. A parent who takes an excessive and often unhealthy interest in the life of their child may be categorized as a(n) _____ parent.
   a. Overprotective
   b. Helicopter
   c. Snowplow
   d. Any of the following may be correct

4. It is helpful for a parent to accompany their child to apply for a job or to attend a job interview.
   a. True
   b. False

5. Offering help that perpetuates rather than solves a problem is:
   a. Being in denial
   b. Enabling
   c. Snowplowing
   d. Helicoptering

Answers: 1b, 2c, 3d, 4b, 5b

62

# Lesson 4

# The Right Job for You

Chapter 2 was all about you—your dreams, values, interests, skills, and preferred working environment. You're now ready to match *who you are* with the types of jobs, or occupations, that are right for you.

Before we talk about specific jobs, it's important to understand what the overall job market looks like. Why should you care about this? Because how the economy is doing has a greater impact on workers age 16-24 than any other age group. I'll explain why.

We'll then look at the most common, and not so common, jobs that are available to young job seekers like you. You'll take the results of your self-assessment from Chapter 2 and research potential jobs. This is the list of jobs you'll use to find job openings in the next chapter.

If you're a minor (under the age of 18), the law places limitations on the types of job duties you can perform and the hours you can work. If you're 14 or 15, those restrictions are even greater. It's important to understand these legal requirements so that you spend your time and effort looking for the jobs that the law allows you to have.

Finally, we've been talking a lot about part-time, paid jobs, but volunteer jobs and internships are several alternatives with advantages and disadvantages of their own. The process of finding these positions is no different than finding a part-time job, as we are discussing.

## KNOW THE JOB OUTLOOK FOR YOUNG WOKERS

When you hear phrases like "our economy is strong" or "the economy is in a recession," what exactly does that mean and, more importantly, who cares? Without going into a complex lesson on macroeconomics, the answers in general terms are pretty simple.

The health of our economy is affected by how much we as consumers spend and how much we as workers make in income. When consumers spend more money on goods and services, businesses have to hire more workers to produce those goods and services. More income among consumers leads to more spending, which in turn leads to more hiring, and so on. This is an example of an economy in *expansion*. If the opposite is occurring, where consumers are spending less money on goods and services, businesses have to lay off workers. This reduces their income which causes them to spend less, and so on. When this occurs, we say the economy is in a state of *contraction* which could lead to a *recession*. The direction in which the economy trends will continue unless our government intervenes, or outside forces — like the collapse of an industry, wars, or even changes in weather — occur. You just learned Macroeconomics 101 in a nutshell!

We care because our ability to find and keep a job depends on the current conditions of our economy. A key measure of economic health is the unemployment rate, the percent of people who are willing and able to work, and who are actively looking for a job. *Figure 5* represents the unemployment rate in the U.S from 1990 to 2018 by age group. The line at the top of the graph is the unemployment rate over time for teens and young adults age 16 to 24, a measurement that is consistently twice that of the national rate.

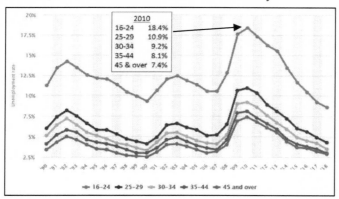

Figure 5 Unemployment Rate by Age Group

Let's look at the year 2010 when the economy was in a severe recession. The rate for 16 to 24-year-olds was 18.4%, more than twice the national rate of 8.6%. Since then the economy has experienced a period of expansion and in 2018, this age group experienced an 8.6% unemployment rate while the national average fell to 3.9%.

So let me ask you this: When the economy is in a recession and many people of all age groups are out of work, who are you competing with for a job? It's not just others your age, but older workers with potentially more skills and work experience than you who may now be willing to settle for one or more low-paying entry-level job rather than no job at all. And because

64

recessions also affect retirement savings and investment accounts, older re-tired Americans tend to re-enter the work force. This is why recessions hit your age group harder than any other. Look at the line at the top of the graph again during the last recession, starting in 2009. Do you notice how much higher the rate goes in proportion to any other age group? Now you know why.

Economic changes are inevitable. But how well you fare through tough economic times is within your control.

### Make yourself valuable to employers.

You do that by building a solid educational foundation and a history of rel-evant job skills, so that you can not only find a job but keep the one you have when the economy slows down and businesses have to lay off workers.

## JOBS FOR WORKERS 16 AND OLDER

If you think that your best shot at finding a job is in a retail store or restau-rant, you're not wrong.

Most part-time, entry-level jobs don't require formal education or exten-sive experience. They're also the jobs that usually require less than a month of on-the-job training. Businesses hesitate to spend more time than that to train young workers because the turnover rate—the frequency of workers starting and leaving a job---for young people is very high.

Here are the top 10 most common jobs for teens. They are in order from highest to lowest in number of workers typically employed.

1. Cashiers
2. Waiters and waitresses
3. Retail salespersons
4. Food preparation workers
5. Hosts and hostesses - restaurant, lounge and coffee shop
6. Customer service representatives
7. Laborers and freight, stock, and material movers (manual)
8. Stock clerks and order fillers
9. Childcare workers
10. Counter attendants - cafeteria, food concession, and coffee shop

Notice that this list includes quite a lot of food service positions. Before I continue, let me say something about this.

**A job in food service is one of the most valuable work experiences a teen can have.**

From my own personal experience working at the Orange Julius in high school and two different restaurants in college, working in food service, especially fast food, is a great simulation of life itself. Regardless of the type of restaurant, customers want their food and drinks fast. Whether you're at the counter taking orders, waiting on tables, or preparing food items, food service jobs involves constant communication with customers, handling of customer complaints, and multi-tasking in a fast-paced and sometimes stressful environment. Later in your life, if and when you move on to other professions, you'll be more likely to give your server at a restaurant or the cashier at the counter the appreciation they deserve for performing a challenging job. I tell students who might otherwise be reluctant, if they can succeed in fast food, they can succeed anywhere.

A more extensive list of entry-level jobs is included below, but it's by no means comprehensive. They don't require a college degree, and in most cases, they don't require a high school diploma. Review the list and circle the type of job you think may be consistent with the results of your self-assessment, i.e., your values, your top three interest areas, your marketable skills, and your preferred work environment. Then, go to O*Net Online and *Browse by Industry* and research the job title. For example, if you want to work as a Pharmacy Aide, search the industry *Health Science,* and select the job title *Pharmacy Aide*. To analyze whether a job is a good fit for you, review the work duties, required skills, pay, and educational requirements.

Since the list below is not comprehensive, I encourage you to use the O*Net *Browse by Industry* feature to review other jobs you believe might be right for you. When you're done with your research, you should have circled several potential jobs and added some of your own. These are the jobs you'll focus your job searching efforts on in the next chapter.

The jobs my students held are indicated with an asterisk (*).

# Entry Level Jobs by Career Area

**Agriculture/Food/Natural Resources**
- Pet Sitter/Walker
- Animal Caretaker *
- Kennel Attendant *
- Nursery Worker *
- Landscaper *

**Architecture and Construction**
- Construction Assistant *
- Carpet Installer *
- Electrician Assistant *
- Painter Assistant
- Land Surveyor Assistant *
- Heating & AC Mechanic Assistant *

**Arts, Audio/Video & Communications**
- AV Equipment Technician Assistant
- Photographer Assistant *
- Writer Assistant *
- Print Binding & Finishing Worker *
- Music, Art, or Dance Tutor

**Business Management & Admin.**
- Bookkeeping & Accounting Clerk *
- Customer Service Representative *
- Data Entry Keyer
- File Clerk *
- Library Clerical Assistant
- Office or Admin Assistant *
- Receptionist *
- Stock Clerk *

**Education & Training**
- Sports Instructor *
- Teacher's Aide *
- Tutor
- Camp Counselor *

**Finance**
- Insurance Broker Assistant *
- Bank Teller *
- Insurance Sales Assistant *

**Government & Public Administration**
- Local, State, or Federal Services Office Assistant *

**Health Science**
- Veterinary Technician Assistant *
- Medical Records File Clerk *
- Medical Office Assistant *
- Pharmacy Aide
- Dental Office Assistant *

**Hospitality and Tourism**
- Baggage Porter or Bellhop
- Building Cleaning Worker *
- Hotel, Motel, or Resort Desk Clerk *
- Amusement Park & Recreation Attendant & Cashier *
- Youth Sports League Referee
- Movie Theatre/Sports Arena Usher, Lobby Attendant, Ticket Taker
- Bakery Worker
- Barista *
- Cook *
- Counter Attendant – Cafeteria, Food Concession, Coffee Shop*
- Dishwasher or Busser*
- Waiter or Waitress *
- Host or Hostess – Restaurant, Lounge, Coffee Shop *
- Golf Caddy or Maintenance Worker
- Grocery Bagger *

**Human Services**
- Childcare Worker *
- Hair Salon Assistant *
- Nail Salon Assistant *
- Barber Shop Assistant *

**Information Technology**
- Web Developer
- Computer Repairperson

**Law, Public Safety, Corrections & Security**
- Law Office Assistant *
- Lifeguard *
- Security Guard

**Manufacturing**
- Small Equipment Repair Person *

**Marketing**
- Cashier *
- Retail Salesperson *
- Telemarketer

**Transportation, Distribution, Logistics**
- Automotive Body Detailer *
- Automotive Service Mechanic *
- Cleaners of Vehicles & Equipment *
- Parking Lot Attendant
- Laborers & Freight, Stock, and Material Movers (manual)*
- Food Delivery Person

67

Once you complete your list, you have to make sure there are no legal restrictions that apply to you based on your age. If you're 18 or older, the law allows you to work at any job, even those that are deemed hazardous, with no limits on the number of hours you can work. But if you're still a minor, it's important to know the legal restrictions and how they apply to you.

## WORKING TEENS AND THE LAW

The Secretary of Labor and the Fair Labor Standards Act (FLSA) establish the following basic guidelines for teen workers.

- The minimum working age is 14 for non-agricultural jobs.
- Minors are prohibited to work in hazardous occupations.
- There are no hours of work limitations for 16 and 17-year-olds at the federal level. However, some states have restrictions.
- Workers ages 14 and 15 have significant job restrictions as well as hours of work restrictions.

I'll discuss the general guidelines here, but details can be found on Youth-Rules! at www.youthrules.gov. It's an excellent resource sponsored by the Wage and Hour Division of the U.S. Department of Labor.

**Minors under the age of 18 may not work in hazardous occupations.**

All workers by law are entitled to work in a safe and healthy environment. The Occupational Safety and Hazard Administration (OSHA) is the federal agency responsible for ensuring that employers adhere to strict safety standards. However, if you're under the age of 18, the safety standards for you are higher. Federal child labor laws require that you may not work in an occupation that's deemed hazardous which, in general, involves working above or below the ground, the handling of dangerous material, and the operation of power-driven equipment. Because of the popularity of teen jobs in the food industry, it's important to note that deli meat slicers, bakery mixers, and automobiles used for deliveries are off limits. There are 17 hazardous occupations that minor workers must avoid. See www.youthrules.gov for a complete list and explanation of each.

**Hours of work are limited for 16 and 17-year-olds.**

68

While federal law does not limit hours of work, many states have number of hours, time of day, and number of *days per week* restrictions, depending on whether school is in session or not. The Wage and Hour Division of the U.S. Department of Labor provides a state-by-state synopsis of these limitations at www.dol.gov; search "State child labor laws".

### Jobs duties are limited for workers 14 and 15 years-of-age.

In general, this age group can work in the following locations and jobs:
- Offices
- Grocery and retail stores
- Restaurants
- Movie theaters, amusement parks, and sports arenas
- Gasoline service stations – limited to dispensing gasoline or oil and washing or hand polishing
- Landscaping - limited to clean-up and yard work which does not include using power-driven mowers, cutters, trimmers, edgers, or similar equipment
- Intellectual or creative work such as computer programming, teaching, tutoring, singing, acting, or playing an instrument.
- Errands or delivery work by foot, bicycle or public transportation
- Lifeguard duties at traditional swimming pools and water amusement parks (15-year-olds only)

### Hours of work are limited for 14 and 15-year-olds.

The FLSA places strict limits on this, as do child labor laws in most states. In situations where both state and federal laws apply, employers must meet the higher minimum standard. In other words, the stricter law must apply. FLSA states that 14 and 15-year-olds may work:
- Outside school hours (unless student is enrolled in an approved Work Experience or Career Exploration program)
- After 7 a.m. and until 7 p.m. (hours are extended to 9 p.m. June 1 through Labor Day)
- Up to 3 hours on a school day
- Up to 18 hours in a school week
- Up to 8 hours on a non-school day

69

- Up to 40 hours in a non-school week

## What children age 13 and under can do.

In general, this age group can perform the following job duties.
- Babysit on a casual basis
- Deliver newspapers
- Work as an actor or performer in movies, TV, radio, or theater
- Work for a business owned entirely by their parents as long as it isn't in mining, manufacturing, or any of the 17 hazardous occupations.

## IF YOU'RE 14 OR 15 AND "NO ONE WILL HIRE" YOU

My 14 and 15-year-old high school job seekers as well as their parents are often frustrated because "no one will hire" them during the school year. To understand why, you have to look from the employer's point of view. Employers are bound by state and federal Child Labor Laws that are in place to protect your health, well-being, and your educational opportunities. This means that your job should not interfere with your responsibilities as a student.

## School comes first.

That's why you may not work past 7:00 p.m. on a school night. Limitations like this aren't just restrictive for you, but they can be inconvenient for employers. For example, if you can only work 3 hours during a 5-hour shift, the employer now has a scheduling issue. What are they going to do, bring in another worker for the remaining 2 hours? Here's how one business owner explained it to me.

> We'd like to hire more 14 and 15-year-olds but it's very hard if we can't schedule them past 7:00 p.m.—we close at 10. So they get to leave while everyone else has to stay and do all the clean-up duties before closing. This causes hard feelings among the staff and that's a situation we try to avoid.
>
> Glenn Wagner
> Franchise Owner, Rita's Water Ice

Employers have a second concern about hiring 14 and 15-year-olds.

## Are you mature enough?

It sounds condescending but it's not meant to be. It simply means that we all mature and develop socially, emotionally, and psychologically at different rates. It takes time and experience for young people to adapt to the workplace because being at work is very different than being at school. Issues that come up aren't necessarily about the job skills but those soft skills like getting along with your boss and your co-workers or taking constructive criticism. The biggest concern regarding your level of maturity? Whether you'll show up for work when you're scheduled or whether you'll call out for unexcused reasons. Lack of maturity as well as staffing related issues like the one above can cause a lot of drama in the workplace, and the one thing employers hate is drama.

If no one will hire you regardless of your age, then how do you get the experience that employers are looking for?

## GET A VOLUNTEER JOB

Companies and non-profit organizations are continuously looking to fill volunteer positions for summer camps, libraries, nursing homes, hospitals, and many more. When you volunteer, you're helping a worthy cause right in your community. It'll also make you feel good to know you're helping others.

Getting a volunteer job also has benefits for you, the most important of which is to give you an opportunity to explore a potential career. For example, health care is the fastest growing industry due mainly to our aging population. In 2016 it was projected that the employment rate in health care will increase 18%, more than double the 7.4% average for all industries. This equates to 2.4 million new healthcare jobs in that time frame. This is fantastic news for young people aspiring to enter this field. Unfortunately, if you are under the age of 18, your ability to work directly with patient care may be severely limited due to the liability that comes with hiring minors. That's why hospitals, doctors' offices, and nursing homes are hesitant to hire young workers for anything other than food service, for fear of getting sued. They will, however, offer volunteer positions that don't require direct patient care, but allows experiences in the same work environment. So while you won't be paid, you're gaining something much more valuable for your future — work experience in the career field of your choice.

If you do a good job, you'll also gain a potential reference for a resume or job application. That's why it's called volunteer *work* or a volunteering *job*. A future employer won't care whether you made $15 an hour, $5 an hour or $0 an hour. They care that you wanted to work, you had the initiative to go out and get a job, you maintained a regular work schedule, and you did a good job even without getting paid. You now have a clear advantage over other applicants that don't have that experience.

## DO AN INTERNSHIP

Internships and paid jobs are similar in that they are both great ways to gain work experience, learn the expectations of the workplace, and explore your future potential career. They're very common for college students but are becoming more popular among high school students.

They do however have some notable differences.

While a job provides you with short term training to get you up to speed, an internship is more about learning. That's why your school coordinates internship programs and gives you course credit for them. That's also why some internships may be unpaid — the employer is expending time, money, and resources to educate you without necessarily reaping the benefits of your productive services to the business.

One of the greatest benefits of college internships is that almost 60% of interns are offered a full-time job after graduation. It's a great way for both employers and interns to test out the employment situation and learn about their expectations of each other before making a full-time commitment.

Finding an internship is no different than finding a part-time job. If your school offers internships, they may help you find openings for intern positions, but you have to apply and interview for them like any other job.

### Next Up...

By now, you should be getting pretty confident about the occupations you've chosen to pursue. You're now ready to find the businesses or organizations looking to fill those open job positions. I'll give you two tips that will give you an advantage over other applicants. The first will bring your

72

application to the top of the stack; the second will get your application to the hiring manager even before the stack begins to form. Those tips and more are next.

## CHAPTER SUMMARY QUIZ

The following quiz summarizes the chapter.

1. During a recession, teens and young adults compete with who for jobs?
   a. Adult workers who have lost their full-time jobs
   b. Other teens and young adults
   c. Retirees who re-enter the workforce
   d. All of the above.

2. What types of jobs do teenagers typically find?
   a. Jobs that require a high school or college degree
   b. Jobs that don't require any formal education or training
   c. Jobs that require 3-6 months of on-the-job training
   d. Jobs in the manufacturing industry

3. Working conditions and hours for minors are covered under:
   a. Civil Rights Laws
   b. Child Labor Laws
   c. Americans with Disabilities Laws
   d. Minimum Wage Laws

4. Employers may be reluctant to hire teens under the age of 16 because:
   a. Child labor laws significantly limit their work hours.
   b. 14 and 15-year-olds lack work experience.
   c. Employers question their level of maturity.
   d. All of the above.

5. All are advantages of volunteer jobs or internships *except*:
   a. They provide you with work experiences.
   b. They may provide you with a job reference.
   c. They are always paid.
   d. They offer opportunities to explore a potential future career.

Answers: 1d, 2b, 3b, 4d, 5c

# Lesson 5

# Search for Job Openings

With your list of occupations in hand, you're now ready to look for some jobs. Notice I said, "look for some jobs" and not "look for some job ads." That's because I want you to look for jobs where they're advertised as well as where they're not advertised, for two reasons. First, the average job opening receives 250 resumes or applications. By responding to a job ad, your application will be somewhere in a large stack. Second, 75% of all job openings in the U.S. are not even advertised because employers prefer to have their current employees refer a friend or relative. The advantage you'll have over your competition is that you'll be looking for openings in places where they won't.

## ARE YOU QUALIFIED?

Being qualified means that you have the skills the job requires, or you can learn them quickly. If you're not qualified, you won't get the job. Or worse, this could happen.

> I once posted a position on my job posting board for a Writer's Assistant. A college professor was writing a book, but he had minimal computer skills and English wasn't his first language. The job ad, therefore, clearly requested applicants to have excellent writing and computer skills. He advertised a $15/hour pay rate and unfortunately hired the first student that contacted him on her word that she had the required skills. According to the professor, his new assistant had adequate computer skills but very poor English; the work she did for him was filled with typos and misspellings. Needless to say, the student didn't work out because she was not qualified for the job. The experience wasted everyone's time and I had to re-advertise the job.

If there's a required skill that you don't have, you can state that you have a similar or related skill, which implies that you can learn the required skill with minimal training. For example, if a position for an Accounting Clerk requires you to know the software application called QuickBooks, but you have experience with Quicken, the implication is that by already knowing one, you can learn the other relatively quickly. But in the example above, if you have good math skills but poor writing skills, your math skill are not going to compensate for your poor writing skills.

Being qualified isn't just limited to your skills or educational background. It also means you're able to meet the requirements of that specific job position. Watch for prerequisites of your availability (*Must be able to work weekends*), age (*Must be 18 or over*), certifications (*Must have driver's license*), or materials (*Must provide own tools*).

While a job ad won't state it explicitly, it's assumed that when you apply for a job, you've researched its location and worked out reliable transportation to get there on time. If you drive and have a car at your disposal, great. If not, can you walk to the job? Is there public transportation like a train or bus that will coincide with your work schedule? Do you have a reliable person, like mom, dad, or a grandparent who is available to transport you 100% of the time? Make sure the logistics of getting to and from work are thoroughly worked out before applying.

If you apply for jobs that you're clearly not qualified for, you too will waste everyone's time.

## NETWORKING IS YOUR BEST SHOT AT FINDING A JOB

Now let's talk about the different methods of connecting with companies to look for jobs.

You're five times more likely to be hired by a company if a current employee refers you. Many employers even offer *referral bonuses* to their employees for recommending a friend or relative who eventually gets hired. On average, 70% of new employees are hired because of someone they knew in the company. Why do employers hire this way? Say you have a friend who's doing a good job at a company you'd like to work for. Ask your friend to put in a good word about you to the hiring manager, and even ask them to pass along your resume. By referring you in this manner, the employer will assume that because of your association with an excellent worker, that you'll be an excellent worker too.

**You are who you associate with.**

There were rumors at school that the local mall was expanding, and that new stores were hiring. The idea of working at a retail store or restaurant appealed to me very much at the time, and after turning in a few applications, I found myself at the Orange Julius, a stand-alone structure in the middle of the mall. I loved the vibe immediately, with the activity of shoppers maneuvering around, the sound of the blenders, and the smell of hot dogs. I sat on a bench and filled out the applications, and when I was done, I handed it to the woman in charge. Her name was Crystal and she owned this franchise with her father, she offered without looking up from my application. Suddenly her face lit up and she looked up at me and smiled. "Are you Ro's sister?" Well, yes, I am! She and Ro, she explained, worked together at the Thom McAn shoe store, and she just loves Ro, and if I'm half as wonderful as Ro, and on and on she went. I'm being generous when I say she glanced through the rest of my application, then beamed at me as she offered me the job right there and then.

Now I'm not going to say that I got the job only because I was Ro's sister. My application showed that I was a good student, I was active in school, and I had work experience from two prior summer jobs. I was qualified for this job. But the fact that I was associated with someone who had a good reputation as an employee certainly helped. What's more, it helped Crystal by making her decision an easy one.

**I discovered the power of association when I was 16 years old.**

The fact that Ro was my brother and was an excellent employee worked out well for me. But be careful because the power of association works both ways.

**Choose your friends and acquaintances wisely.**

If your friend who's referring you isn't doing well at work, the employer will assume that you won't do well either. You may have been an excellent candidate for the job, but as unfair as it seems, you'll fall victim to *guilt by association* because of your friend's poor reputation. Remember your resume is one of 250 in a stack. The employer has no reason to take a risk on you.

Finding a job through someone you know involves networking, which simply means to interact with other people to build relationships. The people in your network can not only help you find a job now, they can also help you progress through your career.

I find that students are generally reluctant to speak to people about things like this, but before you shy away, keep this in mind.

**People love talking about themselves.**

Talk to your friends, classmates, neighbors, relatives, friends of your family, and the families of your friends.

Talk to your teachers at the end of class so they can get to know you better. I can't tell you how difficult it is to write a letter of recommendation for a student who never said a word to me privately over an 18-week semester. But those who give me the opportunity to get to know them better enable me to comment not only about their academic performance, but also their character.

The next time a guest speaker comes to a classroom, on your way out stop and introduce yourself, shake their hand, and thank them for their time. Always ask for a business card from a professional contact so that you have their name, the company they represent, and all their contact information.

If your school or community offers a career fair or a career day, take advantage of this situation where professionals representing numerous careers are all gathered in one place. Not only can the exhibitors answer your questions about careers, they can be a valuable resource for your job searching efforts right now. It's okay to ask an exhibitor if their company is hiring; many of the exhibitors that come to our annual career fair come prepared with a stack of blank job applications.

You may not realize it, but every contact you make, whether at school or church, or shopping at the grocery store for that matter, is a potential opportunity to expand your network. Every encounter you have with the people around you tells them who you are.

Are you an upbeat, positive person or are you a complainer?

Are you humble and respectful or are you demanding and entitled?

Are you honest and hardworking or do you do the minimum to get by?

77

Do you look people in the eyes when you speak to them or do you avoid making eye contact?

People will remember you if you make a positive impression on them. They'll also remember you if you don't.

> A few years ago I posted a summer internship position on my job posting board for an architectural firm. So that I could screen candidates for the company, I didn't post the company's contact information; just a note to "See Mrs. Purdy in room D206." If I felt that if the student was a suitable candidate, I would give them the company's contact information, and even call the company to introduce the student. One candidate who came to see me about the position didn't know who I was, but I certainly knew who he was. I never met him personally, but I had a good idea of the type of person he was because for years I had watched this kid sit on a bench during tennis drills while the rest of the kids picked up balls. Do you remember this story from Chapter 3? When his tennis instructor, Sal, solicited his mother's help, instead of correcting her son's bad behavior she enabled it by putting him in a different drill. Here he was now, standing in front of me, asking me to vouch for his work ethic and character to a potential employer.

How you conduct yourself in your personal life and at school is a good indication of how you'll conduct yourself at a job. It's my experience that adults will look for opportunities to help young people like you. They'll advocate for you if they believe you'll make them proud. But you have to deserve that consideration. You don't have to change who you are, but *who you are* should be presented in the most positive light at all times. You can't just pretend to be nice; you have to *be* nice. Adults know a put-on when they see one.

One more thing. Networking is powerful, but it can only get you so far towards your goals. You've heard people say that finding a job is "all about *who* you know." I disagree. It's also about *what* you know and *how* you present yourself. While a contact can help you get a lead on a job, getting it and keeping it is all up to you.

## DIRECT INQUIRIES

Contacting a business directly is another effective way to get ahead of your competition, because like networking, it enables you to learn about an open position before it's advertised. Start by contacting the businesses you know and trust—your favorite restaurants and retail stores, your doctor or dentist's office, the ballpark, the swim club, and so on. If you enjoy being a customer there, you'll probably enjoy working there too.

The next option is to go to the Yellow Pages website and search by type of business, like "restaurants," "sporting goods", or "dental." Contact the companies that interest you either in person, by phone, by letter, or by email, depending on the company contact information provided. While you may not have any indication whether an open position even exists, you'd be surprised how many hits, or responses, my students and I had using this method, where the person on the other end said, "Why don't you come in and pick up an application."

### Walk into a place of business whether they have a "Now Hiring" sign or not.

Appearing in person to inquire about a job is the best way to contact a business for several reasons. First, when you're standing in front of someone, it's much harder for them to turn you down than if you sent them an email. It establishes a personal connection and gives you an opportunity to make a good first impression. What should you say? How should you dress? What should you take with you? It's critical to plan ahead because what starts out as a walk-in to pick up an application can turn into an interview. For these reasons, Chapter 8 – The Walk-In Inquiry, is dedicated to this method.

### Make some *cold calls*.

Cold calling is a marketing term that means to call someone unexpectedly to sell them a product or service. Except in this case, what you're trying to sell is *you*. Cold calling is not as effective as appearing in person, but better than sending a letter or email.

If my Co-op students hadn't found a job within the first two weeks of school, I'd have them make cold calls right in front of me so I could coach them through it. The script I made for them is below; use it as a template to make your own. Make sure you practice first with someone and have pencil and paper handy before you call.

> **Introduce yourself:** *Hello, my name is <your first <u>and</u> last name>. May I please speak with the hiring manager?*
>     **State why you are calling:** *I'm calling to inquire if <business name> currently has any open positions for <job position>.*
>     **If hiring:** *That's great. <Explain any relevant skills or previous experience>. May I stop by to pick up an application?*
>     **If not hiring:** *May I apply or send my resume in case a position does become available?*
>     **End the call:** *Thank you for your time and the information.*

Keep the following things in mind:

- Do not eliminate your last name. Introducing yourself with only your first name is too informal and shows a lack of confidence.
- Try to find out the name of the hiring manager before you make the call. It shows that you cared enough to do some research. Otherwise, just say "the hiring manager."
- If you do talk to the hiring manager, get their first and last name so you know who to contact in the future.
- Use the name of the business. It shows that you want to work there specifically, and not just anywhere. Definitely don't say, "I'm calling to see if you guys are hiring." It's too informal and unprofessional.
- If you don't get a manager initially, ask if there's a better time to call back. Try not to leave a message for them to call you. More than likely, you'll never get that call.

No two calls will go exactly the same way, but the script will get the conversation started.

### Send a letter of inquiry via snail mail or email.

If a business isn't open to the public and there's no phone number to call, your last option is to send a letter of inquiry. It's identical to a cover letter that you'll send with a resume, with one main difference. A cover letter references a known open position:

> *I learned of the open position for a part-time Office Assistant at your insurance firm through my high school's online job posting board. I would like to apply for the position.*

80

A letter of inquiry, on the other hand, asks whether an open position exists for which you may be qualified:

*While I am unaware of any open positions at your insurance firm, I am writing to inquire whether you are seeking a part-time Office Assistant.*

If you know the email address of the hiring manager, you may send an email instead. Review the sample cover letter and email in Chapter 7 – Create Your Resume and Cover Letter and adapt it as I've specified above.

The advantage of sending a letter or email is that it demonstrated your initiative of researching the company and making contact. It also allows you to send your resume, either on paper or as an email attachment. The disadvantage is that it's not very effective; you have about a three percent chance of getting a callback. Sending an unsolicited mailing like this, called direct mail, is not much different than sending customers a flyer or a coupon in the mail. And you know where most of *that* mail goes. So why should you bother with this method? Because it may be your only option if going in person or calling isn't possible. If you don't do it, your chance of getting a response goes down to zero percent. Three percent is greater than zero percent.

## LOOK FOR JOB ADS

Local businesses still post job openings in local newspapers, so don't discount them. However, savvy companies who want to fill job positions quickly will use faster and more efficient methods.

### Online job sites

There are dozens of job sites like LinkedIn, Monster, Indeed, Glassdoor, and ZipRecruiter. They have powerful filtering capabilities so that you can narrow down your search to just about anything—job title, location, industry, skills, educational requirements, part-time versus full-time, etc. There are some that serve a niche market like yours. Snag specializes in part-time, hourly workers. CoolWorks focusses on summer and seasonal jobs. Idealist specializes in jobs as well as internships and volunteer jobs for non-profit organizations. While College Recruiter specializes in entry-level positions for recent college grads, it also advertises internship positions for college students. Some job sites are even industry specific. For example, Dice specializes in technology jobs, ECO Jobs specializes in environmental jobs, etc.

You'll also see postings placed directly by the hiring company. Regardless of where the job ad appears, go to the hiring company's website and look for other job openings on their *Career* page. In the next chapter, you'll learn how to engage with the company through their social media sites.

## School job posting boards

Employers know to call high schools in their local area when they are looking for teens to hire. My job posting board is on my school district's website, which means it's open to the whole community. Your school may have jobs posted online or even on paper on an actual bulletin board. Check your Career Services or Guidance Counseling office.

## EMPLOYER REVIEWS

Before you apply for a position, check out the employer so that you know whether it's a good company to work for. The most reliable way to review a company is by asking someone in your network who has direct knowledge of the company. You can also see company reviews directly on job sites like GlassDoor, Great Place to Work, Comparably, or CareerBliss. They provide all kinds of information on things like compensation, employee reviews, diversity, work environment, and much more. Some can even give you details down to the department level.

I learned to do company reviews the hard way.

> Do you remember my Co-op student, Andie, whose job at a veterinary hospital didn't work out? Here's why.
>
> Andie had been working as a Kennel Assistant for almost three weeks when she expressed concerns to me that she hadn't gotten paid. Her supervisor had assured her that while the payroll system was slow, her paycheck would ultimately come.
>
> So when the time came for me to make my visits to all my students' employers, I made my first visit to the vet hospital—or so I tried. All my attempts to schedule an appointment failed; despite promises that Andie's supervisor would call me back, I couldn't even get past the receptionist. After a few days of getting the runaround, I left my fifth and final message stating

SEARCH FOR JOB OPENINGS

that if I didn't receive a call from the supervisor by the end of the day, Andie would not be returning to work. Well, not too surprisingly, the owner of the hospital returned my call within the hour, and after scheduling an appointment with her for the next day, I asked about Andie's pay.

In an annoyed tone of voice, she responded, "I started this business to help animals and I expect my employees to do the same." She went on to tell me that she expected her employees to work on a "voluntary basis," and that if Andie had a problem with that, she should have never taken the job. Surprised by this, I asked, "If that were true, why was Andie assured by her own supervisor that while the payroll system was slow, she would ultimately receive her paycheck." She stood by her claim that Andie knew the job was unpaid, and I explained to her that Andie would not be returning to work.

After verifying with Andie that she had, in fact, been told during her interview that she'd be making the minimum wage, I had real doubts about the legitimacy of this business. I turned to my computer and entered the company name into the search bar and couldn't believe what I saw: page after page of employee complaints about not being paid and accusations of the business owner being a scam artist.

Not even a month went by before I noticed the empty parking lot and the vacant building that used to be the veterinary hospital where Andie worked.

You should conduct employer reviews regardless of whether it's a well-known company or not. You may not discover a scam like I did, but you'll certainly find out if it's the kind of place you'd like to work or avoid. At a minimum, you might see things—good or bad—that you may want to discuss in an interview.

### Next up...

Of all the options of where to find job openings, which one should you use? The answer of course, is all of them. In the next chapter, I'll tell you how to maximize the connections you made using the technology you love.

## CHAPTER SUMMARY QUIZ

The following quiz summarizes the chapter.

1. What is the most effective method of finding a job?
   a. Tell those in your network that you're looking for a job.
   b. Check your school's job posting board.
   c. Search job sites on the internet.
   d. Make cold calls.

2. Which of the following best indicates that you're qualified for a job?
   a. You have a connection in the company.
   b. You have a college education.
   c. You have the relevant education, skills, and qualifications.
   d. You have a high school diploma.

3. Which website will provide information on companies in your area, by the type of business they're in?
   a. Your state's Labor Department
   b. Your local public high school
   c. Google Docs
   d. The Yellow Pages

4. Why is conducting employer reviews a good idea?
   a. To confirm whether it's a good company to work for
   b. To know which companies to avoid
   c. To give you information to use during an interview
   d. All of the above

5. Do not apply for a job if you have no way of getting there.
   a. True
   b. False

Answers: 1a, 2c, 3d, 4d, 5a

# Lesson 6

# Let the Technology You Love Work for You, Not Against You

Personal devices like smartphones and tablets have really expanded our ability to communicate. We can reach anyone, anywhere, at any time. While technology has encouraged us to communicate quickly, it hasn't necessarily encouraged us to communicate well. The fast and easy interactions it's created can often enable bad writing habits and diminish the quality with which we communicate. While this is harmless when you're speaking to your friends and family, it's not appropriate in many situations. Your speaking and writing skills have to be professional for you to be taken seriously in the business world.

In addition, just as important as *how* you communicate is *what* you communicate. Your online presence must be just as professional as your resume, because hiring managers will closely examine both. Unprofessional or inappropriate online content could end your chances of getting a job before they even begin.

While technology, if used inappropriately, can cause you problems, it can also drastically improve your ability to sell yourself in the job market. Social media can be used to connect with your network as well as the businesses you want to pursue for a job.

## IT'S CALLED A CELL PHONE FOR A REASON

We use the term cell phone, but we know it's much more than that—it's really a pocket computer with all the tools that keep us organized and connected with the world. It's a smartphone, and the feature that you probably use the least is the one that it originated with—a phone.

Now that you're leaving your cell phone number to potential employers, understand that most businesses won't text you, they'll call. If you don't pick up, they'll leave a voice mail message. So before we go any further, I want you to pick up another phone right now, call your cell, and listen to the message your callers are hearing.

> I always called my Co-op students—I never texted—to get them into the habit of speaking on the phone for business. I'll never forget the voice mail greeting I heard from my student, Teresa, when I called to give her a job lead. It was an excerpt from the rap song, *Stupid Hoe* by Nicki Minaj. It started out like this:
>> I get it cracking like a bad back
>> Bitch talkin she the queen when she looking like a lab rat
>> I'm Angelina, you Jennifer come on bitch you see where Brad at?
>
> It went on like this for about 30 seconds, and then in a sleepy voice, "Leave a message."

I have to laugh when I think about that crazy message, but it wasn't funny at the time. Not only was it inappropriate, it was also incredibly annoying to be forced to listen to a nonsensical greeting for 30 seconds just so I could leave a 10 second message.

If you're still in high school, employers will understand that you're still in transition from being a teenager with limited work experience to a young adult looking for more responsibility. For making a poor decision like this, you may get some slack. But if you're in college, you're older and have more life experience, and so better judgement will be expected of you.

Regarding Teresa and her voice mail message, no one was trying to strip her of her personality or individuality. But who you are is not defined by the greeting on your cell phone. You will, however, be judged for it. Don't let something like a silly voice mail greeting prevent you from being taken seriously.

Here are some tips for making and receiving phone calls.

- Make sure your voice mail greeting is short, simple and professional: "Hi it's Teresa. Please leave your name, number, and a message and I'll return your call as soon as I can." That's a five-second greeting.
- Cell phone etiquette dictates that you respond to a message in the same manner in which you received it. That means if you receive a text, it's okay to text back. But if you receive a phone call, that means that the caller wants to talk and not text. You not only need to call

back, but an unwritten rule in business says you should return that phone call within 24 hours.

- Move your voice mail app to your main home screen so that even if you miss a call and the notification, you'll see how many messages are waiting for you.

Finally, here's an obvious piece of advice but one that gets overlooked. Whenever you're interacting with a business, whether it's to pick up or drop off your application, or certainly during an interview, put your phone on silent or turn it off completely, and put it away. Don't let an incoming call or text interrupt you while talking to a potential employer.

## USE YOUR COMPUTER

When you're communicating for business via email, always use your computer and not your phone for several reasons. First, using your thumbs can result in too many errors. And second, email editors on your cell phone are very basic and don't allow for proper formatting. Even the email editor on your computer isn't as robust as a word processing app like Microsoft Word or Google Docs. Line spacing, tabbing, bullet and numbered list formatting are not properly supported. For this reason, type up your correspondence in Word or Docs first, do a thorough spelling and grammar check, and then copy and paste it into the email. If you absolutely have to use your phone, remove any digital signatures like "This message was sent from my iPhone." Otherwise, an employer will think you didn't care enough to take the time to get on a computer.

## KEEP TEXT LANGUAGE CONFINED TO TEXTS

Some students think that unless they're writing a paper for English class, anything goes. It doesn't. While writing for business should be formal, it should also be concise and to the point. But don't confuse *concise and to the point* with the text language. While it's perfectly acceptable to use *omg* or *lol* for casual writing, keep business writing to standard English. Be especially careful of using *u* instead of *you* – I see that creep into my students' writing from time to time.

## BE A FOLLOWER

Roughly 80% of employers use social media to promote their brand, so you should follow the companies you're interested in applying to. If you see something you like or can make a personal connection with, leave an occasional comment. Maybe they're involved in a charity or community outreach program. Maybe they're introducing a new product or service. Responding to their posts in a meaningful, well thought out way will show that you have a genuine interest in their company. But make the comments all about them, not you; this is not the platform to sell yourself, ask if they're hiring, follow up on your application, or request an interview. As always, write professionally and in standard English, even though it's social media.

## YOU MAY ACTUALLY NEED *MORE* SOCIAL MEDIA

Facebook is no longer the most popular social media site for teens, but I probably don't need to tell you that. It is, however, the number one social media marketing site for businesses in the world, with over 200 million users, 60 million of which are businesses. Instagram is number two, with over 150 million users.

As *Figure 6* from the Pew Research Center shows, while more than 70% of teens use Instagram, only about half use Facebook. For users 18-29, Instagram usage falls slightly to 67%, but Factbook usage jumps considerably to 79%. When you're ready to follow the companies you're interested in and the hiring managers you may meet, you may want to have a Facebook account, an Instagram account, or both.

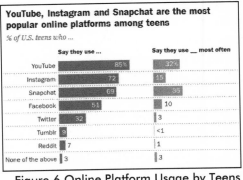

Figure 6 Online Platform Usage by Teens

Another site, LinkedIn, is a social media platform geared for professionals, and many recruiters use it to look for qualified candidates for jobs. As you can see from the chart above, it's not a platform used often by teens and only about 29% of ages 18 to 29-year-olds are users. While it hasn't quite caught on with high schoolers, college professors are making a big push to convince their students to start connecting with their contacts on LinkedIn. As you expand your professional network, having a LinkedIn account will become more and more important for you. The minimum age you can join is fourteen.

You probably already know 100-200 friends, family members, family friends, or acquaintances that you may want to connect with on LinkedIn. If each one of them has 100-200 professional contacts of their own, imagine how large your network could be in a very short period of time. Make sure your LinkedIn profile picture is a high-quality headshot of you wearing something presentable and update your site often with your latest skills and accomplishments.

Don't be too generous with your personal information on any of your profiles. Don't provide your cell phone number unless it's just for the site's security. No one should need your mailing address, and definitely do not provide your date of birth. Recruiters don't need to see how old you are, and identity thieves would love to open up a credit card in your name and go shopping. If receiving birthday wishes is important to you, only include your birth month and day but exclude the year.

## PREP YOUR SOCIAL MEDIA ACCOUNTS

Just as you'll be checking out the companies you're interested in, they'll be checking you out too. Employers and recruiters want to look at your social media content to do background checks, explore your area of expertise, and review your online reputation. What's more, you want to let them, because having a positive social media presence allows the people in your network to look deeper into who you are professionally.

Most employers will look for you on social media before bringing you in for an interview. Almost all will check before extending you a job offer. Be warned that 70% of employers say they've turned down candidates because of something negative they found online. Top reasons for disqualifying you as a candidate? Pictures or posts of you drinking or partying, especially if you're underaged. Foul language or just plain poor English. Cyber bullying or making discriminatory comments. And the craziest one of all? Bad-mouthing employers, teachers, coaches, or anyone in positions of authority.

> I recently got a call from a recruiter asking me for information about one of my favorite students, Maggie, who had recently graduated from college and looking for her first full-time career job. As soon as she said her name, I responded, "Absolutely...

yes... she's a ten out of ten." I went on to describe my experiences with her in three of my classes, detailing examples of her maturity, work ethic and her playful personality that always made me look forward to her walking into my classroom every day.

Maggie is also one of two former students that I've broken my *Absolutely Positively No Friending Former Students On My Facebook* policy. About a year after she graduated from high school, she posted a beautiful message to me, thanking me for being one of her favorite high school teachers. I was so touched by this gesture, and since it was a moment I'll never forget, I relayed this story to the recruiter with a promise that I would find that post and share it with her as soon as possible.

That very same day, I went to Maggie's Facebook account and did a search on "purdy." I found the post I was looking for, and another one I wish I hadn't. The post I accidentally found was apparently the result of her having received her class schedule while still in high school.

Maggie: "How about purdy, room D206 at West?"

Mike C: "No...no...no! Drop that class she's a bitch!"

Maggie: "Oh great, I always have the worst luck with teachers."

Now let me say that this post was made before Maggie and I met. I'm very happy, as I'm sure she is as well, that she didn't drop my class. The impact she has made on my life is as special as her description of the impact I made on hers. And regarding Mike C.? In my almost 20 years of teaching he was the only student whose behavior was so outrageous that I had to remove him from the classroom on the first day of the semester, before I could even finish reviewing the course outline.

A very important lesson should be clear from this example.

**Choose your online friends carefully.**

While Maggie wasn't the one who used the profanity, she was having a conversation with someone who did, which reflects poorly on her. Remember that you are who you associate with. A potential employer will rightfully assume that if you can participate in a discussion that disparages a teacher, you can do the same to your employer.

And finally, social media can be a useful tool for anything from expressing yourself to getting recommendations on products, classes, entertainment, and so on. However, be very careful when you initiate a post because you have no control over where the conversation will go.

### Block the friends from your social media accounts that could hurt you.

Everyone knows someone who says and does outrageous things on social media. They swear. They post inappropriate pictures of themselves, or worse, inappropriate pictures of you. They rant about politics, share inappropriate relationship information, or complain about employers or teachers.

> Knowing that Maggie was in the middle of a job search, I messaged her immediately and suggested she remove this, and any other compromising post, from her account. The post was gone within the next two minutes and she assured me that Mike C., who she hadn't spoken to since high school, was blocked from all her social media accounts.

### Google yourself.

Do an online search on your name and examine every result that pops up. Here's a cautionary story from a professional recruiter — don't let this happen to you.

> I've been working with a young man for weeks to try and place him in an open position at a construction company. He had already gone through a lengthy interview process and had impressed the interviewers with his qualifications, the manner in which he communicated, and the maturity with which he handled himself. The day before he was to get the job offer, I got an email from the employer. They did an internet search on the young man and discovered a series of YouTube videos of his stand-up comedy act he made during college. The videos were

> laced with political rantings and profanity. The email simply stated, "Take a look at this YouTube video. We are no longer interested."

In addition to doing a Google search on yourself, you can also set a Google alert at www.google.com/alerts. This will send you a notification if someone has done a Google search on your name.

### Scrub, deactivate, or delete your social media accounts.

Before you make any contact with an employer, look through every part of every social media account you own and examine it through the eyes of an employer. Just because you don't recall posting anything inappropriate doesn't mean it's not there. Especially if you're in college or beyond as Maggie was, you may have had your accounts for so long that you've forgotten what they contain from the past. Delete every post, picture, video, or *like* that's inappropriate or even questionable. If an account has too much inappropriate content to scrub, you may want to deactivate to hide it or delete it entirely. You can then create a new account and re-friend or re-follow individuals you feel comfortable associating with.

I know individuals who attempt to maintain two separate accounts on the same social media site, such as one private Facebook account for personal use, and one public Facebook account for professional. You can do this, but I don't recommend it for several reasons. First, it's very easy to mix up the two accounts where personal content ends up on your public professional account. The second reason is much more important.

### Making an account private will not guarantee your privacy.

> There were only a few minutes left before the end of the class and a group of my students were huddled together, talking in hushed tones. One of the girls came over to me, handed me her phone, and said, "Read that." Very few things at school shock me anymore; this was one of them. It was a social media post written by a student I knew well, and it described an incident where the writer of the post had bullied another student, who I

also knew, in a locker room. The post was riddled with profanity with multiple F-bombs. She even called herself the C-word for what she did, all while rejoicing in her own cruelty. There was a steady stream of replies from her "friends" congratulating her for what she did and encouraging her to continue.

According to my student, this was a post on a "private" Finsta account, but the post didn't stay private for long, as the screenshot I was looking at circulated throughout the school. As a result, school administrators got involved to take disciplinary action against the writer of the post, and counselors got involved to console the subject of the post.

The name Finsta is a combination of the words *fake* and *Insta(gram)*. It's a second, hidden account and unlike their real (*Rinsta*) account, is meant to be privately shared among small groups of followers. It took less than a day for this post to go from private to public. How private and hidden is that?

The bottom line is, don't allow anything inappropriate to appear anywhere whether you have public accounts, private accounts, or both.

It's hard to fathom that technology won't play a useful role in your job search efforts. Technology is wonderful, except when it isn't. Don't let the misuse of technology come between you and the job you want. I've always loved the following quote that's often used by Judge Marilyn Milian of the People's Court when litigants present social media posts or texts as evidence of their opponent's wrongdoing:

**"Say it, forget it. Write it, regret it."**

Please live by this philosophy. Every time you go to write, text, email, or upload something questionable, imagine that the person you respect the most in your life is watching you. If you'd do it with them watching, then go for it. If not, then you know that what you're about to do is something you may regret in the future. If your social media contains anything that you might later regret, take it down.

## CHAPTER SUMMARY QUIZ

The following quiz summarizes the chapter.

1.  Which of the following is the only social media account aimed at building professional networks?
    a.  Facebook
    b.  Twitter
    c.  LinkedIn
    d.  Instagram

2.  Never follow the companies you're interested in working for on social media. They will consider it stalking.
    a.  True
    b.  False

3.  Which of the follow is true about your social media accounts?
    a.  You should have a professional account like LinkedIn, Facebook, or Instagram so that you can connect with other professionals.
    b.  You should cross your fingers that you have no inappropriate content, and then make them all public so that others can follow you.
    c.  You should change their setting to private to guarantee that only your friends and followers can see your content.
    d.  You should delete them all and never use social media again.

4.  How do you make sure that your social media accounts are free of any inappropriate content?
    a.  Do an online search on your name and examine every result.
    b.  Review every post, picture, video and "like" for inappropriate content.
    c.  Remove any content that would be considered inappropriate or even questionable.
    d.  All of the above.

5.  If you have friends or followers on social media who post inappropriate comments or pictures, what should you do?
    a.  Block them.
    b.  Ask them to clean up their act going forward.
    c.  Follow them on all your social media accounts
    d.  Use them as references in your job search

Answers: 1c, 2b, 3a, 4d, 5a

94

# Lesson 7

# Create Your Resume and Cover Letter

"How can I write a resume if I've never had a job."

The answer starts with the understanding that the purpose of a resume is not to list all of your skills and past jobs. It's to convince an employer that you have what it takes to bring *value* to the company. It answers the question, "Why should I hire you?" So whether you have previous job skills or not, what you do have are all those marketable skills you identified in Chapter 2, as well as those intangible soft skills like work ethic, reliability, and professionalism. Trust me, you have more experience than you think you do, if not from a job, then from school, home and your community. Your resume has to communicate all of it.

> I hire college students who are studying music, or college graduates with a degree in music to give beginner music lessons. I don't use applications—I ask for a resume to see what they'll come up with. This one young man, I think he was a junior or senior in college, was so excited about the job that he personally came in to drop off his resume. It was in a nice, sealed envelope labeled, "Resume for Guitar Teacher," and his name. But when I opened the envelope, I pulled out four pages of lined manuscript paper on which he'd hand-written various concepts like key signatures, scales, and guitar chord diagrams. The knowledge he demonstrated was very basic; there's so much more to teaching theory than this. And it was all material that can be copied from a book. There was no mention of his experience, education, or length of time he'd been playing. Needless to say, he was not invited to interview.
>
> Barbara Carlin
> Owner, R&M Music Studios

I'll teach you how to create a resume that will make *all* of your relevant experiences and skills stand out to clearly communicate the value you bring.

## A RESUME VERSUS A JOB APPLICATION

"Why do I need a resume if I'll be filling out job applications?" is a question I get from students. There are three good reasons. First, as in the story above, some companies are just too small to have an application process and they'll ask for a resume instead. Second, the company applications you'll fill out have very general information that employers want to know about everyone who applies, whereas a resume will have the information *you* want to convey. For example, if you have absolutely no work experience, parts of your application will look very bare. But with a resume you can convey your skills and accomplishments with experiences you've had at school, your community, and even with your friends and family. You can't do that with an application. Finally, when you ask a contact in your network to put in a good word for you, hand them your resume to submit to their hiring manager. When you send those inquiry letters asking about job openings, you need to attach your resume. If you're completing an application online, it will always give you the option to attach a resume. And here's a great tip: when a contact agrees to be a good reference for you, send them your resume as a reminder of who you are and what you did for the organization.

## MAKE A GOOD FIRST IMPRESSION

Your resume has one shot at making a first impression, and an employer will make it within the first seven seconds. If they see poor formatting, typos, or spelling and grammar errors, they'll assume the quality of your work will be similar to the quality of your resume, and it'll go into the *no* pile. Let's look at my student Kimberly's resume in *Figure 7* below and see what immediately stands out.

- The structure adheres to common standards. Don't get creative with the location of all the information. Managers are busy people and seeing the structure they're familiar with allows them to easily find the information that's most relevant to them. For example, it's clear that Kimberly has prior work experience, but the fact that she listed her education first tells us that the majority of her achievements and skills come from being a student.

96

---

**Kimberly G. Nicklecut**
10 Main Street
Tullytown, PA 19055
215-555-8917 / knicklecut27@serviceprovider.com

Motivated honor roll student with previous work experience and proven organization and multi-tasking abilities. Strong business background and proficient in office productivity tools.

**Education:**
High School Diploma, Pacific High School, Fairless Hills, PA. Will graduate June 2021.
- **GPA:** 3.5/4.0
- **Business Courses:** Investment Management, Introduction to Business, Keyboarding and Word Processing, Microsoft Office Applications
- **Honors:**
  - Honor Roll, 2019
  - Student of the Quarter: English, 2019
- **Clubs:** Yearbook – Writer, 2018-19

**Skills and Accomplishments:**
- Type 50 words per minute with 100% accuracy
- Completed numerous class projects in Word, Excel, PowerPoint, Publisher, and Access

**Work Experience:**
September 2018 – Present: ABC Bookstore, Langhorne, PA
Bookseller
- Sell products and memberships; exceeded membership registration goal by 4.2%
- Provide excellent customer service by assisting customers in finding products and making book recommendations
- Work computerized cash register, answer phone inquiries, run special events and author visits
- Shelve and organize books, conduct zone maintenance, arrange and manage displays

August 2017 – Present: Meadowbrook Nursing Home, Newtown, PA
Volunteer
- Assisted residents in writing letters and emails
- Engage residents during special events by baking cookies, doing arts and crafts, and giving manicures

May 2016 – Present: Various families
Babysitter
- Cared for multiple children ages 9 months to 10 years
- Duties included preparing meals, bathing, playing, and putting to bed

**Other Activities and Qualifications:**
- JV Tennis Team: First Doubles, 2017-2019
- American Red Cross Blood Donor, 2018-2019
- American Red Cross certified in babysitting, 2015
- American Red Cross certified in CPR, 2015

**Figure 7 Resume with Previous Work Experience**

- The formatting makes it easy to read. There's plenty of white space on the page by using indenting, bullet points, double spacing between sections, and a one-inch margin on all sides. Never use full sentences or paragraphs; they take too long to read and make the resume look cluttered. Use brief phrases instead and notice that you don't need periods at the end.

- It's only one page long. Later in your career when you've had lots of relevant professional experience, you can go to two pages.

- The document does not contain any text language, slang, or company jargon—words only an exclusive group of people would understand. The word EOP appears on my students' resumes regularly: "Led staff meetings during EOPs." Only people familiar with our high school would understand that EOP stands for Extra Opportunity Period. We use the term so often that we forget that it's not a word in the English language. Jargon is okay to use if others in your industry will understand it. For example, if you're in the technology field, there's no need to spell out Random Access Memory; everyone will know what RAM is.

- There are no spelling or grammar mistakes, and no typos of any kind. Use your word processor's spelling and grammar check, but because a computer won't find formatting or logical errors (i.e., Mr. instead of Mrs.), have a trusted adult proofread it.

- The font style used is simple and easy to read. If you like serif fonts, those that have the little hairs on the end, try Bookman Old Style, Garamond, or my favorite, Georgia. If on the other hand you like San Serif fonts, those without the little hairs, use Century Gothic, Lucida Sans, or Verdana. These styles are simple but not boring. What's boring is Calibri or Arial, the default fonts for Microsoft Word and Google Docs, respectively. There are literally thousands of interesting fonts and a savvy reader will appreciate your effort to go find one. Above all, don't use Comic Sans—it's not serious enough for business. As the name signifies, it was created for comic books.

- Important text is emphasized using bold, italics, and underlining. However, they are used sparingly. If you emphasize too much, then nothing gets emphasized. Be careful that what you underline can't be mistaken for a hyperlink.

- The font size and color make the text readable. Use a black, 12-point font that's consistent throughout, and never go below 10 points. It's okay if autocorrect underlines hyperlinks such as email addresses and websites and turns them blue.

Now that you've glanced at Kimberly's resume, let me tell you who she is so you can understand the thought process that went into constructing it.

Kimberly was a high school junior who wanted to leave her current Co-op job in retail because of the late-night hours she was required to work on school nights.  The job, coupled with the demands of her junior year, were preventing her from giving school the priority it needed that year. Because she was proficient in computer applications and was considering business as a college major, I helped her find a job as an Office Assistant at an Insurance Brokerage firm. As an extra bonus, she went from making $8.50 to $10.00 an hour with the new job. These were all good reasons to find a new job, and this resume helped her get it.

## BUILD YOUR RESUME

Every section on a resume has a specific purpose. Let's go through Kimberly's resume section by section and discuss how they were constructed. If you follow these guidelines, they will help you construct yours.

### Contact Information

Your name and contact information need to stand out clearly so that it's easy for the employer to find immediately.

- Set the top margin to .5 inches to make room for your contact information.
- Emphasize your name by making it bigger, using a slightly different font, or making it bold.
- Addresses have a very specific format. The street address should be on one line. The city, state and zip code on another properly punctuated with commas as shown. Follow abbreviation rules as follows.
  - ☒ 10 Main St.
  - ☑ 10 Main Street
- Abbreviate the state properly with its two-digit, uppercase code.
  - ☒ Pennsylvania
  - ☑ PA
- If you put the entire address on one line:
  - ☑ 10 Main Street, Yardley, PA 19067

## Summary Statement

The *Objective* section has been replaced by this broader concept that, in a few sentences, summarize your key qualifications and how you will bring value to the company. If it's a well-written statement, it will motivate a hiring manager to keep reading.

Notice that the job title that you're applying for is not mentioned here. Actual job titles are specific to each company, i.e., Sales Associate and Sales Representative are two different job titles for essentially the same job. For this reason, you'll put the job title in the subject line of a cover letter or email.

## Education

As a student or a recent graduate, your education may be more relevant to the job than your work experience, so lead with this section until your work history becomes more relevant and extensive.

- List the degrees, diplomas or certificates you've earned. If you're still in school, state the month and year you plan to earn your degree or certificate.
- Only list your cumulative GPA if it's higher than a 3.0. If it's lower than 3.0, list your college major GPA if it's higher than 3.0.
  - ☒ Cumulative GPA: 2.8
  - ☑ Cumulative GPA: 3.5
  - ☑ Major GPA: 3.8
- Include courses that are relevant to the job you're applying for. For example, for a job in construction, list any woodworking, robotics, or applied engineering classes you've taken. If you're applying to a restaurant, list any culinary courses you've taken, and so on.
- List honors and awards to demonstrate you were recognized for your abilities and achievements. List clubs, especially if you held a leadership position.

## Skills & Accomplishments

This section can be very important for you, especially if you have limited formal work experience. Think about all the things you've learned from school, friends, family members, your community, your church, or any other connections in your life. Maybe someone at home taught you how to cook, fix a computer, or change the oil in a car. Maybe you sold merchandise at a church flea market. If you do have work experience that you'll put on your resume, don't duplicate those skills here.

Use the list of marketable skills you developed from your self-assessment and assign them to the skills category below. Be specific; for example, don't just say "Raised funds for charity." Say what you did that demonstrates that skill and quantify it if you can: "Raised $320 by running a 5k race for the Juvenile Diabetes Research Foundation."

Here are some good examples:

- Creativity skills: Created a dress entirely out of musical instrumental parts and sheet music for a recycling fashion show. Won Best in Show with a $300 prize, May 2019.
- Leadership skills: Assembled a team of 12 students to raise money for the American Red Cross walk-a-thon, Raised $560.
- Communication skills: Won second place prize of $250 for the Princeton University Poetry Contest for High School Students
- People/Social Skills: Peer mentored three transfer students to acclimate to their new school.
- Math skills: Completed my own federal and state tax returns and received a $250 refund.
- Mechanical skills: Changed and rotated the tires on my family car.
- Technical skills: Created a video game in Java called "Corn Maze" with three levels of difficulty.
- Organization skills: Organized a community trash clean-up day.
- Business skills: Developed a business plan and storefront model for a fictitious clothing store.
- Critical thinking skills: Won a debate arguing for stricter gun control laws.

Notice that none of these skills were learned on a job, but that's okay. What matters more is that you have them, not where you got them.

Next, put the skills you came up with on your resume that support your summary statement. The four skills on the sample resume all point to Kimberly's communication, organization, and computer skills, competencies that are necessary to be a good Office Assistant. Kimberly may also be able to ride a horse or groom a dog, but those skills are irrelevant for an Office Assistant and should be left off.

## Work Experience

If you have prior work experience, this is the most important section for you.

- List your jobs in reverse chronological order — most recent first.
- Include unpaid volunteering jobs, internships, and jobs like lawn mowing and babysitting.

> I recently helped a student apply for a job as a server. On her application she had written, "Hostess" as her current job title, and "Seat customers" as her duties. This undervalued her contributions because she doesn't just seat customers, she does much more. She plans the arrival of large parties with reservations, she appeases customers who are upset over a long wait, she problem-solves every time that party of nine walks in without a reservation, and she multi-tasks not only by seating guests but also by bussing tables, folding napkins, cleaning menus, and covering the take-out counter, just to name a few. Don't just think about what you did but the value you brought.

- Be specific. State what you accomplished, not just what duties you performed. For example, don't say, "Performed landscaping duties." Say, "Built a 20-foot waterfall in a newly landscaped backyard."

- Quantify your accomplishments as much as possible.
  - ☑ Exceeded membership sales goal by 4.2% in one month.
  - ☑ Installed 25-foot wood framed counter at a retail store.
  - ☑ Obtained and tested blood samples of approximately 20 dogs and cats.
- Include jobs where you were paid under the table. That means that you were paid in cash, and your employer didn't take taxes out of your pay. It's wrong to not pay your fair share of taxes, but don't eliminate a job from your resume for this reason. Again, employers are looking to see what experience you gained based on what you

did on the job, not how you got paid.

- If you were fired from a job, try not to list it. Assume every employer you list will be contacted as part of an employment background check. If it's the only job you had that's relevant to the job you're applying for, you may want to go ahead and list it, because even if you don't, it may still come up in an interview: "Were you ever fired from a job?" You may need to come up with an explanation sooner or later. I'll help you answer this question when we discuss interviews.

- If you have a history of job hopping, you may want to eliminate those from your resume. List the most relevant jobs to the position you're seeking, and the ones where you worked the longest. If the gaps between jobs are noticeable to the employer and you're still granted an interview, you'll need to address them then. I'll help you do that.

- Notice that the duties you list should start with an action verb. Past jobs should start with verbs in the past tense (i.e., shelved books). Current job duties should start with verbs in the present tense (i.e., seat customers). Use the list of power verbs in Appendix E.

  - ☒ Babysat. Again, this doesn't do justice to the job because good babysitters seldom sit. Put "Babysitter" as the title and list duties and skills like these:
  - ☑ Cared for two children ages 3 and 6.
  - ☑ Engaged them in games and activities.
  - ☑ Prepared meals when needed.
  - ☑ Read to them and put them to bed.
  - ☑ Conversed with family in Spanish and English
  - ☑ CPR Certified - American Red Cross

- If you've had two different jobs for the same employer, you should list two separate job titles and duties for that employer, especially if the change was a result of a promotion.

## Other Activities and Qualifications

Here, list any other activities, clubs, sports, etc. that are not previously listed. List any certifications you hold or education you received not listed above.

## Interests and Hobbies

This section is optional, but you should include it especially if you have no work experience. If you're not sure, check the Interests and Activities list you created during your self-assessment in Chapter 2.

- Employers may want to know what you choose to do in your down time. They will appreciate your revealing something personal about yourself so they can get to know who you are as a person.
- Try to list interests and hobbies that are relevant to the job you're seeking. Gardening, baking, or drawing shows you're creative. Participating in sports or other outdoor activities show you're energetic. Doing puzzles may show you're a good problem solver.

> On my first resume coming out of college, I put skydiving as a hobby; I was a member of the Nittany Sky Diving Club at Penn State. It was always the first thing an interviewer asked me about: "Did you really skydive?" It wasn't just a conversation starter; it was a way for me to show that I was a risk-taker—an important trait for someone going into a career in business.

## References

There's an ongoing debate about whether references should even be placed on a resume. Old school theory says *yes* but the answer today is *no*. You will, however, be asked to provide references when you fill out applications or before you are offered a job. In Chapter 9 – Application Expectations and Preparation, I'll tell you how to gather those references. For now, exclude them from your resume until they are specifically requested. Put a "Professional References" section on a separate page in your resume document and have it printed and available during interviews. See *Figure 8*.

If you're asked for your references after an interview, pat yourself on the back. This means you've made it to the end of the hiring process and are still being seriously considered for the job.

---

**Kimberly G. Nicklecut**
10 Main Street
Tullytown, PA 19055
215-555-8917 / knicklecut27@serviceprovider.com

**Professional References**

Bill McHenry
Teacher, Department of Business Education
Pacific High School
215-555-6780 ext. 20910
bmchenry@serviceprovider.edu

Joseph Minor
Customer Service Manager
ABC Book Store
215-555-2300, Ext.114
jminor@serviceprovider.com

Susan Bale
Guidance Counselor
Pacific High School
215-555-6780 ext. 20934
sbale@serviceprovider.edu

Figure 8 References on Page 2 of Resume

## COMMUNICATE YOUR SOFT SKILLS

At the beginning of the chapter I told you I'd show you how to make your soft skills stand out, and guess what… I already did. Look again at Kimberly's resume, not at the individual sections, but as a whole. It doesn't just communicate her soft skills, it screams them. Then put yourself in an employer's place. What do you think they see? If I were considering hiring Kimberly, here's what I would see:

- From my first glance, the fact that it's formatted correctly, easy to read, and free from typos tells me that Kimberly is conscientious about producing quality work. It looks like she did some research on resume-writing which indicates good problem-solving skills. She has excellent attention to detail, an important quality for an Office Assistant.

- A couple of things on the resume tell me that Kimberly is a very hard worker, and that she's self-motivated, organized, and multi-tasks effectively. First, she's doing well in school, evident by a 3.2 GPA, her honor roll status, and recognition as Student of the Quarter. Second, based on the dates on the resume, I can see that she's been working consistently since she was 13 years old, not just at one but two part-time jobs at a time. Finally, Kimberly is about more than just work and school; she participates in school sports and clubs. That's a heavy load she's carrying yet she appears to be juggling it all very effectively.

- While I don't know for sure, I'd bet that Kimberly goes to work and school regularly and shows up on time. Students with poor attendance don't succeed the way she has. And workers who are habitually late or call out often don't keep their jobs for as long as she has at the bookstore. As a result, I can tell that she's reliable.

I can't tell everything I need to know about Kimberly by her resume, but it's a good start. It's enough to bring her in for an interview so that I can find out more about her in person.

## RESUMES WITH NO WORK EXPERIENCE

While Kimberly was a real student of mine, Joshua is fictitious and created for the purpose of comparing two applicants with similar backgrounds, one with work experience and one without. Let's assume that Kimberly and Joshua are classmates, and they are both applying for the same job.

Take a look at Joshua's resume in *Figure 9* below.

While Kimberly was able to demonstrate her relevant skills from her prior jobs, Joshua on the other hand, has never had a job and will have to find those similar relevant skills and accomplishments in other areas of his life. His resume has lots of space, so his skills are broken out by skill area, making it easy for an employer to match his skills to the requirements of the job.

Based on their resumes only, Kimberly may get the job because of her prior work experience, but Joshua is certainly qualified for the position.

**Joshua R. Leafspire**
401 K Street
Levittown, PA 19054
215-555-1789 / jrleafspire19@serviceprovider.com

Motivated honor roll student with proven organization and multi-tasking abilities. Strong business background and proficient in computers and office productivity tools.

**Education:**
High School Diploma, Pacific High School, Fairless Hills, PA. Will graduate June 2021.
- **GPA:** 3.2/4.0
- **Business Courses:** Investment Management, Introduction to Business, Keyboarding and Word Processing, Microsoft Office Applications
- **Honors:**
    o Honor Roll, 2019
    o Student of the Quarter: Business, Computers & Information Technology, 2019
- **Clubs:** Future Business Leaders of America – Treasurer

**Skills and Accomplishments:**
Computer
- Type 50 words per minute with 100% accuracy
- Completed numerous class projects in Word, Excel, PowerPoint, Publisher, and Access
- Created an income and expenses spreadsheet for FBLA funds using formulas and charts
- Used Publisher to create invitations for my Sweet 16 party
- Used Access to produce mailing labels for my Sweet 16 party

Communication
- Created properly formatted letters, memos, emails, envelopes, and mailing labels for class projects
- Gave speech for FBLA elections and was elected Treasurer

Organization:
- Organized FBLA fundraiser making $1,500 for competition travel expenses
- Formed a study group of 5 people for Investment Management class
- Helped to schedule and organize volunteers and equipment for tennis team car wash fundraiser

Business:
- Placed third in a stock market game for Investment Management class
- Developed a business plan and shoebox storefront model for Introduction to Business class

**Other Activities and Qualifications:**
- JV Tennis Team: First Doubles, 2017-2019
- American Red Cross Blood Donor, 2018-2019
- American Red Cross certified in babysitting, 2015
- American Red Cross certified in CPR, 2015

**Interests and Hobbies:**
- Reading for pleasure, investing in stock market, traveling abroad

Figure 9 Resume with No Previous Work Experience

## SELLING YOURSELF VERSUS EMBELLISHING

Kimberly looked at all of her qualifications, both educational and work experience, and connected them with the requirements of the job. That's selling herself. Embellishment is something different. It's defined as "a detail, especially one that is not true, added to a statement or story to make it more interesting or entertaining." On a resume, it's taking an experience and making it out to be more than it is.

> I once posted a position for a server at a seafood restaurant. My student, Isabel, was applying for it, and I offered to review her application. I knew she had previous hostess experience, so I was surprised to see the job title "Server" at her previous job. Her response when I questioned this? "I sometimes helped servers by taking drink orders, running food to the tables, or bussing their tables." I advised her that while she should certainly list these as the duties she performed as a Hostess, she can't give herself a job title of Server. That's embellishing.

Another word for an embellishment is a lie. Don't lie on your resume.

Don't state you have a degree from high school or college when actually you didn't finish school.

Don't say you have a GPA that's higher than what it is.

Don't say you took courses or have hobbies or interests you really don't have.

If you lie on your resume, two very bad things will most likely happen to you. First, an employer will do a background check on your education and work experience and you'll get caught. Even if you've been working for the company for weeks or months or years, lying about your qualifications is grounds for firing you. No one wants a liar working for them.

Second, if you lie and say you have a skill that you really don't, what will happen when you're asked to demonstrate that skill on the job, or even in an interview? How long will it be before the employer discovers that you lied on your resume? This also is grounds for firing you.

## YOUR RESUME IS A LIVING, BREATHING DOCUMENT

Your resume will undergo major changes throughout your life because you'll change throughout your professional life. You'll have new personal experiences, more education, and new work experiences that you'll want to highlight. As you work more, other qualifications like education, interests, and hobbies will need to have less prominence on your resume. Try very hard to keep your resume to one page for as long as possible.

The most drastic changes to your resume will occur when you change careers. For example, if Kimberly goes to college and becomes a graphic designer, all of the things she has on her resume about her office job may no longer be relevant for a design firm—a job as a graphic designer requires more artistic skills than the business skills she currently possesses.

Every time you have a significant change to your resume, make a new version of it on the computer so you can keep your previous version. You will most likely email the resume to employers or upload it to an online application, so give the file a name that can easily identify you as the author: Resume of Kimberly G. Nicklecut - 2019.

## THE COVER LETTER

The cover letter, also called the letter of application, must accompany your resume even if it's not required by the employer. Think of it as a way to introduce yourself before getting into the details of your resume. While the same resume is used to apply to many different companies for a given position, the cover letter gives you a chance to direct your sales pitch to a particular individual and highlight your most relevant skills and qualifications for a particular position. For example, Kimberly's resume states that she's proficient in Excel, but it doesn't specify what she can do with Excel. So if a job position specifically states that knowledge of Excel was required or preferred, Kimberly would elaborate in the cover letter. Look at the example in *Figure 10* below to see how.

Cover letters are also a good way to explain a problem on your resume. For example, if your work experience shows a lot of job hopping, this is your first opportunity to explain that your sketchy work experiences have made you realize the importance of not taking the first job that comes along and doing a proper job search, which has led you to this company.

10 Main Street
Yardley, PA 19067
August 14, 2019


Ms. Janice Seymour, Office Manager
Cooper and Smith Insurance
27 W. Monmouth Avenue
Langhorne, PA 19047

Subject: Office Assistant Position Reference #2525

Dear Ms. Seymour:

I learned of the open position for a part-time Office Assistant at your insurance firm through my high school's online job posting board. I would like to apply for the position.

While I have not worked specifically as an Office Assistant, I have prepared for such a position through my education and prior work experience as described in my resume which is enclosed.
- I have taken numerous business and computer courses and am proficient in Microsoft Word, Excel and Access. My expertise in Excel includes the following:
  - Created professionally formatted spreadsheets with formulas and functions to compute numbers and statistics. Use advanced functions like PMT to calculate monthly mortgage payments and VLOOKUP to assign grades in a teacher's gradebook.
  - Managed large amounts of data using tables.
  - Displayed data visually by creating charts and SmartArt objects.
- I can type 50 words per minute on a 3-minute timed writing.
- I have good time management skills and can multi-task effectively. I have excelled in school, sports and work for the past four years, all at the same time.
- I have excellent communication skills. I performed extensive customer service duties and helped customers solve problems. I speak effectively with customers, co-workers, and supervisors in person and over the phone.
- I am a fast learner and always eager to learn new things.

May I have an interview to discuss the job and my qualifications in greater detail? I can be reached at 215-555-8917. I look forward to hearing from you soon.

Sincerely,

*Kimberly G. Warner*

Kimberly G. Warner
Enclosure: Resume

Figure 10 Cover Letter Printed to Accompany Resume

**Email your cover letter with your resume.**

If an employer requires you to email a resume to them, put the cover letter directly into the email. Write it first in Microsoft Word or Google Docs, and then copy and paste it directly into the email editor, as *Figure 11* below shows. That way, not only will it be professionally formatted, you'll also have a permanent record on your computer of what you wrote and who you sent the letter to. Make sure you state that the resume is *attached* to an email; state that a resume on paper is *enclosed* in the envelope.

---

jseymour@insurancecompany.com

---

Application for Office Assistant Position #2525 – Kimberley G. Nicklecut

---

Dear Ms. Seymour:

I learned of the open position for a part-time Office Assistant at your insurance firm through my high school's online job posting board. I would like to apply for the position.

While I have not worked specifically as an Office Assistant, I have prepared for such a position through my education and prior work experience as described in my resume which is attached.
- I have taken numerous business and computer courses and am proficient in Microsoft Word, Excel and Access. My expertise in Excel includes the following:
    - Created professionally formatted spreadsheets with formulas and functions to compute numbers and statistics. Use advanced functions like PMT to calculate monthly mortgage payments and VLOOKUP to assign grades in a teacher's gradebook.
    - Managed large amounts of data using tables.
    - Displayed data visually by creating charts and SmartArt objects.
- I can type 50 words per minute on a 3-minute timed writing.
- I have good time management skills and can multi-task effectively. I have excelled in school, sports and work for the past four years, all at the same time.
- I have excellent communication skills. I performed extensive customer service duties and helped customers solve problems. I speak effectively with customers, co-workers, and supervisors in person and over the phone.
- I am a fast learner and always eager to learn new things.

May I have an interview to discuss the job and my qualifications in greater detail? I can be reached at 215-555-8917. I look forward to hearing from you soon.

Sincerely,

*Kimberly G. Nicklecut*

Kimberly G. Nicklecut

---

Figure 11 Cover Letter Email

## COVER LETTER CONTENT AND FORMATTING

As is true of the resume, the cover letter should follow the industry standard guidelines for content as well as formatting.
- As you did in the resume, keep the letter to one page, and use the same font style to keep the two documents looking consistent.

111

- This paper letter is formatted as a block format, which means all the parts of the letter start at the left-hand margin. This letter also has mixed punctuation, which means that the salutation (Dear Ms. Seymour) and the Complimentary Closing (Sincerely) both end with the proper punctuation, as the example shows.

- The paper letter should have a one-inch margin on all sides. However, notice that the sender's mailing address starts about two inches down on the page instead of one inch.

- Letters have rules about line spacing. Notice that everything is single-spaced except for the double-spacing after the date and complimentary closing (Sincerely).

- Date formatting in formal business communications have rules.
    - ☒ 8/14/19
    - ☒ May 14th, 2019
    - ☑ May 14, 2019

- Include a job code or reference number identified in the job ad.

- Don't use a generic salutation like "To whom it may concern." It tells an employer that you didn't bother to find out the name and title of the hiring manager. If this was a referral, ask the contact who referred you. Or search the company's website or call the company's main number. If all else fails, say "Dear Hiring Manager."

- The salutation, "Dear Ms. Seymour:" should be formatted in this way, using a person's last name with their title as Mr., Mrs., Dr., or other. If you're not sure of a woman's title or marital status (Miss vs. Mrs.), use the generic title, Ms. Never address a recipient using their first name in a formal letter like this, even if you know the person.
    - ☒ Dear Janice:
    - ☒ Dear Janice Seymour:
    - ☒ Dear Ms. Janice Seymour:
    - ☑ Dear Ms. Seymour:

- The extra space after complimentary closing is where you will sign your name. If instead of printing the letter you're emailing it or uploading it with an online application as a separate file, "sign" your name using a script font, like French Script. I've used Lucida Handwriting in my example in blue font color to make it stand out.

- If you're printing the letter, sign your name legibly. My students love to draw a scribble for their signature like they often see adults do, like this: ⬛〰️ It's cool, right? If you put a scribble for your signature, you're telling the reader that they should know that it's you from your "mark." They will not think it's cool; they'll think you're being naive.

- Whether you're signing your name using the computer or a pen, use black or dark blue color only. Other colors or gel pens do not copy well on a black-and-white copier or printer.

- Because you're sending another document with this letter — a resume in this case — somewhere in the letter you must state that your resume is enclosed. This is done in the second paragraph when referring to your qualifications for the job.

## COVER LETTER BODY

The body of the cover letter should have three distinct paragraphs.

<u>Paragraph 1:</u> In the first paragraph, tell the reader why you are writing. Come right out and say that you are applying for the position. If you have a personal connection with the company — "I spoke with you briefly at my school's Career Fair last April" — mention it here. Lastly, explain how you learned of the position. If someone recommended you, state that as well but only if you believe that person is highly regarded in the company. Remember that you are who you associate with.

<u>Paragraph 2:</u> This paragraph is your sales pitch; it explains what makes you the best person for the job. To do this, you have to know the requirements of *this particular position* that's been advertised. If the position wasn't advertised, look up the job description and requirements on O*Net Online. Finally, think about the skills you have that may not only satisfy the job requirements but differentiate you from other candidates. For example, a job ad for an Office Assistant may not list multi-tasking as a requirement, but it's certainly a desired quality to have. Explain what you've done that demonstrated this skill.

It's tempting to repeat what's in your resume, but don't. Remember that the reader will be looking at the resume in a moment.

<u>Paragraph 3:</u> Ask for an interview in the last paragraph. Notice I said

"ask" and not "tell." I read a lot of letters that state, "I would like the oppor-tunity to speak with you." I know people think that's being assertive, but it may come across as arrogant or demanding. They are doing you a favor by granting you an interview, not the other way around. You must ask.

Finally, there's a problem with the following statement: "Can I have an interview to discuss my qualifications?" Can you guess what it is? The word *can* implies ability and so you're asking the interviewer if they're able to grant you an interview. Of course they can, but are they willing to? "May" implies permission: "May I have an interview…?"

## Templates are a great starting point.

I've offered you some simple, easy to maintain formats for resumes and cover letters, but there are hundreds more by searching for *templates* on your word processing software. But be careful because not all templates follow the generally accepted guidelines for communicating in business, and I've seen some that don't include all the necessary information.

## Next up…

Creating your resume required you to analyze who you are, and then relate it to the requirements of the job. As a result, you now have your selling points. Having gone through this thought process before filling out job applications should make completing those applications go smoothly. You're now ready to go in person to inquire about jobs, pick up job applications, and talk to the hiring manager. This is the walk-in application method, and it's the focus of the next chapter.

## CHAPTER SUMMARY QUIZ

The following quiz summarizes the chapter.

1. _____ on your resume is grounds for dismissal.
   a. Selling yourself
   b. Having two pages
   c. Lying
   d. Typos

2. Statements on your resume should start with a(n) _____ verb.
   a. Linking
   b. Helping
   c. Passive
   d. Action

3. If a cover letter is not required, don't include one.
   a. True
   b. False

4. The cover letter serves which of the following purposes?
   a. Repeat all the things you've listed in your resume.
   b. Highlight your most relevant skills and qualifications for a particular job.
   c. Tell the employer that you want an interview.
   d. Ask the employer for more information about the job.

5. Which of the following is a good formatting technique for a cover letter?
   a. Use fancy fonts like Comic Sans to differentiate yourself.
   b. Make it at least 1-2 pages to show how qualified you are.
   c. Your signature should look like a scribble and be hard to read. This shows how important you are.
   d. None of the above are good formatting techniques.

Answers: 1c, 2d, 3b, 4b, 5d

# Lesson 8

# The Walk-In Inquiry

The types of jobs most sought after by teens — cashiers, customer service, retail, food service, business offices, childcare, and even warehouses — are all places of business you can walk into, ask if the company is hiring, request an application, and ask to speak to a manager. Next to networking, it's the best, most effective way of finding a job for two reasons. First, you may learn of a job opening even before it's advertised. And second, by appearing in front of an employer, you have an opportunity to make a personal contact and a good first impression.

That's the opportunity you have. The reality can be very different.

> I talk a lot to business owners and managers about the experiences they've had with teen job applicants. I may be in a restaurant or hair salon and when I tell them what I do for a living, I'll casually ask them, "How do you find the high school kids who apply for jobs?" Their initial response may surprise you. It's never about how they interview, or whether they know how to write a resume or cover letter. It's not even about the skills they have or don't have. Without a split second's thought, their response almost always is about what young applicants are wearing and how they present themselves when they come in to pick up or drop off an application.

There seems to be a misconception that the way you present yourself only matters during an interview. But you have to consider every encounter, from the moment you step into the establishment to the moment you accept a job offer, as part of the interview process.

## YOUR FIRST IMPRESSION

While online applications have made employers' lives much easier, I think it's really done a disservice to applicants. Showing up in person at a place of business to pick up an application is your first chance to make an impression. To make a good first impression, it must be planned. It can't be an afterthought.

> Last summer, my daughter Samantha was a hostess at a local restaurant. Knowing what I do for a living, she offered, "So mom, today a girl came in to fill out an application wearing a shirt with a midriff, sweatpants, and flipflops, and her hair was tied back in a messy ponytail." This of course piqued my interest, so I asked her to tell me more. Here's what transpired:
>
> "Can I help you," Samantha asked at the hostess stand.
>
> "Um, yeah, are you guys hiring?" asked the applicant.
>
> "We are. Would you like an application?" Samantha asked. Her response: "Sure."
>
> The young girl spent about 20 minutes filling out the application in the seating area and brought it up to the hostess stand when she was done.
>
> Samantha took the application and said, "Great! I'll give this to my manager and I'm sure he'll be in touch with you."
>
> The response? "Okay." She turned and walked out.

Not surprisingly the manager, in fact, did not get in touch with this applicant. This encounter was a failure from beginning to end. Let's discuss what should have happened.

## DRESS LIKE IT'S AN INTERVIEW, BECAUSE IT IS

Everyone knows it's important to dress up for an interview, but no one really talks about dressing to pick up an application. It doesn't require a suit and tie. If you're over-dressed, it won't go against you. But if you're dressed too casually, it will. Here are a few guidelines.

- Wear what's called your Sunday best, an old phrase which means you should wear what you'd wear to church. That means conservative clothing—nothing flashy or revealing. Khakis and a collared shirt for boys. Nice top and slacks for girls. No jeans, no T-shirts, no leggings, and certainly no flip-flops.
- Dress nicely even for jobs where the dress code is casual, like landscaper, busser, or construction worker. What the employees are

wearing doesn't matter because they're not applying for a job; they already have one. A common problem I see in my profession is when someone is applying for a job as a Phys Ed teacher and they come to the interview in their gym clothes. When in doubt, err on the side of being overdressed instead of underdressed.

- Be neat and well-groomed. This includes your hair, nails, and clothing. If you're sloppy about yourself, you're telling a potential employer that you'll be sloppy about your work.

- Can you show tattoos and piercings? The answer is still under debate but comes down to the culture of the workplace. If it's a trendy clothing store, maybe. If it's a restaurant, bank, or office where you'll be interacting with customers, then maybe not. If you know someone who works there, ask them. Many companies are including specific guidelines for tattoos, piercings, and even hair color into their dress code policies that can be found online. But if you're unsure what's acceptable, why risk it? I've always told my students, "When in doubt, take it out." Once you get the job, stay within the dress code whether it's written or verbal.

I helped my Co-op student, Joe, find a job at a photography studio. Before his interview, I made him remove the piercings from his ears, eyebrow, nose and tongue. I also told him to wear long sleeves to cover up the tattoos on his arms. I explained to him that as a Photographer's Assistant, he'd be dealing with clients and that the heavy piercings and tattoos would not be a good reflection on the photography studio.

It wasn't even two weeks into his job that I received a call from his boss. "He's doing fine as far as the work is concerned. But last week he came in wearing an earring. The next day one earring turned into two. And a few days later there's a stud on his eyebrow. I just want to let you know that I've had to talk to him about this and that if he wants to wear all that on his face, he'll have to find a job somewhere else."

When you're at work, you're a representation of your company. They have an image to portray to their customers, and the way you work, behave and appear must be consistent with that image. Your employer has the right to fire you if you fail to comply to their policies.

- Finally, when it comes to your appearance, remember the acronym, KISS. Although it stands for keep it simple, stupid, I tell my students it stands for keep it simple, students. When you present yourself to a potential employer, do you want them to notice your flashy hair, clothes, nails, make-up, or jewelry? Or do you want them to focus on what you're saying about who you are and what you have to offer? Keeping it simple eliminates the distractions.

## COMMUNICATE LIKE IT'S AN INTERVIEW, BECAUSE IT IS

Let's go back for a moment to Samantha and the applicant in the flip-flops. Before the manager, Isaiah, even looked at the application, he was not impressed, not because she made a negative impression on him but on the hostess who took the application.

> At the end of the shift, Samantha handed the application to Isaiah and reported, "She had an attitude."

It was the attitude that communicated that she didn't really care about working there. She was unprofessional in the way she appeared, the way she talked, and her lack of enthusiasm. I tell students all the time, "Say yes, not yeah. Say no, not nah." Don't say "you guys" to anyone when applying for a job. The people you just met are not your guys. And her last words to Samantha should have been, "Thank you very much," not "Okay." You are not talking to a buddy; you're talking to someone who will determine whether you get a callback or not.

Who was Samantha to the applicant? Was she just someone who was there to pass the application along to the manager? People often treat entry-level employees like hostesses, cashiers, and secretaries without the respect they deserve. Samantha is obviously not making the decisions to hire or fire anyone; she was a 17-year-old at the hostess stand. But Samantha had something that should never be taken for granted — she had the power to influence. As a good employee who was well liked by her managers, her opinion of an applicant will be taken into consideration.

What motivated Samantha to evaluate the applicant as having an attitude? She didn't know her, so it certainly wasn't personal. Put yourself in her place and ask yourself, "Would I want to work with this person? If she doesn't care about her appearance or the way she presents herself even before she gets the job, will she care about doing a good job? What if I have to work side-by-side with her?"

So how should this encounter have gone? Let's play it over again, but this time the right way.

> The applicant should approach the hostess stand properly dressed, with a smile on her face, looking the hostess in the eye:
> You: "Is there a manager on duty I can speak to?"
> Hostess: "Can I help you?"
> You: "Hi, I was wondering if [company name] is currently hiring?"
> Hostess: "We are. Would you like an application?"
> You: "Yes please. Thank you."
> Upon returning the completed application:
> You: "Is there a manager on duty I can speak to?"
> Hostess: "He's not available right now, but I'll be glad to give it to him and I'm sure he'll be in touch with you."
> You: "Awesome. Thank you so much. What's your name?"
> Hostess: "My name is Sam."
> You: "Thanks, Sam. I'm Kelsey. I really appreciate it."

Keep the following in mind when you do a walk-in.

- First, you can't say "please" and "thank you" enough, because the person in front of you is doing you a favor.

- Your nonverbal communication is more important than what you actually say. If your body language or your facial expressions conflicts with your verbal communication, people will always believe the nonverbal. Create a positive vibe by smiling, standing up straight, and looking the person in the eyes as you speak.

- If you don't like using the word "awesome," no problem. "Great", "super", or "terrific" will do nicely. The idea is to show some enthusiasm. If you don't, it becomes obvious that you're just going through the motions.

- Don't use filler words like "um," "uh," "like," or "basically." We use them while trying to think about what we're going to say, but they're very distracting to the listener. It's perfectly okay to pause and be silent during those times; it'll make you appear more thoughtful.

- Be mindful of your use of gender specific language. When referring to an adult female, refer to her as a woman, and not a girl. You wouldn't refer to your male interviewer as "the boy who interviewed me," right? That would be demeaning. So don't say, "the girl who interviewed me." The difference between a girl and a woman is simply age. If she's under the age of 18 you may refer to her as a girl. If you're not sure, say young woman.

- Prepare a script like the one above ahead of time and write it down. Practice in front of a mirror, and then to a friend or family member.

- Go first to the companies that you least want to work for. By practicing on them first, you'll be more polished when you approach your most desired places.

- If you ask whether the business is hiring and the answer is "no," ask for an application anyway. The answer may be "no" today, but "yes" tomorrow.

- Asking for the name of the person you spoke to serves several purposes. First, what would you do if later on you were told that they don't have your application? By getting a name, you'd be able to say, "I gave it to the hostess, I think her name was Sam." That immediately gives you credibility that you did in fact turn one in, and that maybe it was misplaced. Getting her name also helps you connect with her in a personal way. By looking her in the eye and asking her name, and then using it, you showed maturity and professionalism. Now if she asked herself, "Would I like working with this person?" the answer would most likely be "yes."

- Offering your name also helps to make a personal connection. Now the person who took your application can associate the application with a name as well as a face.

Remember that your application will be sitting in the middle of a large stack. If you don't look, speak, or act professionally and other applicants do, why would an employer bring you in for an interview over them?

## MEET THE MANAGER

I've told you before that it's not okay for a parent to drop off your application. It gives the impression that they're forcing you to work. It's always better to hand your application over to the manager on duty as Kelsey should have done: "Is there a manager on duty I can speak to?" If you do get this chance, here are the things you should communicate, both verbally and non-verbally.

- Try not to be nervous. You are simply having a conversation with someone who may need you as much as you need them.
- If you have to wait to speak to the manager, don't be on your phone — it'll make a bad first impression.
- Nothing communicates your enthusiasm more than eye contact and a genuine smile. The way you communicate now is the way this manager will assume you will communicate with their customers.
- Give them a firm handshake and introduce yourself with your first and last name. Introducing yourself with your first name alone shows that you lack confidence in yourself.
- Follow this script:

    *Hello. I was dropping off my application and just wanted to introduce myself. I'm <your first and last name>. I'm very much interested in applying for a <job title> position."*

    *Would it be okay if I checked back in a week or so to see the status of my application?*

    *Thank you so much for your time.*

My students often tell me that they don't want to bother a manager. I think what they mean is that it's scary. But try to look at it from their viewpoint. Managers are responsible for hiring the best people possible. When you assert yourself like this, you've accomplished a few very important things. First, you've demonstrated your genuine interest in the job. Second, you've shown some very important soft skills like communication, maturity, and initiative. Finally, you've allowed this manager to be able to associate the name on the application to a real face. This is huge.

### How will a manager remember you?

Employers meet many people during the course of a day. So when a hiring manager meets you, how will they remember you? The answer is, they probably won't, unless they make an actual note at the top of your application. Notes like "Well-spoken," "Nicely dressed," "Very eager," or just plain

"Yes." When a company is ready to bring in candidates to interview, who do you think they'll bring in first — those with applications that say "Yes" or those that say nothing at all?

Just as a manager will remember you for good reasons, they'll also remember you for bad ones.

> An employer of mine at a big box retail store experienced her fastest hiring decision ever when a young man in his early twenties came in to drop off an application and asked to see the manager. She spoke to the applicant briefly, noted he presented himself well enough, and then was asked this question: "Do you drug test here?" He didn't even make it out the door before the "No" was written at the top of his application.

If you bring in a parent, seem disinterested in working there, communicate poorly, or are inappropriately dressed, it's very likely that the note at the top of your application will say, "No" too. Oh, and don't ask about drug testing; I'll talk about that when we discuss interviews.

### Don't show up during busy times.

Nothing good will happen for you if you visit a store during the holiday season, an accounting office at tax time, or a restaurant on a Friday or Saturday night. First, you'll drastically decrease your chances of actually speaking with a manager because their focus will be on their customers and their staff, not job applicants. But what's even worse is if the manager *does* see you. It tells them that you don't understand the nature of their business, or even worse, that you don't care about inconveniencing them.

> Samantha was one of three hostesses working on a Saturday evening at 6:30 pm. There was an hour-long wait and the restaurant and waiting area were already buzzing with guests when a young woman approached the hostess stand and asked to see the manager. As she was trained to do, Samantha asked what it was regarding, then offered to take her resume and pass it along to the manager on duty.
>
> But the applicant insisted, "I'd like to speak to the manager."

123

> Reluctantly, Samantha went into the dining room to fetch, Rex, the manager who after a few minutes made his way through the crowd of waiting guests to greet the young woman.
>
> "Hi, I'm Rex, the Manager. What can I do for you?"
>
> "Hi, I wanted to introduce myself. I'm looking for a server position." She went on to explain her prior experience in serving while Rex responded, "Yup...yup...yup...."
>
> After about a minute of this, Rex finally interrupted, "Let me stop you, we only take applications online."
>
> "Oh," she replied. "Then I'll apply online but here's my resume."
>
> As she reached into her folder to look for her resume, all three hostesses and Rex exchanged an "Are you kidding me?" look.
>
> She was barely out the door when Rex threw her resume in the trash can and returned to his work.

Showing up on a Saturday night at a restaurant to apply for a job shows that this applicant didn't understand the restaurant business. Then, taking up the manager's time even after seeing they were in the middle of the dinner rush shows that she either didn't recognize or didn't care that she was distracting them from doing their jobs. Just as important as having good body language is reading the body language of others. If you see that you've come at a bad time, get out of there and return when it's not their busy time.

### Next Up...

The applicant in the last story made a mistake even before entering the restaurant; she didn't realize that the company only accepted online applications. A simple review of their website would have informed her of this. Before we actually discuss how to complete an application, there are a few things you must do to get ready. The next chapter will help you do that.

## CHAPTER SUMMARY QUIZ

The following quiz summarizes the chapter.

1. What is the best way to make a first impression on an employer?
   a. Email them a resume
   b. Complete an online application
   c. Call them on the phone
   d. Go in person to the business to inquire about a job.

2. What is the biggest complaints employers have about teen applicants?
   a. They have sloppy handwriting.
   b. They don't return phone calls quickly enough.
   c. They don't dress and speak professionally when they walk in to inquire about jobs, pick up an application, or drop one off.
   d. They don't have the right skills for the job they're applying for.

3. Which of the following would not make a good first impression?
   a. Applying in person instead of online if given the chance.
   b. Showing up at the place of business during their busy times.
   c. Having a clean, professional appearance.
   d. Keeping hair, make-up, nails, jewelry and clothing simple.

4. If you don't know a company's policy on tattoos or piercings, what should you do when contacting the business in person?
   a. Call the employer ahead of time to ask.
   b. Cover up the tattoos and remove the questionable jewelry until you know the answer for sure.
   c. Show tattoos and questionable jewelry. After all, they are an expression of who you are.
   d. Do not apply to this company.

5. Which of the following is an example of good communication?
   a. Eliminating filler words from your speech
   b. Making eye contact when speaking to someone
   c. Introducing yourself
   d. All of the above are examples of good communication.

Answers: 1d, 2c, 3b, 4b, 5d

# Lesson 9

# Application Preparation

In the next chapter, I'll teach you how to respond to every question on an application whether it's online or on paper. But first, you have to be prepared to complete both. While they ask similar questions, how you respond will be slightly different.

You'll be asked to provide references on the application, so you need to establish who they are. Your legal paperwork must be in order before you submit an application. Everyone needs a social security number, and if you're a minor, you may need working papers depending on the state where you work. I'll explain how to get all of that in this chapter.

## LINE UP YOUR REFERENCES

References are people who will testify to your work ethic, performance, and your character. This can be past employers, adult co-workers, teachers, guidance counselors, coaches, clergy members, or any other objective adult who knows your work. Don't use friends or family members because they're not viewed as being objective.

Contact three potential references either by calling them or in person, not by email or text. Don't just ask them to be a reference, ask them if they'll be a *good* reference, and then carefully study the reaction on their face or in their voice: "Mr. Sherk, I'm applying for a job as a Mechanic Assistant. Would you provide me with a good reference?" Their immediate reaction will tell you whether their recommendation will be positive or less than positive. If it's something like, "Are you sure you want to use *me?*", be skeptical. If you don't think it'll be positive, don't use them.

Once someone agrees to be a reference, make sure they know the type of job you're applying for so that they know what aspects of your work to amplify. For example, if it's a job in customer service, ask them to talk about your good communication skills. If it's a job as an Auto Mechanic, ask them to vouch for your technical or problem-solving skills.

Potential employers may also want to talk to your references about an red flags they see on your application, or any concerns they have coming out of an interview. They may ask former employers about your stated work duties, the length of time you worked there, or the reason you gave for why you left. If you lie or mischaracterize yourself to a potential employer, this may also come out during a reference check. If you have concerns about any of this, it's better to talk to your references about what they'll say in a reference check before you decide to use them.

As a manager and teacher, I've been a reference for dozens of my students and my employees, and probably written an equal number of recommendation letters. So I can tell you that while it's easy to give a positive recommendation, it's difficult to provide one that's not positive. Notice that I said *not positive*; I didn't say I gave one that was *negative*. There's a big difference.

### A savvy employer or teacher may not want to give you a negative reference.

Why? Because they are afraid of getting sued. While it's certainly not illegal to give a negative reference, it's illegal if the information provided isn't true. That's why more and more organizations are making it a policy for their managers to only provide facts—like dates of employment, title, and work duties.

So you may be wondering, what's the point of references if all they do is provide the positives and leave out the negatives?

### A reference will express their opinions about you not only by what they say, but by what they don't say.

I've been put in this position twice in my career.

If my opinion of a student is positive, I'll elaborate on their strengths and give detailed examples as evidence. On the other hand, if the experience I had with the student doesn't warrant a positive reference, I would provide only factual information where requested.

To illustrate the difference, here are two actual references I completed for former students.

The first reference is for a former student who was looking for a teaching position. As you'll see, I think very highly of her.

What do you see as the candidate's strengths?

One word - determination. Ever since I knew Melissa back in high school, she had a goal that someday she would work in a profession where she could help young people. She experienced some bumps in the road during her high school years and knew she would be able to reach students like her. In the Co-op program she won numerous awards and scholarships for her service to her peers, her outstanding attendance, improvement in her GPA, and excellence on the job. She is honest and loyal; at her Co-op job she immediately turned in to her supervisor a bank deposit bag she found at her station that a customer left behind. It was filled with over $7,000 of cash and checks. She made that decision in a split second, something that only a person of good moral character would do.

Since high school, I have watched her grow professionally, socially, and emotionally through her college years and now beyond. When I talk to my students today about having goals, accomplishing milestones, and having the determination and drive to reach those goals, I still refer to Melissa.

Alternatively, here is an example of a letter of recommendation for college wrote where I could not in good conscience give a positive reference, like th one I gave Melissa. The student was intelligent but very oppositional. Be havior was a constant issue and I had multiple dealings with his parents. even had to write an infraction for attempting to cheat on a test. Why, you may be wondering, would he ask me for a letter of recommendation? Be cause he was majoring in business in college, and I was the only busines teacher he had through high school.

To the members of the Admissions Committee:

This letter is in support of Dale Barnes who was a student in my AP Macroeconomics class. AP Macroeconomics is a challenging course that introduces students to complex economic and financial concepts. In this class, Dale showed his inquisitive nature by asking questions that demonstrated his intelligence and his desire to learn the subject matter. He did well on tests and quizzes and earned a '5' on the AP Macro-

> economics exam.
>
> Overall, I believe Dale is an intelligent young man who values academic success. If you have any questions, please feel free to contact me at ...

Do you see the difference? While I described his strengths, they were exclusively related to his academics. The fact that I didn't comment on qualities like attitude, cooperation, teamwork, or work ethic is a clear signal to an experienced employer or admissions counselor that according to me, those aren't his strengths.

What should you do if you were in a situation like Dale's and you had no choice but to include a reference from someone who was less than satisfied with your performance?

## Explain the situation to the hiring manager.

Before you provide your list of references, tell the hiring manager your side without badmouthing the reference or calling them a liar. Maybe you were much younger and you're more mature now. You can say that it was a mistake, and then communicate what you learned as a result of the experience. By doing this, you'll be showing your maturity, and a hiring manager will be much more likely to give you chance.

Writing references like Dale's is very difficult. I'd love for every reference I write to be positive because there's no greater joy than to reward a young person who is deserving, and to help them meet their career goals. But we have to be honest, because when we teachers, coaches or employers are asked to give a reference, our good name and reputation are on the line. Take a lesson from Dale and remember what I said earlier—every person you meet is a potential contact in your professional network.

## GET YOUR PAPERWORK IN ORDER BEFORE YOU APPLY

The law requires employers to verify that you have certain documents issued by the government, and their failure to comply can result in substantial monetary fines. While you can accept a job without these documents, you can't begin working. Don't delay your start date, or even jeopardize the job, by not having them in time. Get them now.

129

## Get your social security number (SSN).

Employers need your SSN to report your wages to federal, state, and local governments.

- If you are a U.S. citizen, a legal permanent resident, or a temporary worker authorized to work by the Department of Homeland Security (DHS), you should already have an SSN. If you don't, you must apply for one through the Social Security Administration at www.ssa.gov.
- If you are a recipient of deferred action through the Deferred Action of Childhood Arrivals (DACA) policy, visit the U.S. Citizenship and Immigration Services (USCIS) website at www.uscis.gov for information on how to apply.

## Get your working papers.

If you're a minor, you may need either an *employment certificate* that proves you and a parent or guardian have been informed about limitations of job duties and work hours, or a *proof of age certificate* that tells the employer that you're old enough to work. Which certificate you need under which age limit depends on the state in which you will work. For example, Pennsylvania requires all workers under the age of 18 to obtain an employment certificate but not an age certificate. Florida requires an age certificate but not an employment certificate. North Dakota requires both but only for youths under the age of 16. Arizona requires neither.

Working papers can be obtained either at your state's Labor Department or the local public-school system. For information on your state, do a google search on "us department of labor working papers/age certificates."

## PREPARE YOURSELF FOR ONLINE APPLICATIONS

Before you walk into a place of business, know whether they accept paper or online applications. If you show up to inquire about an open position and you're told they only accept applications online, you'll not only have wasted your time, it'll appear that you didn't do any research on the company.

The best advice I can give you about online applications is to try and avoid them if possible. If given the choice between paper and online, always go for the paper so that you can deliver it in person. Online applications al tend to be very restrictive and won't allow you to continue without entering certain information, and often have no space for writing a note to qualify an answer. Employers tend to get a larger number of online applications than paper ones, so it becomes increasingly more difficult for you to differentiate yourself from other applicants.

Unfortunately, about 50% of companies now only want online applications, so you'll have to make the best of it. Here are some guidelines:

- Online applications will ask you for a lot of information that's already on your resume, so have your resume handy.
- Give yourself plenty of time to complete it. Some sites will allow you to save and continue, and others won't. You don't want to get halfway through and realize you need to stop for the day, only to start all over again tomorrow.
- Employers may receive hundreds of online applications for an open position, so reviewing them individually may not be possible. Instead, their application computer system will automatically review each application by looking for certain key words; use these key words in your application as much as possible. For example, if the position is for a Ride Operator and you have that experience, use the words Ride Operator exactly as the ad specifies. If a required duty of a job involves stocking shelves and you have that prior experience, enter the exact words stocking shelves. If the employer is seeking 3 years sales experience and you have it, use that phrase exactly. This will increase the chance of your application being selected by a computer system.
- Online applications will usually allow you to upload a resume and cover letter. Always attach both.

## PREPARE YOURSELF FOR PAPER APPLICATIONS

Completing an application requires thought, information that may not be readily available to you, and preparation. That's why you should never complete the application at the place of business. Take it home so that you can give it the time and attention it deserves. If you don't, there are lots of things on the application itself that will end your chances of getting the interview.

- Plan to make mistakes by making a copy of the application before filling out, especially if this is your first time. Use one as a rough

131

draft, and the other as a final.

- If you only have one copy of the application, complete it in pencil first and then go over it in pen. If you make a mistake in pen, use white-out. Don't have any scratched-out pen marks on it.
- Write legibly. If you have terrible handwriting, print every word and do it slowly. Don't ask someone else to fill it out for you.

---

While one of my Co-op students was filling out his parking form, I noticed that the handwriting was different than what was on his Co-op application. When I commented on this, he admitted that his mom filled out his application for the Co-op program. If he had done this with a job application, an employer would have thought, "If he can't complete his own job application, how will he perform the duties of his job?" Remember what I told you about your parents being the scaffolding.

---

- Don't bend, fold, or allow the application to crumple. Make sure nothing spills on it. If you turn in an application that's a mess, employers will assume that you'll care about your work as little as you cared about the application.
- Have a copy of your resume with you when completing the application. A lot of the information you'll need on the application will be on your resume.
- Complete every section or question of the application so that nothing is left blank. If a question does not apply to you, write "N/A" for not applicable or draw a small line through it. If you leave it blank, the employer may either think that you mistakenly skipped it or intentionally avoided answering it.
- Use proper, standard English. Check your spelling and grammar. Again, if you're careless on your application, an employer will assume you'll be careless at your job.

## HOW MANY APPLICATIONS IS ENOUGH?

Now that you're all set to fill out some applications, how many should you fill out? Finding a job is a numbers game. You can't fill out one or two and then complain that no one is hiring. That's why it's called finding a job. You have to go find it; it won't find you.

A mother of one of my students was excited to find out about my job posting board. In a Facebook exchange she told me that her son, Blake, has been looking for a job, "but no one is hiring." I knew this wasn't the case because it was spring semester and I had been posting jobs at a rate of one or two a day. So the next day I approached Blake, "Your mom says you've been looking for a job?" He gave me a puzzled look as if he didn't know what I was talking about. He thought for a moment and replied, "Oh, yeah. I put in an application a couple of weeks ago, but I haven't heard back."

There's just no magic number of applications you should fill out, but one is definitely not it. It's not even 5 or 12 or any other number. If you want a job, you fill out job applications until you find a job. Many of my Co-op students didn't have jobs at the beginning of the school year and so their job was to find a job. I required them to contact a minimum of three businesses a day. So, three applications a day for five days a week resulted in most of my students finding employment within the first two weeks of the semester.

### Next up...

Now that you know what to have ready and what to expect, I'll teach you section by section how to complete an application. That's the focus of the next chapter.

## CHAPTER SUMMARY QUIZ

The following quiz summarizes the chapter.

1. What advantages do paper applications have over online ones?
    a. Paper applications are more personal; you have personally contacted the company to submit one.
    b. Paper applications allow you to qualify your responses with notes.
    c. The high volume of online applications received by an employer makes it harder for you to differentiate yourself.
    d. All of the above are advantages of paper applications.

2. Which of the following is *not* a good practice when filling out paper applications?
    a. Complete the application at home, not at the business.
    b. Make a copy of the application before filling it out.
    c. Have a parent complete it if you have poor handwriting.
    d. Never leave a response blank.

3. Which of the following would *not* be a good reference?
    a. A friend or family member
    b. A coach
    c. A teacher or guidance counselor
    d. A former employer

4. How many applications should you complete to find a job?
    a. At least 1 a week
    b. 2-3 a week
    c. 10 – 12 in total
    d. As many as you can until you find a job

5. Where can working papers be obtained?
    a. Your state's Labor Department
    b. The public-school system in your area
    c. Both A and B.

Answers: 1d, 2c, 3a, 4d, 5c

# Lesson 10

# Complete the Job Application

In a previous chapter, I told you about Kelsey, the applicant wearing flip-flops and a midriff who my daughter Samantha helped at the hostess stand. Let's return momentarily to that story and see what happened after the manager, Isaiah, was handed the application.

> After hearing from Samantha that the applicant "had an attitude," Isaiah glanced at the application, looked up at Samantha and said, "Oh, hell no." Something on that application turned him off immediately. What was it?

While no two applications are exactly the same, they all pretty much request the same type of information. I'll go section by section and teach you how to respond correctly and avoid critical mistakes like the one Kelsey made. There are three especially daunting questions I'll help you answer: *desired pay, reason for leaving a job,* and *criminal convictions.* I'll also give you examples of good responses as well bad.

Applicant information is always the first section.

---

**PLEASE COMPLETE PAGES 1-4.**                      DATE _____

Name _____
        Last            First        Middle       Maiden

Present address _____
        Number      Street   City  State  Zip

How long _____           Social Security No. _____ – ____ – _____

Telephone (___) _____          Email _____

If under 18, please list age _____

                     Days/hours available to work

Position applied for (1) _____          No Pref _____  Thur _____
and salary desired (2) _____            Mon _____  Fri _____
(Be specific)                                      Tue _____  Sat _____
                                   Wed _____  Sun _____

How many hours can you work weekly? _____     Can you work nights? _____

Employment desired    __ FULL-TIME ONLY    __ PART-TIME ONLY    __ FULL- OR PART-TIME

When available for work? _____

---

135

## Name

Seems like such an easy section, but believe it or not, this is the first area where I see scratched out pen marks. Some applications will ask for your last name first, so read each question carefully before you start writing.

## Date

This refers to the date you submitted your application, not the date you filled it out. Don't eliminate the year. My students often leave it off thinking, "Everyone knows the year, why do I need to write it?" Your application is a formal record of your employment, and it will remain in your employment file potentially for years.

    ☒  7/18

    ☑  7/18/19

## Address

An application is a formal document, so don't abbreviate.

    ☒  7619 Mountain Ave.

    ☑  7619 Mountain Avenue

Abbreviate the state properly with its two-digit, uppercase code.

    ☒  Ariz.

    ☑  AZ

## How Long [at current address]

The longer you've lived at your current address, the more stable you're considered to be in your life.

If you've been moving around a lot in your past, they'll assume you'll continue to do so in the future, and that will make you appear unreliable. If you're stating on the application that you've lived at this address for less than a year, explain the reason in a note next to this section. You'll hopefully get a chance to elaborate in an interview.

    ☒  6 months

    ☑  6 months – My family just moved here for my mother's job. We were at my previous residence for 12 years.

This was this section that Isaiah reacted to so negatively, because it stated that she was at her current address for only three days with no explanation. This alone may not have been enough to disqualify her, but it may have been strike three. Remember that she was dressed improperly, "had an attitude" like she really didn't care about working there, and now is presenting what looks like instability. The third strike apparently put her into the "hell no" category, according to Isaiah.

## Social Security Number (SSN)

Your social security number is a very precious piece of data. It enables you to prove that you're legal to work. It also allows you to open a credit card, register for college, rent an apartment, or buy a car. There are others who also think your SSN is very precious: identity thieves. They would love to get your SSN and your Date of Birth so they can open a credit card in your name and go shopping. So...

- Memorize your SSN. Do it now. Find a pattern or associate groups of numbers with those that have meaning to you.
- Never carry your social security card with you. That's why you need to have it memorized.

We were taking a family vacation to Hawaii years ago and had taken my mother-in-law with us. Unfortunately, she was pick-pocketed during the trip and her wallet was taken. As we reviewed all her credit cards that were stolen to have them cancelled, I asked her if she was carrying her social security card. "Of course not. I'm not stupid," she snapped. I had obviously insulted her. "I wrote it down on a piece of paper." Guess where she had stored that piece of paper... in her wallet!

- Never write your SSN down on a piece of paper and carry it in your wallet. Your SSN has a very distinct format. It's nine digits long, separated by dashes, like this: xxx-xx-xxxx. Even if you excluded the dashes, how long do you think it would take an identity thief to recognize a nine-digit number as an SSN?
- Don't put your SSN on this job application! Employers will need it

eventually when checking your employment eligibility, doing criminal background checks, and for tax purposes. But an SSN isn't necessary right now, and I recommend that you wait to get further along in the interview process before providing it. Think about all of the public places your application will travel before you even come in for an interview: the hostess stand, the shelf under the cash register, a secretary's desk, and so on. It's just too dangerous, so don't do it. Zero-fill the first two parts of the number, and enter only the last four digits to indicate that you do in fact have an SSN:

    ☒  123-45-6789

    ☑  000-00-6789

- If you're completing an online application, an SSN may be a required field without which you won't be able to continue. Using the zero-filled partial SSN as shown here will allow you to effectively bypass this section for now.

## Telephone

What's the best phone number at which the employer can reach you? This is probably your personal cell phone, so make sure you took my advice on your greeting.

    ☒  An excerpt from the rap song, *Stupid Hoe* by Nicki Minaj.

    ☒  A sleepy voice starting with the word, "Yo..."

    ☑  "Hi it's Teresa. Please leave your name, number, and a message and I'll get back to you as soon as I can. Thanks!"

## Email

If your email address is still based on the nickname your favorite uncle gave you when you were 10 years old, it's time to get a new one. A professional email address should include a portion of your name so that it's easily recognizable as belonging to you.

    ☒  Nickylightening98@someprovider.com (Unless your last name is Lightening, change it)

    ☒  winteriscoming@someprovider.com (Employers don't care that you were a *Game of Thrones* fan)

    ☑  ztaylor123@someprovider.com

## Age

Employers may ask age-related questions for a variety of legitimate reasons. On this application, asking for age "if under 18" may be to ensure a candidate meets a minimum age requirement, or to alert an employer to request working papers. Alternatively, you may be asked to provide your date of birth (DOB) to conduct criminal or financial background checks. While age related questions on an application are acceptable, they are not so during an interview, because you cannot be discriminated against based on age. You'll read more about inappropriate or illegal questions during our discussion on interviews in Chapter 15 – The interview.

☑ N/A (If you're 18 or over)
☑ 16

## Position Applying For

If you're responding to a job ad, list the position exactly as it appears in the ad. If not, Chapter 4 has a list of possible jobs for teens; find the one that most closely resembles the position you're applying for.

☑ "Anything". This not only makes you appear desperate, it tells the employer that you didn't care enough to research the nature of their business.
☑ Sales Associate
☑ Bagger
☑ Warehouse Associate
☑ Ride Attendant

## Desired Salary

Many applicants find this question hard to answer. They're afraid that a number that's too low undervalues them, and a number too high may disqualify them. The truth is that most companies have a set range for each entry level position, and the starting pay may not be negotiable. They do, however, want to make sure your expectations are consistent with theirs.

First, note that this application asks for "salary," which is a number that's quoted as a yearly amount. For example, $40,000 a year is a salary. Part-time, entry-level jobs normally pay by the hour. So here, quote your desired hourly wage.

- If this is your first job and you're applying for a position that requires very little skill or previous experience, you should expect to earn a minimum wage:
- Blank. Many employers will eliminate your application if you leave this blank. Online applications will most likely force you to enter a number. Unfortunately, the zero-fill trick will not work well here.
- "Minimum Wage". This tells the employer that you don't know the minimum wage in your state, and you were too lazy to look it up. Do an internet search on "national conference of state legislatures minimum wage" to see a list of minimum wage information by state. States that do not have a minimum wage will default theirs to the Federal minimum wage, which as of this writing has remained $7.25 since 2009.
- $7.25/hr.
- An exception to the minimum wage law concerns tipped employees, like servers and golf caddies. For them, the federal minimum wage is currently $2.13/hour. This wage plus tips must add up to the minimum wage or else your employer has to make up the difference. The minimum wage for tipped employees by state can be found on the Department of Labor's Wage and Hour division website www.dol.gov/whd/state/tipped.htm. Do a Google search on "DOL minimum wage tipped employees." Whether you're expecting the legal tipped minimum wage or something higher, state it here.
  - ☑ $2.13/hr. + tips
  - ☑ $3.50/hr. + tips
- If you have relevant skills or work experience, you may be justified in asking for more than the minimum wage. This is especially true if you were already making more at a previous job. So that you can discuss the salary after getting the job offer, you have two options here. Be prepared to justify your requirements in an interview.
  - ☑ $8.00 - $8.50/hr.
  - ☑ "Negotiable"
- Another exception to the minimum wage law is the youth minimum wage, or training wage, that employees under the age of 20 may receive for up to 90 calendar days of employment. This wage is currently $4.25/hour. This allows the employer to train you at a lower

140

cost until you get up to speed on the job. In all my years of helping students find jobs, I only knew of one company who offered this rate, and the student who applied there did not accept the job offer.

- Whether you have a number in mind or if you have no idea what a position pays, it's a good idea to talk to the people in your network. Someone may know someone who either worked for the company or worked in a similar job. A line cook in two different but similar types of restaurants in your local area should make similar hourly wages. But wages differ based on individuals' experiences, and also where you're located. Areas of your state or the country with higher costs of living will offer higher wages, and all states have their own minimum wage laws. You can find average wage information by occupation and state at the Department of Labor's Bureau of Labor Statistics site www.bls.gov/oes/current/oessrcst.htm. Do a Google search on "DOL BLS occupational wage estimate."

### Availability

Be as specific as possible when listing the days and hours you're available to work. Employers understand that as a student, you have other commitments. But you must understand that employers will expect you to make your job one of your top priorities. For example, if you're applying to a retail store or restaurant, you have to be available to work on weekends.

- Take into consideration all your prior scheduled commitments like school, sports practices, music lessons, etc. This is not the time to indicate your incidental commitments like a weekend trip for sports or a scheduled vacation with your family. You'll do that when you get a job offer.
- State the number of hours you'd like to work weekly. Keep in mind that if you're under the age of 18, your hours may be limited by the Child Labor Laws in your state.
    - ☒ 0-14 hours. Not only are you telling the employer that the job is a very low priority, your lack of availability will make it hard for your employer to schedule you.
    - ☑ 15-20 hours. This is reasonable for a full-time student.

141

- Be specific about the days and hours you're available to work. Make yourself available on as many days of the week as possible. This doesn't mean that you'll actually work on all of those days. Here is a sample availability schedule.

  ☑ Mon: 3 pm – close      ☑ Fri: 3 pm – close
  ☑ Tue: 5 pm - close      ☑ Sat: All day
  ☑ Wed: Not available      ☑ Sun: Not available
  ☑ Thu: 3 – 5 pm

### When Can You Start?

Employers want to know if you are available to start immediately or whether they would have to wait to get you on board.

- ☑ "Immediately" is the most common answer and the one you want to state. If you have a current job that you'll have to quit, your new employer will assume that you'll be giving them a two-week notice. So "immediately" means *two weeks after I quit my current job."*
- ☑ 6/10/19. If you can't start working until a future date due to a prior commitment, add an explanation next to the date.
- ☒ "Planned Vacation next December." If you know you're unavailable to work in the future for an extended period of time for any reason, this is not the time to bring it up. Those details are best left for after you have an offer and before you accept it.

### Education

| TYPE OF SCHOOL | NAME OF SCHOOL | LOCATION (Complete mailing address) | NUMBER OF YEARS COMPLETED | MAJOR & DEGREE |
|---|---|---|---|---|
| High School | | | | |
| College | | | | |
| Bus. or Trade School | | | | |
| Professional School | | | | |

Employers want to see what stage of education you're in.

- There's a reason why this example specifically states to include the "Complete mailing address." Many applicants take shortcuts by stating the street name and city. Doing this tells the employer that you were too lazy to look up the exact address.

142

- If you're still in school, make sure that you indicate your expected month and year of graduation as well as your expected degree.

  ☑ High School Diploma – will graduate June 2020

- If you're a senior in high school or college and you're close to graduating, be prepared to explain your plans for after graduation. Employers don't want to spend time and money to train you, only to see you quit a few months later to pursue higher education, military, or some other opportunity. So if you plan on staying in the area after graduation, state it here.

### Criminal convictions check

---

HAVE YOU EVER BEEN CONVICTED OF A CRIME?   __ No   __ Yes

If yes, explain number of conviction(s), nature of offense(s) leading to conviction(s), how recently such offense(s) was/were committed, sentence(s) imposed, and type(s) of rehabilitation. _____

---

A conviction means you either pleaded guilty or were found guilty of a crime. This is not the same as being arrested or charged with a crime. If the arrest never led to a conviction, you can check the "No" box here. If, however, you have a conviction in your past either as a juvenile or an adult, this question on the job application may be intimidating.

> Haley was a Sales Associate at a kiosk type store in the mall that specialized in earrings and piercings. Things were going fine until one afternoon shortly after she was hired, the store manager called to tell me that Haley had been fired. The employer had conducted a criminal background check that revealed a conviction on her record. In addition, Haley had lied on her application by checking the "No" box for this question.
>
> To this day, I can't say for sure if the conviction itself was ultimately what led to her dismissal, but the lie that followed certainly was. Lying anywhere on a job application is grounds for immediate dismissal, and not only did she lie to her employer, she lied to me.
>
> When I interview students for the Co-op program, I don't specifically ask about criminal convictions, but I do ask about

> previous disciplinary actions taken against them. This is their opportunity to get their issues out on the table so that I can help them make good decisions, both in school and on the job. By hiding the fact that she was convicted of a crime, she committed a lie by omission. If she had been truthful with me from the beginning, things may have gone very differently.

Here are the takeaways from Haley's story, and some additional advice if you have a conviction on your record:

- First and foremost, don't lie. People assume that by checking the "Yes" box they will automatically be disqualified. This may be true in some cases, but because most companies now conduct criminal background checks as a matter of policy, they're going to find out anyway. On a positive note, if you do admit your conviction, the application will always provide a space for an explanation.

- Some applications will ask more specifically if you've been convicted of a felony, a more serious crime than a misdemeanor. Know the classification of your conviction; it varies by state. In Haley's case in the state of Pennsylvania, her conviction for shoplifting was a misdemeanor because it was her first offense, and the value of the merchandise she stole was under $150.

- It is very possible to find employers that will hire those with a criminal record. Hiring managers are human, and they've made their own mistakes. Some employers will even look for the opportunity to help a young person not just by hiring them, but by mentoring them. I can tell you from personal experience that as a teacher, there is no greater joy than to know that I in some way helped a young person to change their life for the better. Those opportunities are out there.

- If you've been unsuccessful finding a paid job for this or any other reason, get a volunteer job so that you can build a work history and have a reference to put on an application.

- Start networking. People who know you will be more likely to want to help you.

- Don't apply for jobs that put you in a high-risk situation. In Haley's case, she stole merchandise from a clothing store. The last place she should have been working was a retail store selling earrings or anything else for that matter, where she had access to merchandise or the cash register.

- You can have your juvenile criminal record hidden or expunged when you reach the age of majority — when you are no longer a minor. This could be at age 17, 18, or 19 depending on the state where you live. It's a misconception that this will happen automatically when you become an adult. You don't necessarily need a lawyer, but the process does differ by state.

- If you checked the "Yes" box, it's important that you ask to speak to a manager when you submit your application.

> Introduce yourself, express your interest in the job, look them in the eye, and say: "I want to be up front with you. You'll see on my application that I have a criminal conviction in my past. I'm a different person today than I was back then, and I would really appreciate a chance to explain further in an interview."

You have now demonstrated your honesty and maturity, and greatly improved your chances of being called in for an interview.

- Finally, don't just talk about being a different person, be a different person. If you don't like what's in your history, build a new one. In other words, prepare yourself so that a potential employer down the road will see the incident as a mistake and not a character flaw. That way, you'll have a good high school or college transcript and a record of consistent employment as evidence of your new history.

> While Haley made some very serious mistakes, she turned things around for herself. Despite the first setback, she continued her good attendance and kept up her grades. I was convinced that the shoplifting incident was a mistake and not part of who she was as a person. Thanks to my network of employers, I was able to help Haley get a job in an animal boarding facility as a Kennel Assistant. I don't know where Haley is today, but she held that job from October of 2003 to at least June of 2004 when she graduated. I'm sure that during any future discussions with employers about that old conviction, she can truly say that she

turned herself around, and she'd be able to prove it. Haley built herself a new history and so can you.

## References

Please list two references other than relatives or previous employers.

| | |
|---|---|
| Name _____ | Name _____ |
| Position _____ | Position _____ |
| Company _____ | Company _____ |
| Address _____ | Address _____ |
| _____ | _____ |
| Telephone (___) _____ | Telephone (___) _____ |

By now you should have three people who have agreed to give you a good reference. Never use anyone who hasn't explicitly given you their permission.

- Always provide the total number of references the application asks for. Providing fewer than two here implies that you couldn't find two people to say nice things about you.
- Make sure you complete everything including last names and titles.

## Driver's License Information

DO YOU HAVE A DRIVER'S LICENSE?     __ Yes  __ No

What is your means of transportation to work? _____

Driver's license
number _____ State of issue _____ __ Operator __ Commercial (CDL) __ Chauffeur
Expiration date _____

Have you had any accidents during the past three years?          How many? _____
Have you had any moving violations during the past three years?   How Many? _____

This information can be requested for several reasons.

- If driving is part of the duties of your job, like delivering food or taking a deposit to the bank at the end of each day, the employer is responsible for making sure you're legal to drive. They must carry auto insurance to cover you and your vehicle and so they will check your history of accidents and moving violations; having violations like speeding may be enough to disqualify you. As in the case of a criminal conviction, don't lie. The employer will check your driving history once you get the job.

- The employer wants to know that you have a reliable way to get to work. If you don't have a car, be specific about how you'll get to work.
  - ☒ Bus
  - ☑ Septa bus 127

## Employment Eligibility

> Are you legally eligible to work in the United States? Yes ☐ No ☐
> (Federal Law requires proof of identity and employment authorization for all new employees.)

You must be legally eligible to work in the U.S., whether you're a U.S. citizen, permanent resident, or if you have a temporary work visa. Proof of your status will be required once you're hired.

## Military Background

| MILITARY | |
| --- | --- |
| HAVE YOU EVER BEEN IN THE ARMED FORCES? | __ Yes __ No |
| ARE YOU NOW A MEMBER OF THE NATIONAL GUARD? | __ Yes __ No |
| Specialty _____ Date Entered _____ Discharge Date _____ | |

Some employers will look to hire vets, and some will be cautious. If you've served in the military, it's best to answer this section honestly.

## Work Experience

| Name of employer Address City, State, Zip Code Phone number | | Name of last supervisor | Employment dates | Pay or salary |
| --- | --- | --- | --- | --- |
| | | | From | Start |
| | | | To | Final |
| | | Your last job title | | |
| List the jobs you held, duties performed, skills used or learned, advancements or promotions while you worked at this company. | | | | |
| Reason for leaving (be specific) | | | | |

Refer to your resume to complete this section.

147

## Employer Contact Information

- Include your supervisor's first and last name. I'm always amazed when teens tell me they don't know their immediate supervisor's last name, and even more amazed when they don't bother to find out before completing a job application.
- If jobs like babysitting or lawnmowing were done for numerous clients, put "Various families" or "Various customers" for this section. If there's a particular customer you'd like to be contacted, consider using them as a reference.
- Include the entire address and remember to use proper address formatting. Only abbreviate the state.
    - ☒ 360 Middletown Blvd, Langhorne
    - ☒ 360 Middletown Boulevard, Langhorne, PA 19047

## Employment Dates

If you can't remember the exact start and end dates of a job, it's okay to state only the month and year.

- ☑ February 2015 – March 2017
- ☑ 2/2015 – 3/2017

## Pay or Salary

How much you made in a previous related job gives employers an idea of what your expectation might be for your next job.

- ☑ $8.50/hour
- ☑ N/A (If this was a volunteer position or an unpaid internship)

Pay raises show that you did well at the job, so indicate that here.

- ☑ $8.50, $9.50 after 6 months

## Title

Put the actual title of the job that you held. If you don't know it and you put something very generic, you'll undervalue yourself.

- ☒ Worker or Employee
- ☑ Cashier, Bagger, Stock Clerk, Receptionist, Line Cook, etc.

## Jobs Held, Duties Performed, Skills, Promotions

Fill out this section from the "Work Experience" section of your resume.

## Reason for Leaving (Good)

Finally, we get to the question that is the greatest cause of anxiety for candidates, not only here but in an interview. Remember I told you earlier that if a Co-op student quit their job without my permission, they would fail the marking period? This is the reason why: to discourage students from having a knee jerk reaction to a problem at work by quitting.

For now, if you did quit a job because of unresolved issues, try to find another reason, because often it's not just one thing that pushed you over the edge. Did you leave to focus on school? Did you leave due to another commitment like a sport or volunteer activity?

If you're having trouble with this section, is it because you quit a job you shouldn't have? The next time you consider quitting a job, think about what reason you'll give on your next job application. It shouldn't be this hard.

While there are several good answers, there are a whole host of bad ones.

- If you worked for a business that only operates during one season, like amusement parks, nurseries, ice cream shops, or ski resorts, the response here should be:
- Seasonal employment
- Any reason for leaving a job to better yourself should never be held against you. Just make sure that the work history you list is consistent with what you put here.
  - ☑ Return to college
  - ☑ Took a better paying job
  - ☑ Took a job with more responsibility
  - ☑ Took a more challenging job
  - ☑ Took a job more consistent with my future career
- If you were let go from your job because the company was having financial problems, or they moved far away, this is not your fault. Being let go is not the same thing as being fired. "Fired" means your employment was terminated because you did something wrong. If you were let go due to no fault of your own, explain it.
  - ☑ Company downsized (this means the company could not

149

afford to keep their entire workforce)

☑ Company relocated

## Reason for Leaving (Bad)

The three worst yet most common responses I see are these. They don't explain the real reason you left, and you cannot assume that you'll get an opportunity to explain in an interview.

☒ Not enough hours

☒ Not enough pay (without a subsequent job)

☒ Issues with manager (or co-workers)

Let's start with the easiest of the three problems, "not enough hours." If your hours got cut because your company was downsizing, then say so. That shouldn't be held against you.

If you asked for more hours and the employer was unable to do so, and you quit to take another job that gave you more hours, then say so: "Took a job with more hours."

If you quit because your hours were cut, this could be a red flag. Put yourself in an employer's shoes for a moment and ask yourself, why would you cut a worker's hours? Good employees get hours. If you're not working out for whatever reason, employers who hire many workers across multiple shifts won't go through the trouble of firing you; they will simply cut your hours to the point where you'll quit. Hiring managers know this is a common practice, so never, ever put this as the reason for leaving.

"Not enough pay" can go one of two ways. If you left this job without having another one lined up, then "not enough pay" doesn't really make sense, does it? How much more were you making when you didn't have a job at all? An employer will assume you left because of other "issues." If by "not enough pay" you mean that you left this job to take another, higher paying job, then good for you. Make sure this is evident in your work history, and write the explanation, "Better paying job."

Now let's look at the last response, "Issues with manager" and again, put yourself in a manager's position. If you saw this response, would you say to yourself, "Huh, I think I'll bring her in to find out what those issues were"? Or would you pick up the next application in the stack on your desk? While you are claiming that you had issues with the manager, you're also implying that the manager had issues with you.

> When I was a Director of Applications Systems at Saks Fifth Avenue, I was interviewing a candidate for a Programmer/Analyst position. The interview was going well enough, until I asked him why he left his last job. His response: "I had issues with my manager." Bad answer. I pressed further. "Oh? What kind of issues?" He sat back in his chair and explained, "Well, every time I was doing something I wasn't supposed to do, I'd turn around and there he was."

The last thing employers want is drama in the workplace because they have a business to run. This candidate oozed drama, and I ended the interview in the next thirty seconds.

Every job, just like at school and at home, will have issues. It's a given because you are now out there dealing with people and personalities you've never dealt with before. Often when I drill down on these issues, it boils down to a matter of fairness. "I was being picked on for coming in late, but I wasn't the only one. It wasn't fair." But what you think is unfair may be very fair for someone else. So, like anything else in your life, you have to do some problem solving and this involves discussing these issues with the people around you. This can be the scariest thing in the world to do, which is why so many young people, when given the choice between dealing with issues or bolting, will choose to bolt.

Again, if you did quit a job because of unresolved issues, try to find another reason.

If you have problems explaining your reason for leaving your job, you'll also have issues with the next question.

### May we contact this employer?

If you say no, you should provide an explanation, and the only valid explanation here is "Current employer." It will be assumed that your current employer does not know you're looking for another job, and you don't want them to find out this way. Otherwise, you should say "yes." If you say no without an explanation, again, you are leaving it up to the reader to assume that you had unresolved issues at this job.

## Signature

You're almost done, but don't rush through this last section.

- As I explained in Chapter 7, your signature should be legible so that your first and last names are recognizable. Before you sign, practice coming up with a legible but unique signature that you will live with probably for the rest of your life.

  ☒  *Mu fh*

  ☑  *Melissa Michaels*

- Always read what you're about to sign so later on you don't have to say, "I didn't know that." Your signature on the application may acknowledge any or all of the following:

  - ☑ You've been truthful in your answers under penalty of dismissal.
  - ☑ You give permission to this employer to contact your references, past employers, and schools regarding your education and employment history.
  - ☑ You give permission to this employer to do background checks on your criminal history, driving record, and any other information you have provided.
  - ☑ You give permission to this employer to check your credit history, if you have one. Some employers will not hire you if you have substantial debt because they believe you will be more likely to steal from them.

### Next up...

Once you're sure that the application is perfect, have someone you trust look it over. If you first completed it in pencil, go over everything with pen, and then completely erase all pencil marks. Finally, make a copy or take a picture of it. You'll need to refer to it when you follow up on your application, as the next chapter explains.

## CHAPTER SUMMARY QUIZ

The following quiz summarizes the chapter.

1. Which of the following should you do on your application?
   a. Eliminate the year on dates; month and day are enough.
   b. Abbreviate parts of the street address, like Dr. for Drive, and Blvd. for Boulevard. It saves space.
   c. Lie if you have to about a criminal history.
   d. Be honest throughout your application. If you do get the job, lying is cause for immediate dismissal.

2. Which piece of personal information are identity thieves most interested in stealing from your application?
   a. Email address
   b. Phone number
   c. Social Security Number
   d. Credit card number

3. Which of the follow in *not* an acceptable response to "Position Applying For"?
   a. Anything
   b. Landscaper
   c. File Clerk
   d. Sales Associate

4. Admission of a criminal conviction on your application will 100% guarantee you will not get the job.
   a. True
   b. False

5. Which of the following reasons for leaving a job is acceptable to state on your application?
   a. Issues with manager
   b. Left for higher paying job
   c. Didn't get along with co-workers
   d. Not enough hours

Answers: 1d, 2c, 3a, 4b, 5b

# Lesson 11

# Application Follow Up and the 30-Second Commercial

Remember my student, Blake, who submitted only one application and waited for a response? You can't just apply for one, or two, or three job positions and hope something will turn up. You have to apply until you get a job. Blake's second mistake was that he did something almost every other candidate will do. He sat back and waited for *them* to contact *him*.

Other applicants for the job you want may have more job experience, more education, or a more impressive application. But most of them will not have the foresight to follow up on their application like you're going to do. If you submitted a paper application in person, then you've made a personal contact and hopefully spoke to a hiring manager. If however, you applied online, you're among a long list of faceless names, and following up in person is even more important. So whenever it's a business that's open to the public, like a restaurant, hair salon, or retail store, always go in person. Otherwise, send an email. When you do this, you will instantly bring your application to the top of the stack.

## WHY AREN'T THEY CALLING?

Remember the average number of applications an open position receives is 250. So it's very possible that your paper or online application is still in that pile. It's also possible that it's been disqualified for any number of reasons. If you haven't received an invitation for an interview, do a self-evaluation of your efforts so far, and determine if you've made any of the following mistakes that may have eliminated you as a candidate.

- There's no correlation between the requirements of the job and your qualifications. This is the most common reason that applications are rejected.
- The application does a poor job of communicating how your prior work and school experiences will help you succeed in this job.

154

- The application is vague about the position you are applying for and it appears that you didn't care enough to research the open position.
- The application itself is incomplete or filled with spelling and grammatical errors. If you couldn't take the time to complete it properly, why should a manager take the time to read it?
- When presenting yourself to pick up or drop off a paper application, you made a bad impression on the person you spoke to. If it was a manager, your application may say "No" at the top.
- There are plenty of qualified candidates for the position, but your application doesn't stand out. You've never met the hiring manager and so there's no face to associate with the name on the application.
- Your social media sites were visited by the employer and they saw something they didn't like.

If you've made any of these mistakes, correct them now before you fill out another application. If your application hasn't been eliminated, it could still be in the middle of the pile. Letting it sit is not a good idea.

## FOLLOW UP IN PERSON

Regardless of whether you applied online or in person, follow up in person if at all possible, rather than calling or emailing. It allows them to associate a name on the application with a face. It will also do something no phone call or email can do.

**It's harder to say no to someone when they're standing in front of you.**

Following up serves several additional purposes. First, you want to make sure they received your application and that there is in fact still a job opening. Second, it tells the employer that you are very much interested in the position and available for an interview. They now know that a parent isn't forcing you to work, and you haven't taken a job elsewhere. Third, making this effort shows that you were willing to take the extra step that most other applicants won't bother to take. And fourth, there is a reason to follow up that is so important, but so little known, that if more applicants knew about this reason, I'm positive that more of them would follow up in the manner I'm about to teach you. I'll save the reason for a bit later in the chapter.

155

## WHEN SHOULD YOU FOLLOW UP?

Approximately 5-7 days is a reasonable amount of time to wait before following up in person or via email. Try too early and it's possible that the employer hasn't reviewed your application yet. Doing it too late shows you weren't that interested. If after the first attempt you were unsuccessful in seeing a hiring manager or didn't receive a reply to your email, wait another week and try one more time. After that, any more attempts may be futile.

## GO IN PERSON

Take copies of your resume and your references with you. Go first to the businesses where you are least interested in working. This way you can practice on them before you approach the jobs you want the most. If you end up being interviewed and getting an offer, it's okay to ask for time to think it over. I'll help you handle that potentially uncomfortable situation later on.

As when you submitted the application, don't go during their busiest times. Remember to dress, act, and communicate like it's an interview, because it is. Every single person you come in contact with is forming an opinion of you. Ask to speak to the manager on duty, and if they are not available, get his or her name, and the day and time when they'll be available so you can make a second attempt. Most importantly, give your name to the person you're speaking to and ask them to give the manager a message that you stopped by to inquire about your application. Make sure you leave your full name and phone number.

### What you should say.

When you do speak to a manager, be prepared to communicate verbally and non-verbally the way I described in Chapter 8 – The Walk-In Inquiry. Smile, shake their hand, and introduce yourself. Then say the following:

> I submitted an application last Tuesday to Joan at the front desk. I wanted to make sure that you received it.

There. Those few sentences should be enough to get a conversation going. You may be asked some questions, or better yet, they may actually go and retrieve your application. For this reason, make sure you review your application before your follow up. Remember I told you in the previous chapter to keep a copy or take a picture of your application? It's for this reason.

It's also very possible that the manager is dismissive. They may tell you that you'll be contacted once your application is reviewed. You may even be told that they aren't currently hiring. If this happens, remember that while there may be no openings today, that could change by tomorrow. This is where what I call the 30-second commercial comes in.

## THE 30-SECOND COMMERCIAL

I have some good news and some bad news about managers. The good news is that managers are busy people. They are usually highly energetic individuals who are very involved in the running of their businesses, and good at managing and motivating their staff. The fact that they're very busy people is also bad news for you because they simply don't have a lot of time on their hands. For you, this means that when you do get a chance to talk to them, be prepared with what you want to say. You may literally have a total of one or two minutes of their time in which to sell yourself. In that time, they won't know who you are or what you've put on your application. Also, they will likely not take the time to pull that information out of you.

That's why I want you to come up with a *30-second commercial* about yourself. Prepare it ahead of time, write it down, and rehearse it over and over again. Your commercial should go something like this:

1. Express your continued interest in this job, not just a job. "I want to let you know that I enjoy working with children, and I've always wanted to work in a daycare center. I would really love to work here."

2. Make a connection from some prior work experience to the job you want. "I worked as a Camp Counselor for two summers at... working with elementary school-aged children."

3. As in a real commercial, end with what's known as *a call to action*. What is it you'd like them to do? "May I have the chance to talk to you about my qualifications in more detail?" Notice that this is a question and not a statement. Remember to ask, don't tell. I often hear students saying, "I'd like an interview." Remember that you are asking them for a favor, not the other way around. If you come across as arrogant, you won't be invited back.

4. End with a firm handshake, smile and say, "Thank you so much for

157

your time."

Boom! You've just differentiated yourself from all the other applications in that tall stack. What's more, you've given the employer a glimpse into your character. You've shown maturity, good communication skills, and some major problem-solving skills. Nothing impresses an adult more than a young person who knows what they want, and politely goes about asking for it.

I told you above that there was a fourth reason for following up in person.

**A follow-up could very well turn into an interview.**

If you do what I told you above, a follow up can easily turn into an interview, which could end in a job offer. This happened to my Co-op students often. The key as always is to be prepared not just for the follow-up, but also for the interview. The next four chapters will help you prepare to be interviewed, no matter when it occurs.

## SEND AN EMAIL

Some businesses do their hiring from locations that are not open to the public. For example, if you've applied to an amusement park, showing up at the park will not work. The person you need to contact is most likely in an office location that may or may not have been disclosed in a job ad. In these situations, an email is your next best alternative. See *Figure 12* below.

In the email, express your continued interest in the position, remind them of your qualifications, inform them of anything new that was not included in your application, like an award or an increase in your availability, and ask for an opportunity to interview. In other words, give them the 30-second commercial. Keep it brief and attach your resume.

---

jseymour@insurancecompany.com

---

Following up for Office Assistant Position #2525 – Kimberley G. Nicklecut

---

Dear Ms. Seymour:

I submitted a resume for a part-time Office Assistant position at your insurance firm about a week ago. I'm writing to confirm receipt of my resume and to reiterate my interest in the job.

As I have indicated on my application, I have taken numerous business and computer courses in high school, I can type 50 words per minute, and have excellent time-management and communication skills.

I have attached my resume and would be happy to provide any additional information you may require. Thank you for your consideration, and I look forward to hearing from you.

Sincerely,

*Kimberly G. Nicklecut*

Kimberly G. Nicklecut
215-555-8917

**Figure 12: Application Follow-up Email**

## Next up...

If you followed my advice up to this point, it won't be long before you're granted an interview. The next four chapters will prepare you for this next, critical step. Let's start with setting some basic expectations of what an interview is—and isn't—and the different formats you might encounter.

## CHAPTER SUMMARY QUIZ

The following quiz summarizes the chapter.

1.  You only need to follow up on applications you submitted online.
    a.  True
    b.  False

2.  When should you follow up on an application?
    a.  You should trust that your application was received and not follow up
    b.  The day after you apply
    c.  5-7 days after you apply
    d.  Two weeks after you apply

3.  When visiting businesses after you've applied, you should go to your most desired companies first.
    a.  True
    b.  False

4.  Which of the following should your 30-second commercial include?
    a.  Your continued interest in the job
    b.  How your prior work experience relates to the open position
    c.  A call to action to request an interview
    d.  All of the above

5.  If you're unable to speak to a manager, you should do all of the following except:
    a.  Find out when they will be available.
    b.  Leave a message for the manager that you stopped by, including your name and phone number.
    c.  Explain that you'll wait as long as it takes until the manager is available.
    d.  Stop by for a second visit when the manager will be at work.

Answers: 1b, 2c, 3b, 4e, 5c

# Lesson 12

# Interview Expectations

Being interviewed is similar to taking a test in school. You're going to be nervous because something important is at stake. When my students tell me they're nervous about an upcoming test, my best advice to them is to be prepared.

"Is the test gonna be hard, Mrs. Purdy?"

My reply: "Not if you know the answers."

It sounds like a sassy response, but it's not meant to be. It just means that the test will be hard if you're not prepared for it.

An interview is no different. If by now you understand who you are and what you have to offer, you're familiar with the job market for your age group, you created a resume and cover letter, you've applied for jobs, and you've followed up on your applications like I suggested, then you've done your homework and you're very well prepared to enter the next major step: the job interview.

In this chapter I'll clear up some misconceptions about what an interview is and isn't. You'll get familiar with the various types of interview format; will there be only one interviewer or more than one? Where will it take place? Will you have to perform a task or just respond to questions? Might there be a drug or alcohol screening?

## AN INTERVIEW MAY OCCUR WHEN YOU LEAST EXPECT IT

When you're searching for a job, it's possible you may not fill out a job application or be asked for a resume. In fact, an employer may not even have advertised an open job position for which they've ended up hiring someone. Some of my Co-op students went to a business to pick up an application, spoke to a manager, and ended up getting the job on the spot. In other words, they ended up "interviewing" for the job without even knowing it happened.

Being prepared will give you confidence and help you recognize an unexpected opportunity when you see one.

161

I was in a Business Communications class in my junior year of college, and one of the requirements was to participate in mock interviews for a fictitious entry-level management position with companies that came to campus to recruit graduating seniors. AT&T was one of those companies and I signed up immediately. Preparing for this involved buying my first interview suit, creating a resume, researching the company, and practicing interview skills. The interviewer's name was Denise Leventhal and she was the Director of Human Resources and a professional recruiter. Although I was nervous, the interview went well enough and when it was over, she gave me both positive and negative feedback. I don't remember the compliments, but I do remember her telling me that I didn't ask enough questions. She was the first person to ever explain to me that an interview should just be a conversation between two people and that I should have asked questions throughout the interview to better understand what AT&T was doing, and what the open position was all about.

What happened next is what I call the stupid part of the story. We have all gone through it, where the brain doesn't engage for a brief but critical moment and we look back and think, "what just happened?" Before we ended the interview, she casually mentioned, "You know, AT&T is hiring college interns for the summer." She waited a second or two for my response, and all I could come up with was, "Oh." I thought to myself, gosh I wish I knew that; I would have interviewed for *that* position instead. It wasn't until the bus ride home to my apartment that a little voice inside my head started to nag at me. And by the time I got home, the little voice was screaming at me. "I think I just made a big mistake," I confessed to my three roommates who saw the panic on my face. They joined my little voice in screaming at me to get back on the bus, head back to campus, and see if I can catch the interviewer.

When back on campus, I ran from the bus stop to the building where we met earlier, only to see my interviewer leaving the building. I shook off the nerves and the embarrassment I felt for being so stupid, walked up to her, and before I could even catch

> my breath, looked her straight in the eye, and asked her if she was offering me an internship this summer. She smiled and said she was, and I accepted the offer immediately.

I had no idea that AT&T was hiring for summer interns, but I got that internship because of a little courage and a lot of preparation.

## INTERVIEW THEM JUST AS THEY'RE INTERVIEWING YOU

When you come out of an interview thinking, "All we did was talk," that's a good sign.

> Bob Parker was the new Chief Information Officer (CIO) of a company I applied to. He was hired to build a new Information Technology organization that would take the company into the 21st century. If I got the job, I would be part of his new organization. While I can't remember what we specifically talked about, I can tell you that I felt like I was talking to a friend and mentor. I had already made it past the first round of interviews earlier that day, so he must have known that I was qualified for the job on paper, and that his managers felt I would fit into the organization. His reason for interviewing me was to see what kind of a person I was. We talked, we laughed, and most importantly, we saw eye-to-eye on many issues. And before I knew it, our hour was over. I was so impressed with Bob and so excited about his vision for the organization that the next day when I got the phone call with an offer, I accepted the job on the spot.
>
> Ironically, the interview with Bob almost didn't take place. I'll explain why below.

**An interview should be a conversation, not an interrogation.**

While the interviewer is learning about you, you need to learn about the job, the company, and the people you'll be working with. That's why it's critical for you to ask questions about the responsibilities of the job, which can be as simple as a Bagger or as complicated as a Veterinary Tech Assistant. If the job is to bag groceries, are there other duties involved, like collecting carts, or returning grocery items to the shelf? You may also ask if and when there would be opportunities to advance to other positions like cashier. For a job like a Vet Tech Assistant, you've hopefully researched the position on O*Net Online and understand the typical duties of the position. That way if you expect the job to involve assisting in examinations and conducting blood tests but find out it's to walk the animals and clean their cages, you then at least have the information you need to determine if this is the job you want.

## WHAT HOURLY WAGE SHOULD YOU EXPECT?

Review what you indicated as your desired salary on your application because you may be asked about it during the interview. Keep in mind that large companies that hire many people will most likely have a set range for each position, and instead of posing this as a question in the interview, it'll be a statement: "The position pays...." Because of this uncertainty, you should have a range in mind before attending the interview. I helped you come up with this range in Chapter 10 – Complete the Job Application.

There is one exception to the minimum wage rule that may come up in an interview. If you're under the age of 20, an employer is allowed to pay you a training wage, or the youth minimum wage, which is currently $4.25/hour, for 90 calendar days after you're hired. This allows the employer to train you at a lower cost until you get up to speed. In all my years of helping students find jobs, I only know of one company who offered this rate to a student of mine; she didn't accept the job offer for that reason. This wage is not likely to come up for you, but you should be aware of its existence in case it does.

## INTERVIEW FORMATS

For a part-time entry-level job, you'll most likely experience a traditional one-on-one interview format. Sometimes you may be asked to speak with multiple people, usually one after another. This may happen if the interviewer wants a second opinion of you, or if you'll be reporting to more than one person. While a one-on-one interview is the most common format, you should be aware of several others.

**An interviewer may first want to screen you over a phone or video call.**

A phone or video interview is probably not something you'll encounter until you get a full-time job, but it's something you should be aware of. This is a good first option if you and the job are in two different locations. Before a company asks you to travel to them, either at their expense or yours, they'll want to make sure your qualifications are in line with the requirements of the position. And since pay is not usually advertised for a position, they'll also want to make sure your expectations are in line with theirs.

Prepare for a phone interview in the same way you'd prepare for a face-to-face interview. It's a misconception that you can interview over the phone in whatever you're wearing – your jeans and t-shirt or even your pajamas. It may sound silly, but your dress and your body language should be exactly the same as if you were interviewing in person. Because the interviewer can't see you, they'll make their impression of you not on just what you say, but how you say it. By dressing professionally, sitting up straight, smiling as you speak, and having a positive attitude, the person on the other end of the phone will be able to hear your professionalism and enthusiasm.

### The lunch-time interview serves a specific purpose.

Of all the Co-op students I've taught, only one had an interview over coffee at Starbucks. And in all the interviews I've had over the past 35 years, I've only had one interview over lunch. It was for a consulting position at Arthur Andersen, and consulting requires interacting a lot with clients. A lunch time interview was a great way for the interviewer to see how I would conduct myself in a social situation for business.

Here are some guidelines for a lunch-time interview:

- If you are male, hold the door open for the females in your party. When the hostess seats you, allow any ladies in your party to proceed before you. This may sound sexist but if you step in front of a woman to enter the restaurant or to be seated, they won't think you're a supporter of equal rights. They'll think you don't have good manners.
- Table manners matter. Fold your napkin across your lap as soon as you sit down. Sit up straight and keep your elbows off the table. Use a fork and knife properly and when you're finished, lay them next to each other on your plate. This tells the server that you're finished with the meal.

- Be polite to everyone, including the hostess and server. Say "please" and "thank you" when appropriate.
- What will you order to eat? It's a good idea to let your host order first so that you can order something in a similar price range. Don't order the most expensive thing on the menu.
- Don't order anything messy, like spaghetti, or things you have to eat with your hands. Something you eat with a fork, like a salad, is better than a hamburger or sandwich. Avoid foods that may give you bad breath, like raw onions or garlic.
- What would you do if your meal had a problem? Would you keep quiet or say something to the server? The answer should depend on how big of a deal it is. For example, if your food has tomatoes and you said "no tomatoes" because you're allergic to them, then of course say something. If you just don't like tomatoes and it's easy to remove them yourself, then let it go. By sending your food back, you'll be prolonging the meal for everyone, and you want to avoid that if possible.
- Never order alcohol no matter how old you are, even if your host orders it. It would reflect as very poor judgement on your part.
- Since you were invited by the employer, it's okay to assume that they will pay the bill. Accept the treat graciously but make sure you thank them for it.

Just remember, there's a very good reason why a company will interview you over a meal. It's most likely a test. They'll assume that the way you conduct yourself with them is the way you'll conduct yourself with their clients.

While an interview over a meal is fine, be skeptical when your *only* interview takes place away from the company's premises.

I've had only one student whose interview took place over a meal, or more accurately, over coffee at a local Starbucks. As a result, she was hired as an Office Assistant for an Insurance Broker, but when she showed up for her first day at work, she found out it was the owner's "home office." I'm not saying that this type of job isn't legitimate—it may very well have been. The issue was that she didn't know this when she accepted the job.

> This type of arrangement violated the Co-op Program guidelines, and I pulled her out of the job immediately.

It's important to check out the environment where you'll work, so if you've been offered a job, ask if you can stop by the "office" before you accept it.

**Performance interviews test your skills.**

Skills tests are becoming more popular because they dig deeper into what a candidate has to offer. If your resume or application claims that you have a particular skill or experience performing a particular job, you should anticipate being tested on it; you'll most likely not have prior notice. If this happens, don't panic and don't rush it. Take your time to figure out how to handle the test and ask questions if necessary.

> As part of an interview for a server position, my student, Kay, was asked to wait on the manager acting as a customer. She took the time to look over the menu, acquainted herself with the specials, then approached the table to begin the test.
>
> Manager: "Is there gluten in the Chicken Parmesan?" he asked without looking up from the menu. Kay went back to the kitchen to ask the cook, and then returned to the table.
>
> Kay: "There's no gluten in the chicken. Would you like to order it?"
>
> Manager: "No. Are there anchovies in the Caesar salad?" Again, back to the kitchen to ask the cook, and then back again to the table.
>
> Kay: "There are anchovies in the Caesar salad, but we can have them put on the side. Would you like the Caesar salad?"
>
> Manager: "No. I'll have the pasta primavera."
>
> When she served him the pasta primavera, he complained that it wasn't what he ordered.

This is called a stress test and it serves two purposes. The first is to see how you'd treat a difficult customer. The second is to see how you'll perform under pressure. Serving food in a busy restaurant can be a high-stress job, and an employer may want to see how you'll react.

Here are some examples and the reasons behind them.

- Wait on customers at a restaurant.

  *How do you treat people and handle stress?*

- Decorate a cake in a bakery.

  *Do you have the basic skills you claim to have?*

- Sell a pen at a retail store.

  *Can you be persuasive but not pushy?*

- Interact with children at a day care or preschool.

  *If you love children, will you get down on the floor and play with them without being asked to?*

- Set up a product display at a retail store.

  *Can you create something that's functional and visually appealing at the same time?*

- Format and type a letter on word processing software like Microsoft Word or Google Docs.

  *Do you know how to format a letter and use the required software? How fast can you type?*

- Answer the phone to take a customer complaint.

  *Do you know how to answer the phone for business? How will you treat the customer? How good are you at problem solving?*

- Take an online or written math aptitude test.

  *How are your basic math skills that you'll need for this job?*

If you've been honest on your resume and didn't embellish the skills you have, you should feel good about taking a performance test. It's a great way to demonstrate your expertise in the areas the job requires.

**Beware the panel interview (a.k.a The Firing Squad)**

> The worst interview experience I've ever had was with a catalog retail company in southern Pennsylvania, where I was

interviewing for a Systems Analyst position. I had no idea when I walked into the conference room that there would be five people interviewing me all at the same time. Two men and three women sat at a rectangular table, and all stood up at once when I entered the room. I was nervous before I entered the room; now I was absolutely petrified. No one had ever prepared me for this, and I had no idea what to expect. And because there were five of them and only one of me, I didn't catch their names or their titles. I didn't even know which one of them—if any—I'd be reporting to.

This is called a panel interview, but people often refer to it as a firing squad, because that's what it feels like. No one explained to me what the job position entailed, so I couldn't tell who, if any of them, was in charge of running the interview. Each of them had their own list of questions, and the questions came at me from every side of the room. On my left, a woman asked me how long I had been programming, and in which languages. Then, from my right, one of the men asked me to describe my greatest flaw. And then again from the left, another man asked me why I was leaving my current job. Every time I turned to answer a question, I would have to turn my back to half of my audience. At the end, even though I was given an opportunity to ask my own questions, there had been no real discussion about what the position was or how I might fit into the company. Where would I even begin?

Even before the interview ended, I knew I was not interested in the job. The interview was a failure not just because it was so poorly run, but because it felt like it had no purpose. What they learned from me they could have read mostly in my resume, and I was no closer to knowing anything about them, the position, or the company. I had to assume that if this group of managers couldn't manage something as basic as a hiring interview, how good could they be at managing their own departments or the people who work for them? I wanted to leave as soon as possible, but unfortunately I was told to stick around because I had made it to the second round of the interview.

The panel interview is very difficult to organize and conduct, but employers use it either to save time or to see how candidates perform in a group setting. If you find yourself in a panel interview, don't panic and try to figure out who everyone is — their names and especially their titles. When responding to questions, try to address everyone in the group, not just the person asking the question. Most importantly, if the interview doesn't go well, you may still have an opportunity to speak to the hiring manager one-on-one. If you didn't get your questions answered, contact the hiring manager directly afterwards.

The firing squad was a terrible experience, but I'm glad I didn't bolt afterwards. Believe it or not, I actually took this job because the second round of interviews was with Bob, the CIO who I told you about above.

## DRUG AND ALCOHOL TESTS

As a young adult looking for a job, you've committed to taking on adult-like responsibilities. In the seven years that I ran the Co-op program, I've had two students who were fired within a week of being hired — one for failing a drug test and the other for refusing to take one. Having to fire a newly hired employee means that an employer has just wasted a lot of time. It's also embarrassing for the employee.

Employers administer these tests to provide a safe work environment. If you're doing illegal drugs or abusing alcohol, there are two things you should do. First, stop immediately. Don't try products that claim they clean out your system so you can pass a drug test. Many of them don't work, and because they're not FDA approved, they may not be safe to use. Second, check the laws in your state that govern drug testing policies of employers so that you know what to expect. These laws govern the substances employers can test for, how they can test for them, and under what circumstances they can administer the tests.

If you are a legally certified medical marijuana user or live in a state where recreational marijuana is legal, state laws may be in place to protect you from discrimination by employers with a *zero-tolerance policy*. State laws may, however, prevent you from participating in high risk work duties. Do an internet search on "Drug and alcohol tests in [your state]" to learn the laws in your state.

## Next up...

Knowing what to expect during the interview process is only the beginning. Knowing what to say and how to present yourself is critical. You have to be prepared.

## CHAPTER SUMMARY QUIZ

The following quiz summarizes the chapter.

1. Which of the following is *not* true about interviews?
   a. They should be a two-way conversation.
   b. They are all about answering the interviewer's questions.
   c. They are as much about you learning about the employer as it is about the employer learning about you.
   d. All of the above are true about interviews.

2. Which is the most common type of interview format?
   a. One-on-one interview
   b. Firing squad interview
   c. Panel interview
   d. Phone interview

3. Why would an employer want to conduct a phone interview?
   a. You and the interviewer may be in different locations.
   b. To screen your qualifications before making you travel.
   c. To make sure salary expectations are consistent.
   d. All of the above.

4. Which interview format is the most difficult to conduct?
   a. Lunch time interview.
   b. One-on-one interview.
   c. Phone interview.
   d. Panel interview.

5. Why do employers administer drug and alcohol tests?
   a. They have a moral objection to drugs and alcohol.
   b. They are required to do so by state and federal laws.
   c. They want to provide a safe workplace.
   d. To discourage you from taking a job.

Answers: 1b, 2a, 3d, 4d, 5c

# Lesson 13

# Present Your Best Self in the Interview

Interviews can range from the very formal to the very informal. You may be asked a series of interview questions, or it could be a simple meet-and-greet. It could take an hour, or it could take 10 minutes. Regardless of the format, they all have one thing in common: your success depends on how you present yourself.

> We're happy to hire high school students as young as 15. We know they don't have much, or even any, previous experience, but that's okay. We'll teach them what they need to know. So if we like what we see on their application, the interview is just to put our eyes on them. First and foremost, did they show up? You'd be surprised how many applicants say they'll come in for an interview and then don't, without even letting us know. Then we want to see if they come in on time. How are they dressed? How do they talk? Many times you can tell in their body language if they *want* to work or if the parents are making them work. We'll know everything we need to know in about 10 minutes.
>
> Michelle Landis
> Franchise Owner, Salad Works

Your enthusiasm, conversation style, and body language will speak louder than your answers to their questions. This chapter is all about how to show your best, most professional self in the interview.

## DON'T JUST SHOW YOU'RE ENTHUSIASTIC

Savvy interviewers know when someone is genuinely enthusiastic about a job or whether they're faking it. You can't just act enthusiastic, you actually have to be enthusiastic. That may be hard to do if you only equate having a job with collecting a paycheck. It's also hard to do if your parents want you to have a job more than you do. Hopefully, you want the job to learn new skills, meet new people, and most importantly, learn things about yourself that you may not have learned otherwise.

Being enthusiastic was easy for me for one very good reason: I loved to work. I didn't just love learning new things, I loved seeing myself learn new things and getting really good at them. I discovered that I was organized and good at multi-tasking. When I worked at the Orange Julius, running the blender, steaming the hotdogs, ringing up the customer, and answering the phone all at the same time was fun for me. It was like a game: how many things could I do at the same time without screwing things up? So I attribute some of my success in interviews to the fact that I didn't just act like I wanted the job, I really wanted the job. Put yourself in the place of an employer—wouldn't you want to hire someone who wanted to work for you so badly?

My enthusiasm for my work didn't just help me get jobs, it helped me advance in just about every position I held. I was 16 years old when I got my first promotion at the Orange Julius to Assistant Night Manager. What qualifications, you may wonder, can a 16-year-old possibly have to deserve a promotion to a position with responsibilities like having the keys to close the restaurant, handling the cash, and making nightly deposits at the bank? And what would a 16-year-old know about supervising other employees to make sure all the closing duties were done correctly before everyone could leave for the day?

This is how it happened. When I first started working at the Orange Julius in my hometown of Lebanon, PA, stores were not open on Sundays. This was because of Blue Laws that prohibited retail stores from operating on "the day of the Lord." In other words, Sundays were to be reserved for going to church and observing God. Eventually, the mighty dollar won out over religious observation and stores and restaurants all over Pennsylvania started to operate on Sundays. The Orange Julius and the entire Lebanon Plaza mall were no exception.

I first heard the rumors from two co-workers who were

173

complaining about the possibility of giving up their Sundays. One was a team member like me, but the other was our Assistant Manager, Lynn. Soon enough the owner, Crystal, approached me and asked me the question we were all anticipating: "Would you be willing to work on Sundays?" As you can guess, my response was something like, "Yes, absolutely, when can I start?"

Not even a week went by after this conversation that Crystal pulled me aside and asked if I'd be interested in the position of Assistant Night Manager. The reason? Not just because I agreed to work on Sundays, but because I was so eager to work on Sundays. And the irony was that all my co-workers who said "thanks, but no thanks" to Sundays? They ended up working Sundays anyway. Because in the real world, you either make yourself available when the business needs you, or the business will find someone else who will. It was a pretty valuable lesson for a 16-year-old to learn.

While faking enthusiasm is bad, not having any enthusiasm at all is ev worse. Here's how a Human Resource specialist at the theme park, Sesa Place, describes the importance of enthusiasm.

We hire hundreds of employees, mostly high school and college students, in a very short amount of time to get ready for the park's opening in the spring. Candidates who pass the initial screening based on their online applications are invited to attend a hiring workshop. Those who don't respond or don't show up are immediately eliminated from consideration.

In the workshop, we give the applicants an overview of who we are as an employer so that they know what to expect if they're hired. What they don't know is that while they're evaluating us, we're evaluating them. We select who gets called back for the formal interview and who doesn't based on what we observe in this workshop. Candidates who are actively listening, engaged, and even asking questions in the presentation get a call back. Those who are not paying

> attention, talking, or on their phones are not invited to return. For us, how candidates present themselves is one of the most important criteria we look for. It tells us whether they want a job or whether mom or dad is forcing them to get a job.
>
> Rodney Anderson
> Supervisor – Human Resources, Sesame Place

If you're not enthusiastic about getting a new job, you're either applying for the wrong job or for the wrong reason.

## BE A STORYTELLER

Typically, an interviewer will tell you the duties involved in a job. But what if they ask *you* to explain what you thought the duties were? You may be asked a situational question like, "What would you do if...." In both of these situations, you might answer hypothetically, "Well, *if* I were in that situation, I would...." But how powerful would it be if you could describe what actually happened in a similar situation? You could explain what you did, not just what you'd do. Relating your past relevant experiences to the requirements of the job is very compelling, because employers know that the best predicter of your future behavior is your past behavior. When you're asked a situational question, let your experiences speak for themselves.

> It was my junior year in college, and I was interviewing at my favorite restaurant, The Deli—home of the killer cookie. The conversation between the general manager, Dave, and I was unremarkable, until he asked me this question: "What would you do if you saw a co-worker stealing from the restaurant?" I couldn't believe my good luck, because I actually practiced this response! I sat up straighter in my chair and beamed as I responded, "That actually happened to me!" I relayed the following story.
>
> Soon after my promotion to Assistant Night Manager at the Orange Julius, my manager, Crystal, confided in me that someone was stealing from the cash register. She suspected it

was either Randy or Doug, or most likely both since money turned up missing whenever one or the other was on duty. One night I was closing with Randy and another team member, Tanya, and after reconciling the cash with the register receipt, I came up $70 short. I counted again, and again the same result. I then sent Randy to the walk-in to put the food away for the night, knowing it would be at least a 10-minute trip, and asked Tanya to count the cash as I watched. Again, the same result. I called Crystal to report the shortage and within 20 minutes she and her husband were at my side, counting the cash now for the fourth time, with the same results. After that night, I never saw Randy or Doug inside the walls of the OJ again. But they did come around to socialize when Crystal wasn't around to complain how they had been "laid off." Apparently without hard evidence, Crystal felt she would not be successful bringing criminal charges against them, and simply let them go.

Dave sat stone-faced while he listened to my story. I went on to explain to him that while I was never told what to do in a specific situation like this, I just tried to use my best judgement. When I was done, he suddenly smiled, leaned forward, and declared, "You have the job!" I couldn't believe it. Up until that question, I didn't think the interview was going particularly well. But months later he told me how impressed he was that I had done the right thing by reporting the missing cash, while others my age may have covered up for a "friend."

It then occurred to me that all of those little jobs I had through high school and college gave me much more than a paycheck; they gave me valuable experiences that I could refer back to. I grew wiser and more confident because with every job came different situations with co-workers, customers, and managers that I had to deal with.

The next chapter contains the 20 interview questions you're most likely to be asked. As you go through each one to construct your answer, think back to similar situations you were in, whether on a previous job, a club at school, a sports team, or anywhere else. Tell the story of what you *did*, not just what you would do. Be a storyteller.

## YOUR BODY LANGUAGE SPEAKS LOUDER THAN WORDS

Having a meaningful conversation first starts by being a good listener. A significant part of the interview should be where the interviewer tells you some things about the job, like the duties, hours, and who you'd report to. They may talk about the company and its mission, and how the job position fits into that mission. Sometimes we hear something, and we start thinking about what we'll say next. The problem with that is we stop listening. Don't do that. If you have a response and don't want to forget what you want to say, just jot down a note. Ask the interview, "Would you mind if I took notes?"

When you're responding to a question and it raises a related question in your mind, ask it. Maintain good eye contact, have good posture by leaning slightly forward, and never cross your arms. Crossing your arms during any interaction says that you're defensive or closed off to what's being said. By the end, the interviewer should have a good idea about whether you're still a viable candidate, and you should have a good idea whether you're still interested in the job.

Part of being a good listener is having what's called a good *affect*. In this context, the word is a noun, not a verb, and means to show emotion or feeling in response to something or someone else. When someone is talking to you, nodding your head in agreement, raising your eyebrows in surprise, or smiling if something pleases you are good examples of positive affects. Conversely, frowning or furrowing your eyebrows indicate a negative affect. Showing affects like these tells the speaker that you're actively listening and processing what's being said.

> I was interviewing candidates for a Systems Analyst position at Saks Fifth Avenue. The position required not only technical skills, but a close working relationship with our systems users in Manhattan. One of the candidates was a young woman in her 30's named Naomi, who sat across from me, leaning forward in her chair with her hands folded in her lap. She spoke quietly when responding to my questions but other than that, she remained quiet and almost motionless. I, on the other hand, have always talked with my hands. I normally do this

unconsciously, but during this meeting, I became very aware of my hand gestures because her eyes followed my every move. Once in a while, I tested my theory by moving a hand in one direction, and then the other. Sure enough, she couldn't take her eyes off my motioning hands. Later when I relayed this story to my boss, we kidded about whether if I took both of my arms and spread them wide in opposite directions, would her head have exploded?

The hiring decision came down to two finalists, and this woman was one of them. They were both equally qualified on paper, but we passed on Naomi and extended the offer to the other. While we didn't exclude her purely on her odd behavior, it did make a difference. Her lack of affect and enthusiasm — coupled with her strange hand-tracking behavior — demonstrated that she didn't possess the type of personality required to work with our users, and I was concerned she just wouldn't fit in with our team.

## WATCH YOUR MOUTH

Presenting yourself professionally isn't just about what you say, but how you say it. Standard English is the only acceptable form of English to use when communicating for business, assuming both you and your interviewer speak English as your first language.

Swearing even a little bit is not okay, even if the interviewer does it. This may sound obvious, but people sometimes let words slip unconsciously, so be careful. Then there are those words that may not seem like swear words because they're used so often, but they're inappropriate to use in any kind of business setting. For example, "It sucks that I have to wake up so early in the morning." Or, "Part of my chores is to empty all the crap out of our garage from time to time." You may argue that *sucks* and *crap* aren't swear words, but they are too informal to use in an interview. Don't risk having an interviewer question your judgement.

Filler words like *um, uh, like, and basically* also need to be removed from your speech because they distract the listener. I know it's easier said than done. The best way to do it is to see yourself talk. In the next chapter I'll discuss practicing for your interview by recording your responses to interview questions. You may see yourself doing things you never knew you did.

Finally, don't use slang that can be culturally or racially offensive.

> During a practice interview with a student, she described herself as a grammar Nazi. The word Nazi in this context describes someone who's overly strict about something and came into common usage after its appearance in the 1990's sitcom Seinfeld. In the episode, a restaurant owner known as the Soup Nazi would shout, "No soup for you!" and throw the customer out of the restaurant if they didn't order the soup in exactly the way he demanded.
>
> But the use of the word Nazi in this context trivializes who the Nazis were and what they did. So why risk offending someone during something as important as an interview?

## IF YOU DON'T HAVE THE ANSWER, DON'T FAKE IT

If you don't know the answer to a question or even what the question means, the worst thing you can do is fake it. Employers don't expect you to know everything about the job or the specific duties until you're properly trained. What they *do* expect is that you recognize what you don't know and work quickly to learn it.

> I was being interviewed for the job as the Cooperative Education Coordinator at the school where I currently work. It was a panel interview with the high school Principal, the Department Chairperson, and the woman who was vacating the position I was applying for. Unlike the one at the catalog company, this interview was well coordinated and the questions they asked were good. The interview was going well until the principal asked my opinion about the current debate in Congress over the funding of vocational education and specifically about the Carl Perkins Grant. Huh? I had never worked in vocational education before and that question was so specific, I had no idea who Carl Perkins was, or that there was a debate on the subject in Congress. I thought for a moment, then asked, "Can you explain that question some more?" The current program coordinator explained to me what the Carl Perkins Grant was, I asked

questions, and a conversation between the two of us ensued. I was eventually able to express my opinion that federal funding for vocational education in public schools was very important in helping young people get the skills that will be in high demand in the 21st century.

Faking the answer to a question won't hide the fact that you don't know the answer. It will, however, show that you're willing to deceive your future employer to get what you want. If you're in the situation where you have absolutely no idea what the question means, do what I did and simply ask, "Can you explain that question some more?" If, on the other hand, you understand the question but don't know the answer, simply say so.

I'm always impressed by candidates, especially young people, who appear to be very well prepared for the interview. I can tell right away when they've rehearsed their responses to potential questions, and when they haven't. I'm especially impressed when they can admit that they don't know everything.

I was recently interviewing an applicant for a Bakery Associate position. Because it's a position that requires a high degree of skill, I was very pleased that she brought a portfolio of pictures of all the cakes and pastries she had worked on. I started with some basic questions about icing and piping techniques, and then pressed on to more advanced techniques: "How would you make a sugar flower?" She responded, "I don't know. I've never made one myself, but I've seen one made and I'd like to learn how to make them." Her response was exactly what I wanted to hear, because after we spoke, I took her back into our bakery and had her demonstrate her skills for the head of our bakery department. If she had been dishonest with me, I'd have known it before the interview ended.

When we hire for skilled positions like this, we want to see basic skills and understand what they *don't* know. That way we know what they need to be trained on.

Joe DeSimone
Store Manager – McCaffrey's Food Markets

180

It's okay to admit that you don't know the answer or that you don't know how to perform a task because employers know that young workers have a lot to learn. But always follow up with, "But I can tell you that I'm a fast learner and I'll do my best to come up to speed as quickly as possible." This shows that you can admit that you don't know everything, and that you're willing to learn what you don't know.

## THE MOST QUALIFIED CANDIDATE DOESN'T ALWAYS GET THE JOB

How you look on paper may get you the interview. How you connect with the person sitting in front of you will determine if you get the job. Connecting includes everything I spoke about in this chapter, like your enthusiasm, your body language, and the professional way you present yourself. This tells an interviewer how badly you want a job and how hard you'll work to succeed in it. It's what may actually result in a lesser qualified candidate getting the job.

> Large companies like AT&T will perform several rounds of interviews before extending a job offer, so my next interview for the internship was with the manager I would eventually work for. In less than a week I found myself sitting on a couch in a hallway of the company's corporate headquarters in Basking Ridge, New Jersey. Apparently, the person who would interview me was in a meeting down the hallway and would be with me momentarily. Minutes turned into an hour when I finally saw the door to the conference room open, and my interviewer emerge.
>
> She was a tiny woman but with a very big presence and a firm handshake. Her name was Linda, the Director of Call Center Services, and the Intern position would report directly to her, she explained. Then a flood of information poured out of her in the next few minutes. She talked about her organization, what they do, and what she needs from the people who worked for her. After just five minutes of this she looked down at her wristwatch, then up at me, and impatiently asked, "Do you have any questions for me?" I realized very sadly at that moment that the interview was over, and I barely uttered a word. I thought

181

about the days of preparation, the money spent on a new suit I couldn't afford, a day spent traveling to get here. It was all for nothing. I would be going home empty handed, because I wouldn't have the chance to tell her all about who I was and what I can do for her. Then, a thought came to me about the advice my brother, Ro, gave me the night before when he called to wish me good luck. He began by saying, "Don't leave the interview without saying this..." So, I didn't.

"I want you to know that I want this internship very badly. I have no friends or family here in New Jersey, so I would give 100% of myself to this job."

As the saying goes, and the rest is history. I got that internship at a starting salary of $22,000 a year—a lot of money in 1985.

Linda later revealed to me that she had interviewed two Intern candidates, me and an MBA (Master of Business Administration) student from Rutgers. I was surprised that she didn't choose the MBA who obviously had more education and experience than I did. She explained, "It was because of what you said to me in your interview." I had to think back for a moment and all I could remember saying was those few brief words. That's it? That's why you hired me? She went on to tell me that on paper, the MBA was far more qualified for the job, and he did well in his interview. But what I had said to her impressed her more.

**When you really want the job, ask for it.**

The 30-second commercial I've taught you to create was advice borne out of this ten-second commercial that got me my internship at AT&T. Have your 30-second commercial ready for the interview.

**Next Up...**

Having clear expectations and knowing how to present yourself is a good start to understanding the overall interview process. In the next chapter, we'll discuss all the things you need to do to prepare when you've been granted an interview.

## CHAPTER SUMMARY QUIZ

The following quiz summarizes the chapter.

1.  Being a storyteller in an interview means to make up stories of things you did that you didn't really do.
    a.  True
    b.  False

2.  What does good body language look like?
    a.  Being a good listener.
    b.  Having a good affect by showing emotion or feeling in response to the speaker so they know you're listening.
    c.  Maintaining good eye contact and having good posture.
    d.  All of the above.

3.  Which of the following should you avoid when you speak in business?
    a.  Slang words like "sucks" or "crap"
    b.  Filler words like "um," "like," or "basically."
    c.  Language that is culturally or racial offensive, like "grammar Nazi".
    d.  All of the above should be avoided.

4.  What should you do if you don't know the answer to an interview question?
    a.  Act like you know it. Give an answer with confidence and they'll believe you.
    b.  Look it up on your cell phone.
    c.  Ask for clarification of the question. If you still don't know, admit it and state that you'll do your best to learn things on the job as quickly as possible.
    d.  Tell the interview you'll email them the answer later.

5.  It's possible that what a candidate says and how they say it could lead to their getting hired over a more qualified candidate.
    a.  True
    b.  False

Answers: 1b, 2d, 3d, 4c, 5a

# Lesson 14

# Interview Preparation

The day will arrive when you're invited to attend an interview. Once it's scheduled, you have to prepare yourself to discuss the specific job with the specific company you'll interview with. Research the company — who they are and what they do — and practice answering interview questions. Details like how you appear, how you'll get to the interview location, what to take with you, and how to be on time are important. Complete the Interview Preparation Worksheet in Appendix F for every scheduled interview, and I promise you'll be thoroughly prepared.

## BUSINESS 101 - WHO ARE YOU TALKING TO?

> There's a show on TV called *The Job Interview*—a reality show where real companies interview real candidates for jobs. In one episode, an accounting firm was looking for an accountant. During one of the interviews, a candidate explained that she used to work for a public accounting firm, and that she never wants to work in public accounting again. "Well, that might be a problem," the recruiter explained. "We're a CPA firm." CPA stands for Certified Public Accountants.

When you first apply for a job, you should have a general idea about what the company does. But when you interview with that company, having a general idea isn't enough. You need to know who they are and what they do so you can understand how the duties of your job fit into the bigger picture.

### How is the company organized? What is its form of ownership?

First, go to the company's website and read their "About us" page to learn about their history, their products and services, their clients, and their mission statement or business philosophy. It may explain how the company is organized, and what type of ownership it has.

Is it a public company, or corporation, owned by many people who have bought shares of the company's stock? Barnes and Noble for example, is a publicly owned company.

Is it a sole proprietorship that is privately owned by one person, or a partnership owned by two or more people?

A company may be a franchise, a special type of ownership where a company allows individuals to buy specific store locations and run them as their own business. For example, 7-Eleven and McDonald's are both franchises.

Once you understand how the company is organized, browse their products and services to get a good idea of what they offer. There may be a "Community" tab that describes the charities that they support. A "Careers" page will list job openings and instructions on how to apply. As you can imagine, most young people will go into an interview without knowing this basic information about a company. If you can show that you took the time to learn this information, you'll stand out in a big way from your competition.

One word of caution about a company's website — there may be more than one.

### There's a difference between a *brand* and a *company*.

For example, if you search *Burger King* on the internet, you'll find the website that's aimed at customers that provides information on their menu, locations, coupons, etc. But as a candidate for employment, you also need to visit the *company website*. By searching "Who owns Burger King," you'll see that it's owned by Restaurant Brands International (RBI). Then go to the RBI website to research the company itself. You'll find information like the fact that RBI not only owns Burger King, but other brands like Popeyes. Burger King is the brand, RBI is the company.

One last piece of advice about the company's offerings.

### Be a customer.

While this isn't necessary, it would sure help. Imagine being able to say, "I've been coming to Barnes and Noble since I was in kindergarten." It's a powerful statement that tells an interviewer that you like the company and believe in it. If you're not a customer, try to become one. My daughter, Marisa, recently applied for a job at a local restaurant/micro-brewery. She worked in a similar restaurant during college and became very knowledge-able about different types of craft beers. Before submitting her application, she and a friend went there to eat and to sample the home-made brews. She loved the experience, which not only made her excited to want to work there (there's that *enthusiasm* I spoke about earlier), but also enabled her to talk about her first-hand knowledge of the restaurant in the interview.

## PRACTICE DOES NOT MAKE PERFECT

The phrase that follows is *perfect practice makes perfect*. But there's no such thing as a perfect interview. At first, you'll make some mistakes and that's to be expected because interviewing is a learned skill that improves with practice. While practice won't make you perfect, it'll certainly help you think through what you want to say, how you want to say it, and give you some confidence when you're saying it in an interview. Do the following to prac-tice your interview questions and take notes as you construct your answers.

1. Start your practice by looking over your resume or application to freshen your memory. You need to know exactly what the inter-viewer has in front of them.
2. Come up with the key points you want to make about your job skills, soft skills, and other experiences.
3. Read the interview questions in the next chapter and think about your answer. Don't forget to be a storyteller and support all your claims with examples of *what you did* and not just *what you would do*.
4. Practice your responses in front of a mirror and record yourself with your cell phone. You'll be surprised at what you see. When I first saw a recording of me teaching a lesson, I noticed that I never smiled, I talked with my hands, and I spoke too fast.
5. And finally, role play questions and answers with someone with lots of interviewing experience. Face them directly and practice using positive affect and body language.

The more you practice, the more opportunities you'll have to make adjust-ments as you go. But don't memorize your responses word for word or you'll come across stiff or insincere. Most importantly, ask your practice in-terviewer for honest feedback; they'll hear and see things that you don't.

## MAKE YOUR FIRST INTERVIEW A PRACTICE INTERVIEW

Every year one of the most valuable activities I organized for my students was the *mock interview,* like the one I had in college with AT&T. I had recruiters and hiring managers from my Co-op employers and my own school district volunteer their time to conduct the interviews. The students were dressed professionally, had created their resumes, and prepared for their interviews. Unless you have this type of opportunity at school, your first interview will be a real one, and you won't get to practice. But don't worry, I have a tip that will help you. It's the same tip I gave you for when you followed up on your application.

**Try not to schedule your first interview for the job you really want.**

Over the course of my career, I've been in plenty of interviews when on the drive home I've said to myself, "I should have said this," or "I shouldn't have said that." You'll be rusty at first but as you get more experience, you'll get better at it. So, say you have three companies that have invited you for an interview. Rank them in order of your preference, #1 being your favorite and #3 being your least favorite. Try to schedule company #3 first and #1 last. By the third interview, you'll have rehearsed what you want to say and what you want to avoid. As a result, I guarantee the interview for the job you really want will go smoother than the ones you practiced on.

## YOUR PHYSICAL APPEARANCE

For the interview, dress for the job you're applying for. I discussed these points in detail in Chapter 8 – The Walk-In Inquiry:
- Be neat and well-groomed overall.
- Wear your *Sunday best.* Never wear jeans, t-shirt, sneakers, or flip-flops regardless of how the employees are dressed. And of course, nothing torn, dirty or too revealing.
- Cover up excessive tattoos and remove excessive piercings.
- Keep hair, clothes, nails, make-up, and jewelry simple so that the interviewer focuses on you without those distractions.

One more piece of advice that affects your appearance. Watch what you eat or drink prior to an interview. Some foods and especially carbonated drinks may cause gastro-intestinal issues or give you bad breath. These are distractions for the interviewer you don't want.

## DON'T BE LATE

Plan out your transportation before the day arrives, whether you're driving, walking, biking, or taking public transportation. If you're unfamiliar with the exact location, do a practice run the day before, and do it around the same time of day as the interview so you know what traffic will be like. Note how long it took to get there and figure out where you'll park. Whatever it takes, don't be late.

> My principal and I were conducting interviews for a Phys Ed position and our next applicant was a young man right out of college. When he came into the room, he was nicely dressed in a suit and tie, but he was all sweaty and his shirt was badly wrinkled. Worse than that, he was 25 minutes late. "I'm sorry I'm late, but I couldn't find you," he explained. We continued with the interview.
>
> After all the interviews were over, the principal and I discussed our thoughts on each of them. When this young man's name came up, the principal responded, "Nope. He was late." When I reminded him that the candidate couldn't find us, he physically turned in his chair, looked me in the eye, and with finality said, "He could have if he tried yesterday."
>
> **Carol Czumbil**
> **High School Physical Education Teacher**

Arriving on time means walking through the door 10 minutes early. If you're traveling by car, use the GPS app on your phone well before you leave for the interview to confirm the travel time and ensure there are no traffic delays. There's a saying about getting to work on time: *If you're early you're on time. If you're on time you're late. If you're late you're fired.* If you're late for the interview, it'll be assumed you'll be late for work. Absolutely, positively, don't be late for the interview.

### What if you're late?

As hard as we try, sometimes bad things happen which we can't avoid. If you're running late, call the interviewer, apologize, and give an estimated time of arrival: *"I'm so sorry but I'm going to be 20 minutes late."*

188

If your lateness is due to no fault of your own, say so when you call: *"There's a very bad accident on 95 and the traffic is all backed up."*

If, however, your reason for being late is that you couldn't find the building, you didn't know where to park, you overslept, you had to stop for gas…you get the idea, don't offer an excuse, just the apology.

When you arrive, apologize again and tell them lateness is not a habit of yours: *"I am so sorry again for inconveniencing you. I want you to know that I'm usually a very punctual person."* And then mean it!

Finally, if someone is driving you, don't let them enter the building with you. Remember that employers want to see that you are your own person. If you come in with a parent, the employer will wonder if they'll be dealing with just you, or with you and a parent.

## WHAT TO TAKE

I have a leather portfolio that I've taken to every interview since college. If you don't have one, a new, clean manila folder will do. My portfolio has a notebook on one side, a pocket on the other, and a loop for a pen or pencil. Inside the pocket, I keep copies of my resume, including my references.

> My interview for the Co-op Coordinator position was with three interviewers. Each of them should have had a copy of my resume provided by Human Resources, but as soon as I sat down in the principal's office, I noticed right away that they had a pad of paper in front of them, but no resume. Luckily, I had brought enough copies with me to give to each of them.

A notebook or a pad of paper should contain a list of the questions you want to ask, as well as your 30-second commercial. Your questions may be answered during your conversation, but it's a good idea to check the list before the interview is over. I'll give you that list in the next chapter.

### Next up…

The next chapter contains not only the questions you need to practice, but the entire interviewing experience, from the time you walk in to the time you leave.

## CHAPTER SUMMARY QUIZ

The following quiz summarizes the chapter.

1. What's the best place to find out about a company's history, products and services, clients and business philosophy?
   a. Their Facebook page
   b. The Better Business Bureau
   c. Ask a friend who works there
   d. Their "About Us" page on their company website

2. Why should you practice your interview questions?
   a. To think through what you want to say
   b. Because practice makes perfect
   c. To make a recording and email it to the interviewer
   d. To have your responses memorized word for word.

3. You should wear whatever clothing, jewelry, hair, make-up, and body art that makes you comfortable. Employers like you to show your individuality and reject business etiquette.
   a. True
   b. False

4. You should arrive at your interview at least 10 minutes early.
   a. True
   b. False

5. What should you take with you to an interview?
   a. A notebook on which to take notes during the interview
   b. A folder or portfolio
   c. A list of questions to ask, and your 30-second commercial
   d. All of the above

Answers: 1d, 2a, 3b, 4a, 5d

# Lesson 15

# Nailing the Interview

All the work and preparation you've put into job hunting was for the purpose of getting the interview, and so you've arrived at your final and most important chance to make a good impression. How you present yourself and how well you sell yourself will help the interviewer(s) determine if you're a good fit for the job.

Interview questions fall into three categories: the good, the bad, and the tricky. It's important that you anticipate these questions and have a response prepared. Finally, you'll have to anticipate the possibility of leaving the interview with or without a job offer.

## MAKE A GOOD FIRST IMPRESSION TO *EVERYONE*

When you arrive on time, smile and be polite to everyone, not just the interviewer. Don't make the mistake of thinking that entry level workers like hostesses, cashiers, and secretaries aren't important to your success. They have the ears of higher-level managers and they can influence a manager's hiring decisions. Entry level workers can be very, very powerful, so treat them with the respect they deserve.

## ASSESS YOUR ENVIRONMENT

Observe your surroundings carefully to see if it's a place you'd like to work. Are the employees upbeat, smiling, and looking happy to be there? Or do they look like it's all business? Is the location clean and comfortable or is it disorganized or messy?

One of my Co-op students, Alex, had an experience with an employer that was so bizarre that I never sent another student to apply there again. The interview was with a local accounting firm who had recently called looking for high school students to work during tax season. It was a great job for Alex—he had already taken several business courses and intended to be a

Business major in college. The day following the interview, I called him into my office to see how the interview went. I'll never forget the look on his face as he raised his eyes to me, and said almost in a whisper, "I sat in cat piss, Mrs. Purdy." He then looked back down in his lap. According to Alex, part of the building was an accounting office, and part of it was the owner's home. What he also observed was that there were cats everywhere—outside the house, inside the house, and all over the furniture. I removed the accounting firm from my employer list, not just because my poor student sat in cat urine, but a messy, dirty, disorganized work environment is a good indication that the employer will have the same disorganized work habits and management style. It's not a good environment for anyone, especially a young person who's anxious to learn good work habits.

During the interview, also observe the dress code. What are the employees wearing? Unless the job requires a uniform, you'll have to create your own workplace wardrobe. Does the dress code seem casual or formal? If it's casual, how casual? Are the women wearing jeans and leggings or dress pants and skirts? Are the men wearing t-shirts or collared shirts? You don't want to show up for your first day of work underdressed or overdressed.

## INTRODUCTIONS

Greet your interviewer with a smile and make eye contact. After that, let them lead your interaction.

**Follow their lead.**

Wait for the interviewer to offer a handshake and give a firm handshake in return. There's an old and very wrong theory that if you're a male, you should give another male a firm handshake. But you should offer a gentle, "half handshake" to a woman by offering only your fingers and not the palm of your hand. Don't do that; it's demeaning to women. You are now entering the world of business and a firm handshake is expected for everyone you meet, regardless of gender.

During the introduction, listen carefully for the interviewer's name, and then refer to him or her by that name. For example, if the interviewer introduces himself as Dan, you may call him Dan. If he says Mr. Smith, call him Mr. Smith. But what if he introduces himself as Dan Smith? Proper business etiquette dictates that you refer to people in higher level positions by their formal names, in this case Mr. Smith, until he gives you permission to call him Dan: "You can call me Dan."

## THE GOOD: 20 COMMON INTERVIEW QUESTIONS

There are three basic things an employer wants to know about you.
1.   Are you qualified for the job?
2.   Will you be a good fit for their team?
3.   Do you really want the job?

The fact that you've been invited to the interview means that based on these three questions, the employer thinks you may be a good candidate for the job. However, how you perform in the interview will help them determine if you're the *best* candidate for the job. The following is a list of typical questions for entry-level positions. Remember that past experiences can come from jobs, school, extra-curricular activities, your community, church, or any other areas of your life. Above all, remember to be a story teller.

WATRA stands for "what are they really asking."

### #1 - Tell me about yourself.

WATRA: What do you think is important for me to know about you so I can get to know you better?

In interviews that are very informal and very brief, this may be the only question you're asked, so make your response great. Talk about your past experiences, skills, and accomplishments as they may relate to the position — not your family, your favorite color, or any other personal details that are on your resume. You can talk about your interests or hobbies that may show your personality, if they're relevant to the position.

### #2 - What do you think your responsibilities will be in this job?

WATRA: Have you done your homework? How well do you know about the position you're applying for?

Give details and examples to demonstrate that you have experience with the job duties. If you don't have the experience, tell them what you know them to be from your research of the job position. Remember O*Net Online.

### #3 - What are your major strengths?

WATRA: What can you do for me?

Your strengths are probably what others have said about you. Don't give vague answers like *"I'm a fast learner"* without providing examples as evidence.

*I learned how to make sugar flowers when I first started working there, and within three weeks, I was training other Bakery Associates to make them too.*

### #4 - What is your greatest accomplishment?

WATRA: What are your past achievements as they are a good predictor of your future performance?

*I graduated high school with a 3.8 GPA while holding down a part-time job to help support my family financially.*

### #5 - What are your major weaknesses?

WATRA: Do you acknowledge that you have things to learn and areas where you can develop and improve?

Common advice is to offer a strength disguised as a weakness. Don't do this. It's insincere and tells the interviewer that you believe you have no weaknesses. Be honest, but not too honest.

Not honest: *"I work too hard."*

Too honest: *"No matter how hard I try, I'm always late for work."*

If you can't think of anything, a great age-appropriate answer is, *"I sometimes lack self-confidence, but I think it's because I know I have a lot to learn."*

Don't leave a weakness hanging in the air; always go on to explain how you're improving on it. *"I think I'm getting better at this. The more I see myself succeed at the new things I try, the more confidence I gain."*

### #6 - Why do you want to leave your current job? Or, why did you leave your previous job?

WATRA: Did you have problems and issues at your old job that you'll be bringing to your new job?

Look back at your response for this on your application. Remember that if you've already left your previous job because you didn't have enough hours or you weren't making enough money, how much are you making now with no job? Don't use these as excuses and don't blame others for why you left, especially your former boss. Instead, focus on why you're looking for a new job. For example:

*I was doing the same thing for over a year and I'm looking for more responsibility. Or…*

*This job is more in line with my career goals.*

Now let's talk about the problem of job-hopping. I told you that if you left a job within six months, leave it off your application or resume. If that was your only experience and you had no choice but to include it, you'll have to address it now. The fact that you were invited to the interview means that the employer likes what they saw on your resume but wants you to explain why you left after such a short period of time. For example:

*I made some mistakes before when I didn't really know what kind of job I wanted. This time it's different because I went through a process of matching my interests and skills with the requirements of this job. I discovered that I'd rather work with my hands than work with customers. I'm convinced that this job is a good fit for me.*

### #7 – What is your GPA?

WATRA: Do you meet the company's minimum GPA requirement?

You may get this question if you left your GPA off your application or resume. If your cumulative GPA is lower than a 3.0, offer your major GPA. If they are both lower than 3.0, you need to explain the reason in a way that doesn't make excuses. Were you working while in school? Did you take on too many extracurricular activities? If you made a mistake by not making school your top priority, own it, but explain what you learned from it. If your grades improved after these issues, say so. For example:

*My overall GPA is 2.8. I will admit that I had some challenges getting adjusted in my freshman year in college, but since then I've brought up by grades, and*

195

*my major GPA is a 3.0.*

### #8 - How were your math grades in school?

WATRA: How are your problem-solving skills?

Be honest if they were good. If not, say your basic math skills are good. That's what most jobs at your age require.

### #9 - What is your favorite subject in school? Why?

WATRA: What are your key strengths?

The answer doesn't have to be an academic class like science or math. It can be art, music, or physical education as long as you can relate it to the job you're applying for.

### #10 – What is your least favorite subject in school?

WATRA: Are the school subjects you dislike related to the job?

Explain that although a subject was difficult or unpleasant, how did you persevere?

### #11 - What kind of hourly rate are you looking for?

WATRA: Are your expectations in line with ours?

By now you should have a range in mind. Give them the range and explain why you're deserving of it.

### #12 - Why do you want to work here? What interests you about our product or service?

WATRA: Do you want this job, or just any job?

Show that you have taken the time to learn about the company and the responsibilities of the job. If there's a personal connection to the company or products, mention it now.

### #13 - In one sentence, state why our company should hire you?

WATRA: Sum up your qualifications for me. How good are you at selling yourself?

Deliver your 30-second commercial.

## #14 - What is your availability?

WATRA: Will you be able to work when we need you?

The interviewer knows that as a high school or college student, you have other commitments. However, depending on the nature of the job and their hours of operation, your schedule has to fit into their requirements. Answer this question not only by giving them your availability, but also the blocks of time you are unavailable. Be specific:

*I can work Monday through Friday after school, except on Tuesdays I'm not available. I'm available most Saturdays. I can work Sundays after 1 pm.*

## #15 - What have you learned from some of the jobs you've held?

WATRA: What do you have to contribute?

Discuss your soft skills, not your job skills. Are you open to constructive criticism? Are you better at dealing with difficult customers or other situations? What problem-solving experiences did you gain?

## #16 - Do you prefer working with others or by yourself?

WATRA: Are you right for this type of position?

Be honest or you may work in a situation you don't like. However, if you're just starting out in the workforce, try to be open to either situation until you have a strong opinion about how to answer this question. For example:

*Both. In school I work very well on group projects, but I'm also good at taking responsibility for my own work.*

## #17 - How would you deal with an irate customer?

WATRA: How well do you handle stress?

The best answer here is to describe a situation where you actually had to deal with an irate customer. The interviewer wants to know if you stayed calm, were polite and sympathetic to the customer's issue, and helped the customer actually resolve their problem. If you couldn't resolve the problem, did you escalate the issue to your manager? If you've never dealt with an irate customer, explain how you dealt with an irate co-worker, classmate, or someone else you were trying to help.

### #18 - Have you ever been fired?

WATRA: Will I have reasons to fire you?

If you've been fired, you have to tell the truth because the employer that fired you may be contacted for an employment background check. Keep the explanation short, and don't blame anyone else. Instead, be honest: *"I was late more than I should have been."* Explain what you learned from the experience, what you should have done differently, and that you've grown professionally as a result.

### #19 - Have you been convicted of a crime?

WATRA: Do you have a criminal history that will put my business at risk?

Again, tell the truth. You may have seen this question on the application. Explain what happened and what you learned from the experience. If it was just a mistake, say so. Saying you were just at the wrong place at the wrong time shows you haven't taken responsibility or made amends for what you did. Ask them to give you a chance to demonstrate that you're a different person. And remember that there's a difference between being charged with a crime and being convicted.

### #20 - When can you start working?

If you have a current job, you must give two weeks' notice to your present employer to give them time to find your replacement. They may only need one, or none at all, but you must make the offer. If you aren't leaving another job, the best answer is "immediately."

## THE BAD: INAPPROPRIATE OR ILLEGAL QUESTIONS

While the questions above are typically the ones you'll encounter, you have to be prepared to answer questions that should never be asked, and those that seem irrelevant.

Anti-discrimination laws are there for our protection so that employers don't discriminate or harass based on certain criteria. These laws are governed by the U.S. Equal Employment Opportunity Commission (EEOC) and you should familiarize yourself with these laws by going to their website, www.eeoc.gov. Company job ads and websites may state that they are an "Equal Employment Opportunity Employer." But if that phrase isn't mentioned, that doesn't mean that these laws don't apply to them, because all companies by law must offer "equal opportunities" to all employees. Not only do these laws protect employees, they protect job applicants like you.

While these laws exist, it's very likely that you'll encounter forbidden questions throughout your professional career. But before you write off the employer, determine whether the question is an honest mistake or an indication of a problematic company culture. It's important to understand that many employers won't even realize that what they're doing is illegal. Hiring employees may be a new job duty for a particular manager. As you interview more, you'll see that hiring managers have differing levels of ability, experience, and maturity, so an inappropriate comment may not be a big deal to them. Realize also that this may not be the only interviewer you'll speak with. Remember my experience at the retail catalog company? If I bolted after the firing squad, I wouldn't have met the CIO and accepted the job offer. Try to be patient and see the interview process through.

I'll tell you how to handle these questions in a moment, but here's what you definitely shouldn't do.

### Don't refuse to answer the question.

Saying "you're not allowed to ask that" will make things very awkward very quickly.

There are two better alternatives. The first is to answer the question honestly. There are questions below that you might even wonder why they are illegal. Questions about your age while you're young, marital status while you're single, and citizenship if you're a U.S. citizen may seem completely innocent. If you're comfortable answering them, go right ahead, but know that from a legal standpoint, these are all forbidden interview questions.

If you're uncomfortable with the question, the second way to handle it is to do what politicians do, and that's to *pivot*. That means change the subject slightly by answering a related question that wasn't asked. Try to determine why the question was asked; in other words, what does the interview really want to know? Then, pivot the discussion back to your qualifications for the job, leaving out the part that's inappropriate or illegal. As a result, the interviewer may get the hint and change their line of questioning. If this strategy doesn't work and the inappropriate line of questioning continues, then that's a valuable piece of information to consider when determining if you want to work for this company.

Let's break down these laws, the illegal questions that might be asked, what are they really asking (WATRA), and possible responses.

### Age discrimination is prohibited under the Age Discrimination in Employment Act.

Before you get too excited about being protected by this law, understand that it only covers individuals over the age of 40. My students often complain that they didn't get the job because they were too young, or that if there's an issue or conflict at work, the manager always takes the side of the adult. They point to these as examples of age discrimination because of their youth. While I can sympathize that they may have been treated unfairly, from a legal standpoint, this is not age discrimination. It's possible that their youth is a factor in the manager's decision. It's also possible that lack of experience and maturity also play a part.

### Bad Question #1: How old are you?

WATRA: Will your age restrict your hours of work and the duties you can perform?

While providing your age in a job application is needed for the employer to conduct a background check on you, asking this question in an interview is forbidden. While your lack of experience may disqualify you, your age shouldn't. But at your young age, they're most likely asking whether you're old enough to work in the job you're applying for, or to determine if your workdays and hours will be restricted due to your state's child labor laws. You should go ahead and answer this question.

*I'm __ years old and I do have my working papers.*

### It's unlawful for an employer to discriminate based on a disability according to the Americans with Disabilities Act.

200

In other words, you can't be denied a job because of a disability or family medical history, but you can be denied if those things prevent you from performing the essential duties of the job.

**Bad Question #2: I see you're walking with a limp.
Do you have a disability?**

WATRA: Are you able to perform the required duties of the job?

*At my current job, I work about 25 hours a week and spend most of that time standing at the register or helping customers look for merchandise. I was never late and only called out once when I had the flu. Last October I received the Employee of the Month award.*

Did you recognize the pivot?

**Sex discrimination based on your gender or
sexual orientation is illegal.**

A furniture retailer called me about several job openings in their warehouse. "I need guys on the floor to pack and load the furniture into the trucks. I need gals in the office helping the secretaries. The warehouse guys get $9.50 an hour. The office job pays $8.50 an hour."

Labeling certain jobs for males versus females is the most blatant form of sex discrimination. Who's to say that a young man who's taken business classes and is proficient with computers can't work in an office? Why would you assume that a young woman who has the strength and skills can't do a physical job in a warehouse? And the dollar difference in their hourly wage? That's just salt in the wound. There is one exception to this law though; the entertainment industry is allowed to discriminate based on sex for models and actors for obvious reasons.

**Bad Question #3: How do you feel about working for a woman?**

WATRA: Have you ever had an issue or conflict with a manager and if so, how did you resolve it?

*I've worked well under all kinds of managers. There was this one supervisor in particular who was difficult for a lot of us to work with. Here's what happened and how I resolved the situation....*

### Sexual harassment in the workplace is illegal.

Sexual harassment takes sex discrimination to a whole new level. It constitutes any unwanted advances, behaviors, or innuendos. It can be verbal — something that's said. It can be graphic — something written anywhere like a poster, an email, or on clothing. It can be physical — the only acceptable physical contact in an interview is the handshake. And it can be non-verbal — a long look at a body part or a violation of your personal space.

For a behavior to be considered sexual harassment, it has to be repeated and have a negative effect on your performance at work or in the interview. A dirty joke may make you uncomfortable (as it should!) but may be too trivial to meet the standards of sexual harassment. Keep in mind that sexual harassers can be men or women, heterosexual or homosexual.

### Bad Question #4: What are you doing later tonight? How about dinner?

This is a totally inappropriate question to ask.

*I'm working later tonight. At that job, my responsibilities are....*

### Bad Question #5: I like those pants you're wearing.

Personal comments like this should be kept out of an interview entirely because it can be taken one of two ways. It's either a genuine compliment or a come-on. This answer will address either scenario.

*That's a good point. What is the dress code for this position?*

If you believe this comment had sexual overtones, as the saying goes, where there's smoke there's fire. Just as you are expected to show your best side during an interview, that's equally true of the employer. If he or she behaves inappropriately during an interview, what must they be like at work? If you do get a job offer, this behavior is an important factor to consider before you make your final decision.

**It's unlawful to discriminate based on race, color or religion.**

**Bad Question #6: What religion do you practice?**

WATRA: Will your religion prevent you from working on certain days of the week?

*If you're asking about my availability, I'm available to work after school Monday through Friday, and all-day Saturday. I'm not available Sunday afternoons when I have practice for the county youth orchestra.*

**It's unlawful to discriminate based on nationality.**

Employers can be fined for hiring workers that are not allowed to work legally in the U.S. You don't have to be a U.S. citizen, but you do have to be authorized to work here. If you're hired, you'll be required to produce a photo ID to prove your identity (like a driver's license or student ID), and proof of authorization to work in the U.S. (like a Social Security card, birth certificate, or an employment authorization document issued by the Department of Homeland Security). A passport serves as proof of both. A list of all the documents that meet these criteria are on IRS tax Form I-9 which your employer must complete for all new employees.

**Bad Question #7: Are you a U.S. citizen?**

WATRA: Can I legally hire you?

*I have a driver's license and social security card to show I can work legally.*

**It's unlawful to discriminate based on marital status, pregnancy, or childbirth.**

An employer must treat issues around pregnancy, like time off or medical issues, the same way they must treat a temporarily disabled person.

**Bad Question #8: Are you married?**

WATRA: Will you get pregnant and miss a lot of work, or quit your job?

*Having a job is a high priority for me. Last year, I only missed two shifts at my old job, and both times I found my own replacement.*

## Bad Question #9: Do you have children?

WATRA: Will your family obligations get in the way of your job?

*One of the things I'm very good at is separating my personal life from my work life. When I'm at work, I'm 100% at work.*

### Employers in certain states must not request your online account login information.

In Chapter 6, I suggested that you set your scrubbed, professional, social media accounts to public so that the people in your network, especially recruiters, employers, and co-workers can follow you freely to learn more about you. If you have accounts that are set to private, they have to be totally free of inappropriate or even questionable content. This interview question is a good example of how privacy settings will not guarantee your privacy. About half of states have laws making it illegal for an employer to ask an employee or applicant for their login information, or to pull up their account in the employer's presence. This also means that the other half do not.

### Bad Question #10: I see your Instagram is set to private. Can I have your login information?

WATRA: What type of reputation do you have online? I want to know who I'm hiring.

*I really don't use it much, but I'll be happy to set it to public when I get home so you can access my information.*

## THE TRICKY: RANDOM OR QUIRKY QUESTIONS

Every now and then, you may get a question that outwardly appears to have nothing to do with anything job related. They're intended to see how you react to a question you didn't expect to be asked. How you answer will give some insight into your personality, problem-solving skills, or your ability to handle stress.

A former student came to visit me last June after finishing up his freshman year in college. He relayed some of his college experiences and wanted me to know how the things he learned in my Introduction to Business class had already helped him after high school:

"Do you remember telling us about how some employers ask crazy questions? I was interviewing for a job as an attendant at a rock-climbing gym, and the guy asked me, "If you were a car, what kind of car would you be?"' At first, I was shocked. But then I remembered what you said about why they ask those questions, and it helped me to stay calm. After thinking about if for a minute, I told him I'd be a Hummer."

The answer to questions like, "what car would you be" may provide a hint about your personality. Are you flashy or conservative? Are you a risk taker or are you risk averse? Questions like, "why are manhole covers round?" may be asked to ascertain your intellect, creativity, or problem-solving ability. Questions like, "How do you think this interview is going?" are meant to put you on the spot to see how you react under stress. Think about how you might respond to questions like the following:

*If you were a [car, fruit, flower, pizza topping, etc.], what would you be and why?*

*If you had to sing a song in front of the entire staff, what would you sing?*

*What's your favorite movie quote?*

*What's the last book you read?*

*If you could have any superpower you want in the world, what would it be and why?*

*You've been given a giraffe. You can't sell it, give it away, or in any way get rid of it. What would you do with it?*

*How lucky are you on a scale of one to 10?*

I can't prepare you for all the possible quirky questions you may be asked. Just know that questions like these are gaining in popularity, so don't let them surprise you or get you rattled. First, stay calm and know that there's no right or wrong answer. Then, take your time to think about the answer: *"That's an interesting question. Let me think about that for a moment."* Next, think about why this question is being asked. What's the relationship between this question and the job you're applying for? Is it to assess your personality, critical thinking skills, or ability to handle a stressful situation? Finally, answer the question in a way to provide the interviewer with the insight they're looking for. The answer my student gave in the rock-climbing interview was excellent. The fact that a Hummer is an adventurous but safe vehicle is very relevant to the job he was applying for.

I truly hope you don't get questions like this when you are just starting out in the workforce. If you do, remember that just as they're assessing you, you should be assessing them. If your interviewer is asking more stress-inducing questions than traditional questions, you should question the stressful nature of the job you're applying for. That's another valuable piece of information you now have about whether it's a job you want to take or not.

## ASK QUESTIONS AND YOUR 30-SECOND COMMERCIAL

The last question you'll be asked is, "Do you have any questions for me." Remember that the purpose of an interview is just as much about you learning about the job as it is about the employer learning about you. You will potentially be spending 15-20 hours per week at this job. Before you take a job, don't you want to know what to expect from that job?

### How will this job meet your needs?

Remember Maslow and his hierarchy of needs? Your job must provide the hourly wage you have in mind, but it must do much more. How will your skills and experiences bring value to the employer? Will you be able to perform the required duties of the job and if not, how will you learn? Will you enjoy working with the kind of customers and co-workers the business attracts? This is potentially your last chance to determine whether this job will not only satisfy your survival and safety needs, but also your social and esteem needs. While you've researched the company on your own, you have someone sitting right in front of you who can answer your questions directly.

The best candidates come into the interview with expectations. That means they've thought about what working for us might be like, and so they come in with questions. When I interview candidates, I ask pretty much the same questions and get pretty much the same answers. It's what they *ask* that makes them stand out.

"What would I be doing?"

"How will I be trained?"

"Who will I be working with?"

When a candidate comes in knowing what they need to know about the company or job, I know they're really interested in the job.

One of the best questions I was ever asked was a personal one. As a result of attending one of our pre-interview workshops, the candidate knew that I started here as a teenager and worked my way up. She asked me questions like, "What did you do when you first started here? What did you like about your job? What didn't you like about your job?" I was very truthful about my answers. Some candidates think that if they ask questions, it's more likely that they won't get the job. It's exactly the opposite. If they ask questions and then accept the job offer, I know that their expectations of the job were met.

Rodney Anderson
Supervisor – Human Resources, Sesame Place

If during the course of the interview you didn't get all of your questions answered, ask them now.

- What are the duties of this job?
- Would I report directly to you or to someone else?
- How will I be trained for the job?
- What days and number of hours can I expect to be scheduled?
- What do you like about working here?
- What do you dislike about working here?

Regarding your pay, if the company has a set range for each position, that amount may have already been disclosed to you. If you haven't had that discussion yet, this is still not the time to bring it up. Many companies that do not have a set range will wait to see who they're making an offer to before offering the hourly rate.

And there's one other situation you should take advantage of if you ever get the chance. If the person you're replacing is in the interview with you, there's a very important question you should ask.

---

When I was interviewed for the position of Cooperate Education Coordinator, the woman I was replacing was on the panel of interviewers. When the principal introduced her to me, he announced that she would be moving into a new job as a Guidance Counselor in the coming school year. Before the interview concluded, I was asked if I had any other questions. "Just one," I said as I turned my attention to the woman I was replacing.

"Why are you leaving this job?"

I'll never forget the expression on her face and her response. She smiled warily, "I've been doing this for 13 and a half years, and it's enough." The tired expression on her face and those two words, *it's enough,* confirmed for me everything I had heard about this job position: the stress, the long hours, and most of all, the unpredictability of the employment situations that was simply the nature of the program.

As a result of the interview, I learned everything I felt I needed to learn to make a decision. I, of course, accepted the offer and went into the job with my eyes wide open.

---

Getting truthful answers to your questions allows you to make a fully informed decision. If after you understand what's good as well as what's not so good about the job, and you still take it, that means you're going into a job with realistic expectations. You have now exponentially increased the likelihood that you'll find enjoyment and success in this job. And employers will appreciate your savviness in how you went about making your decision.

### End with your 30-second commercial.

Finally, ask for the job.

*I want to say that after this discussion, I think I'm even more interested in the*

*Teaching Assistant position. As I've explained, I have over 3 years of experience in programming a number of different languages, and I have a 3.6 GPA in all of my Computer Science related classes. I'm organized and detail oriented. My class schedule is flexible for next semester to work around your schedule, and I can be available most evenings and weekends. I want this position very badly and if I got it, I promise to give 100% of myself to the job.*

It's a powerful way to end an interview and will leave a lasting impression on the interviewer.

## ENDING THE INTERVIEW

You'll know that the interview is coming to an end when you're asked if you have any other questions. Then, as during your introduction, follow their lead. Wait for the interviewer to stand, then stand. They may walk you out or to another room, so wait for them to offer a handshake. Shake their hand firmly and thank them for their time.

If you're not offered the job on the spot, it's very possible that the company still has other applicants to interview before a decision is made. The interviewer may tell you that they'll be in touch with you within a certain time frame; if they don't, ask if you can call to inquire about their decision. Even if you have the interviewer's name, title, and email address, ask for a business card now. You'll need it for following up.

If on the other hand you're offered the job on the spot, congratulations! You did it! You now have a decision to make: will you accept the job or are you not sure? After all, just as the employer may have other candidates, you may have other interviews or even job offers. Or, maybe you discovered something during the interview and now you're not so sure you want this job. I'll help you navigate all of these options in the next chapter.

### Next up...

The interview may be over, but there's more to do to reach your final goal. Whether you received an offer at the end of your interview or not, you need to have an appropriate response for any situation that arises after the interview. I'll help you do that in the next chapter.

## CHAPTER SUMMARY QUIZ

The following quiz summarizes the chapter.

1. Which of the following will make a poor first impression?
   a. Arriving on time for your interview.
   b. Being demanding of entry-level employees like secretaries.
   c. Addressing your interviewer with a proper greeting.
   d. Giving your interviewer a firm handshake.

2. Interview questions are primarily asked to trip you up.
   a. True
   b. False

3. What would an employer be trying to ascertain by asking seemingly irrelevant and tricky questions?
   a. Your personality.
   b. Your intellect.
   c. Your creativity.
   d. All of the above.

4. What should you do if you are asked inappropriate or illegal questions?
   a. Refuse to answer them.
   b. End the interview and leave immediately.
   c. Threaten to call the EEOC and file a complaint.
   d. Pivot by answering a related question that wasn't asked.

5. What's the best way to end an interview?
   a. Ask for the job.
   b. Ask about what the job pays.
   c. Let the interviewer know that you'll get back to them if you want the job.
   d. Let the interviewer know what days off you'll need.

Answers: 1b, 2a, 3d, 4d, 5a

# Lesson 16

# Interview Follow-up

At the end of the interview, one of two things happened. You may have received a job offer and you'll either accept it on the spot or you'll ask for some time to make your decision. Or you were told that you'd be informed of a decision in the near future. In this chapter, I'll help you respond to each of these outcomes. If an offer is made and you still haven't discussed your pay, do if before you accept the offer. And finally, make sure you work out the details of starting the job.

## EVALUATE YOURSELF

After you go through the interview process a few times, you'll begin to know right away whether you nailed it, or you didn't. You'll come out of the interview thinking, *I forget to tell them this,* or *I shouldn't have said that.* It's a good idea to reflect on your performance so you can make some adjustments going forward. When my Co-op students completed their mock interviews, I had them use a self-evaluation checklist for this purpose. One is included in Appendix G, and you should complete it after every interview. Critiquing your last performance will help you do better on the next. It will also help you identify issues or topics to communicate when you contact the employer on the follow up.

## GET YOUR REFERENCES READY

If at the conclusion of the interview you were asked for a list of your references, this is a great sign. That means you're being seriously considered for the job. When this happens, contact your references to give them a heads up, because after the interview you should know a lot more about the position. Let them know who the company is and what the job entails: "I'll be dealing with customers," or "I'll be on the computer a lot." This way your references will be prepared to provide feedback about you *as it relates to the specific job* you just interviewed for. Send them you're most up-to-date resume if they don't have it. If you know that a reference was contacted, follow up with a thank you note or email whether you got the job or not.

## FOLLOW UP AFTER THE INTERVIEW

Once again, here's some advice that will make you stand out from other applicants because it's done so seldomly. Immediately when you get home, send an email to every interviewer you met to thank them for their time. In addition to demonstrating your appreciation and professionalism, this will serve several important purposes. First, it'll help them remember you and keep your interview fresh in their mind. Second, it's a great opportunity to reiterate the key qualifications that you believe you'll bring to the job. Third, if you either forgot to mention something in the interview or need to clarify something you said or didn't say, do it in the email. And finally, it demonstrates just how much you want the job. Believe me when I tell you that going the extra distance here will exponentially increase your chances of getting the job. See *Figure 13*.

Structure the email as follows; put "Thank You" in the subject line.

- <u>Paragraph 1:</u> Thank the interviewer for their time. Use your own words but phrases like *so much* will communicate your enthusiasm.
- <u>Paragraph 2:</u> List the key points that make you highly qualified for the job but keep it brief. If you forgot to mention something relevant in the interview, state it here. If there were concerns brought up during the interview, address those here also.
- <u>Paragraph 3:</u> Close by expressing your continued interest in the job.

### Call to follow up.

If the employer gave you a timeframe in which they'll make their decision and you haven't heard from them within that time period, you should call them. This may be difficult, and you may want to avoid a conversation and send a text or email instead. But calling them tells them that you're willing to take the extra step no matter how uncomfortable it may be. This demonstrates persistence and maturity. Just follow the script below.

*Hello Ms. Johnson, this is John Goldberg. We met last week when you interviewed me for the Teacher's Aide position. I just wanted to thank you again for your time and let you know that I am still very much interested in the job if it's still available.*

pjohnson@childcarecompany.com

Thank you

Dear Ms. Johnson:

Thank you so much for taking the time out of your busy schedule to meet with me today. I really enjoyed meeting you and discussing the Teacher's Aide job responsibilities and rewards.

As I mentioned in the interview, I have two years of experience working in childcare, and I have taken numerous child development courses in high school. In the interview you expressed some concern about my leaving the local area after graduation this June in order to attend college. I can assure you that my plans to attend the local community college and live at home have not changed. I truly believe that my education and work experience, coupled with my love of children, make me well suited for the position of Teacher's Aide.

I am very interested in the position we discussed, and I would be happy to provide you with any additional information that you might need. Feel free to call me at 215-555-1212 at any time. Thank you again for your time and consideration.

Sincerely,

*John Goldbery*

John Goldberg

Figure 13 Interview Follow-up Email

If no decision has been made:

*I understand. Is there any more information you need from me?*

*Would it be okay if I followed up again in a week or so?*

If your attempts to contact the interviewer by phone are unsuccessful, then follow up with a second email.

## FOLLOW UP AGAIN

If it's been a week after your first follow up and you still haven't received an answer, follow up a second time in an email as shown in *Figure 14*.

---

pjohnson@childcarecompany.com

---

Checking in

---

Dear Ms. Johnson:

I hope all is well!

You mentioned that you would be finalizing your decision for the Teacher's Aide position by this week. I'm very much interested in the position, and eager to hear if a selection has been made. Please let me know if there's anything I can provide to assist you in your decision-making process. Feel free to call me at 215-555-1212 at any time. Thank you again for your time and consideration.

Sincerely,

*John Goldberg*

John Goldberg

**Figure 14 Interview Follow-up #2**

Checking in this way, with a short and simple message, will not annoy the employer. It will show your continued interest in the job.

## GETTING DISAPPOINTING NEWS

Whether it's during your interview or during a follow-up, when the employer's decision has been made to extend the job offer to someone else:

*I understand. Thank you for considering me. If another position becomes available, would you please keep me in mind? I'd be very interested in applying for the position again.*

If this happens, don't be too hard on yourself. As the saying goes, *a winner is just a loser who tried one more time.* If you completed the evaluation after the interview like I suggested, you should know where you can make improvements. Did you make mistakes in communicating, dress, or business etiquette? Were you unprepared with responses to certain questions? Are you sure you're applying for jobs for which you're qualified?

It's also possible that you did everything to the best of your ability, but another candidate was simply a better fit for the position. Above all, don't get discouraged. If you followed my advice, the right job is still out there for you.

## AN OFFER IS MADE THAT YOU WILL ACCEPT

Whether the offer is made at the end of the interview or sometime later, this is the news you've been waiting for.

*Really? That's great! Thank you so much!*

In your excitement of getting a job offer, don't forget to ask any outstanding questions you may have about the job.

### Negotiating your pay.

If the issue of pay has never come up, now is the time to ask.

> I had a Co-op student who came into my office the day after her interview to tell me she got the job but didn't know the pay rate.
> "Didn't you ask?"
> Her reply? "No, I was too scared to ask."

Young people sometimes feel that it's an imposition, or somehow impolite to ask about money and that the employer will think they're entitled. Well, guess what? In this case, you *are* entitled... to make an honest wage for the services you provide to a business. The economy doesn't work without workers like us, and businesses must treat us fairly and pay us accordingly.

*May I ask what the position pays?*

In Chapter 12, I told you to have a pay range in mind. If the stated pay is below your range, be prepared to justify why you deserve more. You may be able to negotiate a higher rate if you can convince the employer that your past relevant job experiences, acquired skills, and education make you more valuable.

*I made $7.50 an hour at my last job, and I was hoping to make $8.50. Here's why....*

If you succeed, good for you! If all your questions are answered and you are ready to accept the offer:

*Thank you for the offer. I'm so happy to accept it!*

215

If the offered pay is not within your desired range and you need some time to think it over, ask for it. I'll help you do that in the next section.

### Get all the information you need to start.

You may have questions about how you'll be trained or who you'll be reporting to.

*Where should I go and who should I report to?*

Before agreeing to a start date, remember that you need to give two weeks' notice to a current employer if you have one. Enter the start date and time into your calendar app on your phone.

*When would you like me to start? I'm available immediately after I give two weeks' notice to my current employer.*

Are there things you'll need to bring with you like your working papers, identification, and proof of eligibility to work in the U.S.? Some jobs even require workers to bring their own tools.

*Should I bring anything with me?*

Finally, ask any questions you have regarding the dress code. Certain jobs require you to wear certain colors or special types of shoes. If your job requires you to wear a uniform, what arrangements will be made for you to receive yours?

*Is there a dress code or anything specific I'll need to wear to work?*

### Confirm your availability.

If the days or times you're available to work have changed for any reason, you must disclose that now. Remember that making yourself available during the days and times you provide doesn't mean you'll be scheduled during all of those times. The more available you are to your employer, the more valuable you are to them.

*As I stated on my application, I'm available every weekday after 3 p.m. other than Tuesdays. I'm available all-day Saturday and Sundays after 1 p.m.*

If you have previously scheduled incidental commitments for which you cannot make yourself available to work, disclose that now as well.

*I have a family vacation scheduled during the last week in March.*

*I have a mission trip to Honduras scheduled for the first two weeks in May.*

Employers are generally open to honoring your prior commitments if you give them plenty of notice.

## IF YOU'RE NOT SURE YOU WANT THE JOB

If this is the case, it's okay to say so. Maybe the pay is lower than what you expected. Maybe you're waiting on other offers. My advice is to stall a bit but be honest.

*Thank you so much! Would you mind if I took a few days to think it over? May I let you know by Friday?*

Employers won't be upset with you for asking for some time to think it over. They *will* be upset if you accept the position, and then a week later tell them that you're no longer interested in the position.

In the end, whether you decide to take this job or not, make sure you follow up with a phone call to let them know of your decision.

*I really appreciate having had the opportunity to interview for the Teacher's Aide position and I'm very excited to accept the position!*

## TURNING DOWN A JOB OFFER

Call the person who interviewed you directly.

*I really appreciate having had the opportunity to interview for the Teacher's Aide position. Unfortunately, I did accept another position that I think I'm better suited for. Thank you for the offer.*

If you're unable to get them on the phone, leave a voice mail message and ask them to return your call if they have any questions. I know an email would be easier, but when you speak to a real person, you can have a conversation where they can actually hear the sincerity and the appreciation in your voice.

No one likes getting bad news or giving it. But the response you'll get from the other end of the line will be something like this:

*I understand. I really appreciate you calling and letting me know.*

A less mature and less professional person would have simply not followed up at all, leaving the employer hanging. That's called *burning your bridges,* because if you ever apply there again, they'll remember how you ended the relationship and you won't be welcomed back. The world is smaller than you think, which means people talk and you may get a reputation for being unprofessional. And that's not how you build a strong professional network.

**Next up...**

If you've accepted a job offer, congratulations! I hope it's a job you'll love and an experience you'll grow from. But your job-searching journey isn't quite done. If you have another job that you have to leave, you must take care of that next. And all of those individuals that helped you along the way need to be contacted. The next chapter will help you tie up those loose ends and prepare to start your new job.

## CHAPTER SUMMARY QUIZ

The following quiz summarizes the chapter.

1. What are the proper ways to follow up after the interview?
   a. Send a letter or email to thank them for their time, restate your qualifications, and reiterate your interest in the job.
   b. Make a comment on the interviewer's LinkedIn profile to ask how you did.
   c. Stop by business every day until they get back to you.
   d. All of the above are good ways to following up.

2. What is the best format of an initial follow-up to find out the status after your interview?
   a. Send a letter in the mail
   b. Send a text message
   c. Call them on the phone
   d. Send an email

3. When accepting a job offer, what must you do?
   a. Confirm your pay if the subject has never come up
   b. Get information like start date, time, and location.
   c. Confirm your work schedule and your availability.
   d. All of the above.

4. If you ask for time to think about a job offer and do decide not to accept it, you do not have to tell the employer. Your lack of communication is enough to give them the hint.
   a. True
   b. False

5. The best way to tell an employer that you're turning down the job offer is by text.
   a. True
   b. False

Answers: 1a, 2c, 3d, 4b, 5b

# Lesson 17

# You Got the Job? Time to Quit and Tie Up Loose Ends

So you've worked hard to get a job. You should be proud of yourself. However, if you have a current job that you have to quit, you must resign properly so that you maintain a good relationship with your former employer. Don't diminish all of things you just achieved by doing the wrong things to the people who helped get you here. While it's exciting to look forward to a new beginning at a new job, right now you have to look backwards and take care of some responsibilities. If there were others who helped you find your new job, you must contact them as well. When you tie up these loose ends and fill out the paperwork for your new employer, your new job is official.

## WHY ARE YOU LEAVING?

Before you quit, make sure you're leaving for all of the right reasons. As a reminder, good reasons include:

- Taking a better paying job.
- Taking a more challenging job or one with more responsibility.
- Taking a job that's more consistent with your future career.

If you're leaving for those other, not-so-good reasons we discussed as you were completing your application, like not getting along with your boss or co-workers, I hope you can try to resolve those issues if you really like your job. You shouldn't let someone else drive you out of a situation, whether it's a job or a club or anything else, that you enjoy. If, on the other hand, you've made a mistake and realized the job is just not for you, that's understandable. I hope the advice I've given you will help you avoid this situation in the future. In either case, I hope you were able to stick it out for at least 6 months. The older you get, the harder it becomes to explain gaps in your employment history, especially when you're no longer a full-time student.

## NOW LET'S QUIT

Your goal is to resign in an appropriate manner so you can leave your job while still maintaining good feelings between you and your former company. Not giving two weeks' notice, quitting over text, or worst of all, ghosting your employer by just not showing up for work, would be a very bad decision on your part. Even if you're leaving because you didn't get along with your manager or feel you were treated unfairly, quitting without proper notice is unprofessional, immature, and it *will* come back to haunt you. Here's what a local employer describes happens to him repeatedly.

> We had a wonderful young girl who we really thought was a potential shift leader. She had taken a week off for a family vacation, but the Friday before her vacation, she called out sick without finding a replacement. I told her she was really putting us in a bad situation and asked her to come in. She didn't and my wife, who is a co-owner, had to go in to cover her shift. I knew I had to speak to her about this and planned to sit down with her when she returned. On the first day she was to return, I think it was a Wednesday, she never showed up for her shift. No phone call. No text. She just disappeared.
>
> **Glenn Wagner**
> **Franchise Owner, Rita's Water Ice**

I'd love to say stories like these are rare, but I hear them too often. Not only can this young girl never use this employer as a reference, she should try not to put this job on her list of prior work experiences. A simple phone call to do an employment background check would be detrimental to her job searching prospects. Furthermore, she didn't just leave her boss high and dry; she also abandoned her co-workers who now may be asked to do extra duties or work longer hours until her position is filled.

People talk. If you develop a reputation for leaving a business high and dry, you may have a very tough time finding your next job. Here's a better way to leave your job.

> One of the hardest things I had to do in college was to quit my job at The Deli after I was offered the internship with AT&T. I

dreaded having to resign, partly because I loved the job and partly because I knew I was about to disappoint my manager who had been good to me. To make matters worse, I had only been there for six weeks, two of which were for my training. I went to the restaurant, walked up to Dave, and in a nervous voice asked him, "Can I talk to you for a minute?" His whole demeanor changed in an instant. His face fell and his shoulders slumped. Before I said another word, he just knew. As I fought back tears, I told him about my summer internship and the opportunity it presented for my future career in business. I tried to express how much I appreciated the opportunity he gave me and how much I had already learned, but I was having a hard time keeping it together emotionally. When I was done talking, he said something to me I'll never forget.

"I'm not going to tell you that I'm not disappointed because I am. But I'll never hold a grudge against someone who leaves to better themselves."

Well, that did it for me and I couldn't hold back the tears. At that moment I realized that Dave wasn't just my manager—he was a person who genuinely seemed to care about me. I think most employers who hire high school and college students feel this way. They enjoy being a mentor as well as a boss.

Every contact you make is a potential resource in your professional network. Leaving a job does not mean you have to lose a valuable contact, but how you leave a job will make a difference.

### Make it formal.

Put your resignation in writing so your employer has record of when, why, and more importantly, how you left. Follow this process:

1. Putting your resignation in writing doesn't mean via text or email. It means type up a resignation letter like the one below. Date the letter with the date of your verbal resignation and address it to your immediate supervisor. It will stay as part of your permanent record with the company.

2. On a day that you're not scheduled for work or well before your shift starts, ask your supervisor to speak privately.

3. Look your supervisor in the eye and thank them for the job and tell them that you are resigning.

   *I really appreciate the opportunity to work here but unfortunately, I need to give my two weeks' notice. I've enjoyed working here and so this was a difficult decision.*

4. Explain why you're leaving, but don't complain or talk negatively. If you are leaving because of a problem, focus on the positive aspects of the new job.

   *I've been offered another opportunity that I can't pass up. It's a job with more responsibility as a crew leader.*

5. Larger companies will offer you an exit interview with the Human Resources department, the purpose of which is to identify reasons why their employees quit and to address any issues going on in the workplace. Be positive and tell them how the job has been a good experience for you. If you're leaving because of a bad experience with the employer, you can be honest if you believe this information will help the company. If you just want to vent to make yourself feel better, hold your tongue.

6. Give two weeks' notice. Your employer may not need two weeks, but it's expected that you offer it. In that two weeks, be available as much as you can to help your employer transition your duties to someone else. If you reduce your availability in those last two weeks because you suddenly became "busy," all of the good feelings you worked hard to cultivate will go out the window.

   *My last day will be [no less than 2 weeks from the day you give notice]. I'll do whatever you need me to do to get someone else trained.*

7. Hand them your letter of resignation after you've spoken with them. See the example in *Figure 15*.

104 Heartfelt Drive
Princeton, NJ 08540
July 16, 2019


Mr. Ron Letterman
Taco Tower
2121 Olden Avenue
Princeton, NJ 08540

Dear Mr. Letterman:

Please accept this as my letter of resignation, effective two weeks from today.

I cannot begin to express my gratitude for all that you have done for me for the past 10 months of my employment. Thank you for your flexibility in scheduling me around my busy school schedule. Most of all, thank you for giving me the opportunity to gain valuable skills and experiences at this job.

The decision to leave was very difficult, but the job I have accepted will offer me greater responsibility as a crew leader. I could not have gotten this job without all the things I learned from working for you at Taco Tower.

I wish you and the rest of my co-workers all the best.

Sincerely,

*JoAnne Clark*

JoAnne Clark

Figure 15 Resignation Letter

## TELL THE PEOPLE IN YOUR NETWORK

In your excitement about getting a job, don't forget to tie up this loose end. Contact your references first, tell them about your new job, and thank them for being a reference. If there are other people who helped you, let them know that you are now employed. This could be friends, family members, teachers or others.

If you recall, I gave my former student, Maggie, a glowing recommendation to the recruiter who was helping her find a job. A few weeks passed, and just as I started wondering if she got the job, the headhunter reached out to me, "Have you heard

> from Maggie? I've texted her, called her, and left several voice messages and she's not getting back to me."
>
> It was unlike Maggie to be irresponsible, so I reached out to her on a messenger app to make sure she was okay. She responded immediately, and we chatted about how things were going. When I asked her how the job search was going, and not to forget to check her voice messages, she suddenly went silent.
>
> I couldn't figure it out, until one day a few weeks later, a Facebook notification popped up on my phone. It was from Maggie: "Now that the paperwork is done, I'm happy to announce that I have accepted a full-time position as a...."

That post certainly explained why she didn't need the recruiter's services anymore. It doesn't explain, however, why she never bothered to return a phone call, text, or email to this day. Not only was ghosting the recruiter in this way unprofessional, it was self-destructive. Because guess who else got that notification: the recruiter. How many employers and other recruiting firms in the local area do you think this recruiter knows? As I said before, people in business talk to each other and behavior like this can earn you a reputation for being unprofessional.

### Turn down your other job offers.

If you previously received other job offers, make sure you call — don't email — those companies, thank them for their time and let them know you won't be accepting their offers.

> *I told you I'd let you know by Friday about my decision about the Warehouse Associate job. I want to tell you how much I appreciate having had the opportunity to interview for that position. Unfortunately, I did accept another position that I think I'm better suited for.*

Again, you can add that employer to your professional network because of the way you handled turning down their offer.

### Make the news public.

Once you accept a job offer, it might be tempting to announce it on social media or start friending and following your new co-workers. Don't do it

225

yet—not unless you've officially resigned from your old job and started your new one. That's not how you want your previous employer to find out that you're leaving. Once you fill out paperwork, that's when your employment is "official." Then, and only then, should you make it public by updating your social media sites with your new employment information. Most importantly, send all of those contacts you made—the interviewers, references, friends of friends who gave you job leads—an invitation to connect on your newly updated LinkedIn.

## CHAPTER SUMMARY QUIZ

The following quiz summarizes the chapter.

1. Which of the following is not a good reason to quit your job?
   a. You don't get along with your co-workers.
   b. To take a job with more responsibility.
   c. To take a better paying job.
   d. To take a job that's more consistent with your future career.

2. How much notice should you give when quitting your job?
   a. 1 week
   b. 2 weeks
   c. 1 month
   d. 3 days

3. If you and your employer used texting to communicate for work, it's perfectly okay to resign over text.
   a. True
   b. False

4. Who should you contact to inform them about your new job?
   a. Contacts that helped you in the job-hunting process
   b. Your references
   c. Businesses that offered you a job that you need to turn down
   d. All of the above.

5. Once you start your new job, update your professional social media profiles with your new information and invite all your new contacts to connect on LinkedIn.
   a. True
   b. False

Answers: 1a, 2b, 3b, 4d, 5a

# Afterword

Finding a job you love as a young person is a great beginning to a life filled with satisfying work experiences. But equally important is keeping the job you worked so hard to find. Employers report that while hiring workers is easy, keeping them is very difficult. Help wanted signs are on storefront windows in perpetuity. Job postings that are on my online job posting boards are requested by employers to stay there indefinitely.

Soft skills like communication, problem-solving, taking constructive criticism, work ethic, team work, and many more have to be taught.
And now that you're making your own money, what will you do with the money you earn? How much will you make, how much will go to taxes, and what will you do with what's left. These things need to be learned to help you succeed in the work place, even at a young age.
For now, have confidence in who you are and what you know about job searching and go find that job you'll love. You've got this!

# Acknowledgements

I learned so many things from my predecessor, Kim Krajci, who devoted thirteen and a half years to make the Cooperative Education Program the wonderful experience it was when I took over. So much of the valuable information and insights in this book are a direct result of her innovative program development skills and her love for our students.

For inspiring me to begin writing this book, a big thank you to Mike Zisa, a fellow teaching colleague, skilled Certified Financial Planner, and author of *The Early Investor* and *The Family Investor.*

To my parents, Adi and Mithoo Katrak, who emphasized the value of a good education and the importance of a strong work ethic. They sacrificed so much so that the lives of their children could be built on a solid foundation.

To my brother, Ro Katrak, who tolerated his annoying little sister his whole life. I'll never let on how much I look up to him and value his advice.

Thank you to my content editor, Bobby Peters, for reviewing my manuscript so thoroughly and keeping me focused on my target audience.

To my daughters who generously shared the details of their experiences at school and work. Their stories will help give readers the insight they may not have otherwise gained. To my eldest, Marisa, a voracious reader and talented designer who helped me understand what attracts and deters young readers. To my youngest, Samantha, for using her sarcasm, quick wit, and sense of humor to critique my work and set me straight in a way only she can.

And finally, I am so grateful to my husband and best friend, Steve, who even with his crazy schedule always made time for me and my book.

I started this project almost 4 years ago, undeterred by the "experts" who warned about how hard it was to write a book. As it turned out, it *was* hard. As a first-time author, I had no professional editors, no illustrators, no agents. All I had was my family who spent countless hours reading and re-reading each chapter as they unfolded, offering me encouragement when it was good and honesty when it wasn't. I may be the author, but this book was a family project.

# Appendices

# Appendix A

## IDENTIFYING YOUR VALUES

Rate the importance of your values to make sure they are consistent with your job or career goal.

| Value Statement | Definitely True | Mostly True | Undecided | Mostly False | Definitely False |
|---|---|---|---|---|---|
| 1. I will take my children to religious services regularly. | 10 | 7 | 5 | 3 | 0 |
| 2. I enjoy attending music concerts. | 10 | 7 | 5 | 3 | 0 |
| 3. It is important to me to have a lot of friends. | 10 | 7 | 5 | 3 | 0 |
| 4. I envy the way movie stars are recognized wherever they go. | 10 | 7 | 5 | 3 | 0 |
| 5. I would rather spend an evening at home with my family than out with friends. | 10 | 7 | 5 | 3 | 0 |
| 6. I enjoy making decisions that involve other people. | 10 | 7 | 5 | 3 | 0 |
| 7. If I had the talent, I would like to write songs. | 10 | 7 | 5 | 3 | 0 |
| 8. I have a close relationship with at least one of my parents. | 10 | 7 | 5 | 3 | 0 |
| 9. I am willing to spend time helping fellow students who are having difficulty with their studies. | 10 | 7 | 5 | 3 | 0 |
| 10. Even at the same salary, I would rather be the boss than just another worker. | 10 | 7 | 5 | 3 | 0 |
| 11. I have a special appreciation for beautiful things. | 10 | 7 | 5 | 3 | 0 |
| 12. If I had the talent, I would like to appear regularly on television. | 10 | 7 | 5 | 3 | 0 |
| 13. I would like to counsel people and help them with their problems. | 10 | 7 | 5 | 3 | 0 |
| 14. I would enjoy associating with movie stars and other celebrities. | 10 | 7 | 5 | 3 | 0 |
| 15. I have a dental checkup at least once a year. | 10 | 7 | 5 | 3 | 0 |
| 16. I enjoy writing short stories. | 10 | 7 | 5 | 3 | 0 |
| 17. I would rather spend a summer working than going on a paid vacation. | 10 | 7 | 5 | 3 | 0 |
| 18. I like to go to parties. | 10 | 7 | 5 | 3 | 0 |
| 19. I believe in a Supreme Being. | 10 | 7 | 5 | 3 | 0 |
| 20. I would rather be an officer than just a club member. | 10 | 7 | 5 | 3 | 0 |

| Value Statement | Definitely True | Mostly True | Undecided | Mostly False | Definitely False |
|---|---|---|---|---|---|
| 21. I would rather spend my last $100 for needed dental work than for a vacation at my favorite resort. | 10 | 7 | 5 | 3 | 0 |
| 22. I enjoy giving presents to members of my family. | 10 | 7 | 5 | 3 | 0 |
| 23. If I were a teacher, I would rather teach poetry than math. | 10 | 7 | 5 | 3 | 0 |
| 24. I often have daydreams about things that I would like to do if I had the money. | 10 | 7 | 5 | 3 | 0 |
| 25. I enjoy giving parties. | 10 | 7 | 5 | 3 | 0 |
| 26. It would be very satisfying to receive a lot of publicity for acting in movies or television. | 10 | 7 | 5 | 3 | 0 |
| 27. When I feel ill, I usually call a doctor. | 10 | 7 | 5 | 3 | 0 |
| 28. I believe that it is important to support a religious organization by giving time and or money. | 10 | 7 | 5 | 3 | 0 |
| 29. I enjoy having discussions at the family dinner table. | 10 | 7 | 5 | 3 | 0 |
| 30. I enjoy visiting art museums. | 10 | 7 | 5 | 3 | 0 |
| 31. I like to be around other people most of the time. | 10 | 7 | 5 | 3 | 0 |
| 32. I like to be the one who decides what we will do or where we will go when I'm out with friends. | 10 | 7 | 5 | 3 | 0 |
| 33. Someday I'd like to live in a large, expensive house. | 10 | 7 | 5 | 3 | 0 |
| 34. Each day I try to set aside some time for worship. | 10 | 7 | 5 | 3 | 0 |
| 35. If I knew a family that had no food for a holiday dinner, I would try to provide it. | 10 | 7 | 5 | 3 | 0 |
| 36. I like to spend holidays with my family. | 10 | 7 | 5 | 3 | 0 |
| 37. I would rather take a class in freehand drawing than a class in math. | 10 | 7 | 5 | 3 | 0 |
| 38. I do not like to spend an entire evening alone. | 10 | 7 | 5 | 3 | 0 |
| 39. If the salary were the same, I would rather be a school principal than a classroom teacher. | 10 | 7 | 5 | 3 | 0 |
| 40. I have expensive tastes. | 10 | 7 | 5 | 3 | 0 |
| 41. I can tell the difference between a really fine painting or drawing and an ordinary one. | 10 | 7 | 5 | 3 | 0 |
| 42. I expect to provide music lessons for my children. | 10 | 7 | 5 | 3 | 0 |
| 43. It is important to me that grace is said before meals. | 10 | 7 | 5 | 3 | 0 |
| 44. I sometimes miss sleep to visit late with company. | 10 | 7 | 5 | 3 | 0 |
| 45. I usually get at least eight hours of sleep each night. | 10 | 7 | 5 | 3 | 0 |
| 46. I like to design things. | 10 | 7 | 5 | 3 | 0 |
| 47. I would rather be well-known throughout the country than highly respected by my co-workers. | 10 | 7 | 5 | 3 | 0 |
| 48. I would get a sense of satisfaction from nursing a sick person back to health. | 10 | 7 | 5 | 3 | 0 |
| 49. I care what my parents think about the things I do. | 10 | 7 | 5 | 3 | 0 |
| 50. I daydream about making a lot of money. | 10 | 7 | 5 | 3 | 0 |
| 51. It is thrilling to come up with an original idea and put it to use. | 10 | 7 | 5 | 3 | 0 |

| Value Statement | Definitely True | Mostly True | Undecided | Mostly False | Definitely False |
|---|---|---|---|---|---|
| 52. I believe there is life after death. | 10 | 7 | 5 | 3 | 0 |
| 53. If someone is hard to get along with, I try to be understanding. | 10 | 7 | 5 | 3 | 0 |
| 54. If I were in the television field, I would rather be a celebrated actor than a scriptwriter. | 10 | 7 | 5 | 3 | 0 |
| 55. I enjoy decorating my room at home. | 10 | 7 | 5 | 3 | 0 |
| 56. I enjoy a picnic with my family. | 10 | 7 | 5 | 3 | 0 |
| 57. As an adult, I want to earn a much higher salary than the average worker. | 10 | 7 | 5 | 3 | 0 |
| 58. I am careful to have a balanced diet each day. | 10 | 7 | 5 | 3 | 0 |
| 59. I often influence other students concerning the classes they take. | 10 | 7 | 5 | 3 | 0 |
| 60. I read the writings of my religion regularly. | 10 | 7 | 5 | 3 | 0 |
| 61. If I were in the clothing industry, I would enjoy creating new styles. | 10 | 7 | 5 | 3 | 0 |
| 62. I look forward to an evening out with a group of friends. | 10 | 7 | 5 | 3 | 0 |
| 63. When I am with a group of people, I like to be the one in charge. | 10 | 7 | 5 | 3 | 0 |
| 64. I dislike being financially dependent on others. | 10 | 7 | 5 | 3 | 0 |
| 65. If a friend is in trouble, I feel I must comfort them. | 10 | 7 | 5 | 3 | 0 |
| 66. I love my parents. | 10 | 7 | 5 | 3 | 0 |
| 67. I almost never skip meals. | 10 | 7 | 5 | 3 | 0 |
| 68. I would enjoy for people to recognize me wherever I go. | 10 | 7 | 5 | 3 | 0 |
| 69. I do not smoke. | 10 | 7 | 5 | 3 | 0 |
| 70. I feel good when I do things that help others. | 10 | 7 | 5 | 3 | 0 |
| 71. Someday I would like to write a novel. | 10 | 7 | 5 | 3 | 0 |
| 72. I would put up with undesirable living conditions in order to work at a job that paid extremely well. | 10 | 7 | 5 | 3 | 0 |
| 73. I belong to several clubs and organizations. | 10 | 7 | 5 | 3 | 0 |
| 74. I believe in the power of prayer and meditation. | 10 | 7 | 5 | 3 | 0 |
| 75. I would enjoy having my picture in the yearbook more than it has been in the past. | 10 | 7 | 5 | 3 | 0 |
| 76. When I see a newly constructed building, I consider its beauty as much as its practical use. | 10 | 7 | 5 | 3 | 0 |
| 77. Some of the hobbies I'd like to have are expensive. | 10 | 7 | 5 | 3 | 0 |
| 78. I enjoy classical music. | 10 | 7 | 5 | 3 | 0 |
| 79. I would never use harmful drugs because of what they might do to my body. | 10 | 7 | 5 | 3 | 0 |
| 80. I am kind to animals. | 10 | 7 | 5 | 3 | 0 |

## VALUES HAND SCORING GUIDE

For each value, record the rating (10, 7, 5, 3, or 0) that you circled for each statement number. Then add the numbers to find your total for each area.

| 1 Fame | |
|---|---|
| Statement Number | Value Circled |
| 4 | _____ |
| 12 | _____ |
| 14 | _____ |
| 26 | _____ |
| 47 | _____ |
| 54 | _____ |
| 68 | _____ |
| 75 | _____ |
| TOTAL_____ | |

| 2 Money | |
|---|---|
| Statement Number | Value Circled |
| 24 | _____ |
| 33 | _____ |
| 40 | _____ |
| 50 | _____ |
| 57 | _____ |
| 64 | _____ |
| 72 | _____ |
| 77 | _____ |
| TOTAL_____ | |

| 3 Power | |
|---|---|
| Statement Number | Value Circled |
| 6 | _____ |
| 10 | _____ |
| 17 | _____ |
| 20 | _____ |
| 32 | _____ |
| 39 | _____ |
| 59 | _____ |
| 63 | _____ |
| TOTAL_____ | |

| 4 Religion | |
|---|---|
| Statement Number | Value Circled |
| 1 | _____ |
| 19 | _____ |
| 28 | _____ |
| 34 | _____ |
| 43 | _____ |
| 52 | _____ |
| 60 | _____ |
| 74 | _____ |
| TOTAL_____ | |

| 5 Humanitarianism | |
|---|---|
| Statement Number | Value Circled |
| 9 | _____ |
| 13 | _____ |
| 35 | _____ |
| 48 | _____ |
| 53 | _____ |
| 65 | _____ |
| 70 | _____ |
| 80 | _____ |
| TOTAL_____ | |

| 6 Family | |
|---|---|
| Statement Number | Value Circled |
| 5 | _____ |
| 8 | _____ |
| 22 | _____ |
| 29 | _____ |
| 36 | _____ |
| 49 | _____ |
| 56 | _____ |
| 66 | _____ |
| TOTAL_____ | |

| 7 Health | |
|---|---|
| Statement Number | Value Circled |
| 15 | _____ |
| 21 | _____ |
| 27 | _____ |
| 45 | _____ |
| 58 | _____ |
| 67 | _____ |
| 69 | _____ |
| 79 | _____ |
| **TOTAL** | _____ |

| 8 Aesthetics | |
|---|---|
| Statement Number | Value Circled |
| 2 | _____ |
| 11 | _____ |
| 23 | _____ |
| 30 | _____ |
| 41 | _____ |
| 42 | _____ |
| 76 | _____ |
| 78 | _____ |
| **TOTAL** | _____ |

| 9 Creativity | |
|---|---|
| Statement Number | Value Circled |
| 7 | _____ |
| 16 | _____ |
| 37 | _____ |
| 46 | _____ |
| 51 | _____ |
| 55 | _____ |
| 61 | _____ |
| 71 | _____ |
| **TOTAL** | _____ |

| 10 Social Contact | |
|---|---|
| Statement Number | Value Circled |
| 3 | _____ |
| 18 | _____ |
| 25 | _____ |
| 31 | _____ |
| 38 | _____ |
| 44 | _____ |
| 62 | _____ |
| 73 | _____ |
| **TOTAL** | _____ |

List your top 3 values here:
1. _____
2. _____
3. _____

# Appendix B

Rate your interests from 0 (not interesting) to 5 (extremely interesting). Add an interest of your own that is not listed.

__ Animals
__ Anime
__ Archery
__ Art
__ Astronomy
__ Backpacking, hiking
__ Ballets or operas
__ Baseball
__ Basketball
__ Biking
__ Billiards
__ Bowling
__ Boxing, kickboxing
__ Building models
__ Camping
__ Canoeing
__ Chess/board games
__ Child care
__ Collecting (coins, stamps, etc.)
__ Comedy
__ Cooking
__ Crafts
__ Cross training
__ Dancing
__ Debating
__ Disc Golf
__ Extreme sports

__ Fantasy Sports
__ Fishing
__ Frisbee
__ Flying
__ Football
__ Gardening
__ Go carting
__ Golf
__ Gymnastics
__ Hockey (ice)
__ Field hockey
__ Hunting
__ Knitting/crocheting
__ Ice skating
__ Lacrosse
__ Magic
__ Martial arts
__ Mechanics
__ Movies
__ Motorcycles
__ Music (instrument)
__ Music (vocal)
__ Paint ball
__ Painting
__ Party planning
__ Photography
__ Plays or concerts
__ Politics

__ Rafting
__ Reading
__ Puzzles
__ Religious activities
__ Running
__ Sailing
__ Science projects
__ Sewing
__ Skateboarding
__ Snow skiing
__ Snow boarding
__ Soccer
__ Softball
__ Sports cars
__ Swimming
__ Table tennis
__ Tennis
__ Travel
__ Video Editing
__ Video games
__ Volleyball
__ Volunteer work
__ Water sports
__ Woodworking
__ Wrestling
__ Writing
__ Yoga
__ _____

List your top three favorites interests here.

Interest #1: _____

Interest #2: _____

Interest #3: _____

# Appendix C

## MARKETABLE SKILLS

Marketable skills can be both job skills as well as soft skills. Identify the skills you possess based on your natural and learned skills.

**Creativity/Artistic skills:** Use imagination to create and solve.
\_\_ Baking food
\_\_ Compose music
\_\_ Cooking meals
\_\_ Creating things
\_\_ Drawing, illustrating
\_\_ Dressing models
\_\_ Ensuring people obey the law
\_\_ Imagining creative things
\_\_ Interior decorating
\_\_ Inventing
\_\_ Making designs
\_\_ Matching colors together
\_\_ Modeling clothing
\_\_ Playing musical instruments
\_\_ Putting on make-up
\_\_ Sewing/making clothes
\_\_ Singing
\_\_ Speaking different languages
\_\_ Taking pictures

**Leadership skills:** Guide processes, initiatives, and others to achieve goals.
\_\_ Competing with others
\_\_ Evaluating work of others
\_\_ Delegating work to others
\_\_ Leading groups
\_\_ Managing or motivating people
\_\_ Selling and persuading
\_\_ Showing someone how to do a job
\_\_ Supervising people
\_\_ Teaching people

**Communication skills:** Exchange, convey, express knowledge & ideas.
\_\_ Advocating for yourself
\_\_ Answering questions

\_\_ Answering telephones professionally
\_\_ Being courteous to others
\_\_ Communicating on social media
\_\_ Conversing with strangers
\_\_ Editing groups of words
\_\_ Explaining or teaching to others
\_\_ Finding errors in writings
\_\_ Following directions
\_\_ Interviewing others
\_\_ Listening to others
\_\_ Making a presentation
\_\_ Public speaking
\_\_ Reading articles
\_\_ Spelling words
\_\_ Starting a conversation
\_\_ Talking on TV, radio, or internet
\_\_ Talking to people on the phone
\_\_ Writing articles or speeches
\_\_ Writing letters, memos, and reports

**People/Social Skills:** Communicate and interact with others.
\_\_ Advocating for others
\_\_ Caring for children
\_\_ Caring for the sick/elderly
\_\_ Counseling others and giving advice
\_\_ Offering to help others
\_\_ Giving recommendations
\_\_ Guiding people on a tour
\_\_ Listening to people
\_\_ Meeting new people
\_\_ Working with people

**Math skills:** Use numbers to solve problems.
\_\_ Balancing a checkbook
\_\_ Computing & comparing numbers

___ Memorizing numbers
___ Using a database program
___ Using percentages and decimals
___ Using a spreadsheet
___ Other(s):

**Mechanical skills:** Use of machinery or tools.
___ Building or putting parts together
___ Fixing a leak
___ Fixing cars, trucks, or boats
___ Handling tools
___ Measuring shapes and sizes
___ Moving heavy objects
___ Operating a bulldozer or backhoe
___ Painting rooms/applying wallpaper
___ Repairing electric wires
___ Using a hammer and nails
___ Using underwater equipment
___ Working with very small objects

**Technical skills:** Perform specific tasks.
___ Being athletic/coordinated
___ Cutting hair
___ Drive a car, truck, or boat
___ Experimenting with chemicals
___ Giving first aid
___ Judging entries in a contest
___ Making things grow
___ Manicuring nails
___ Preparing medicine for patients
___ Serving people food
___ Taking people's blood pressure
___ Testing a new product
___ Working with animals
___ Working with nature
___ Writing computer programs

**Organization skills:** Efficiently manage time, workload, and resources.
___ Checking your own work

___ Combining people to form a team
___ Doing chores at home
___ Following directions
___ Fundraising
___ Organizing files
___ Planning special events
___ Prioritizing tasks
___ Scheduling activities
___ Sorting items

**Business skills:** See the big picture of organizational and consumer behavior.
___ Attending to details
___ Managing money
___ Making agreements
___ Promoting/selling product
___ Running a business
___ Taking inventory
___ Telling how much a house is worth
___ Using a cash register
___ Using a computer
___ Using a copying machine
___ Using a phone for business
___ Working with budgets
___ Working with financial data
___ Other(s):

**Critical thinking skills:** Actively and skillfully conceptualize, apply, analyze, synthesize, and/or evaluate information.
___ Being eager to learn
___ Collecting information
___ Coming up with strategies
___ Debating an issue
___ Diagnosing an illness
___ Analyzing reports
___ Researching a subject
___ Solving problems with others
___ Using your mind

236

# Appendix D

## WORKING ENVIRONMENT

The following is a list of typical characteristics of working conditions. Place a checkmark in either column A or B based on your preferred working environment.

I would enjoy a career that...

**Pick this...**                or        **This...**

| | |
|---|---|
| ____ requires taking risks | ____ offers security |
| ____ gives authority over others | ____ doesn't involve supervision |
| ____ is very competitive | ____ is not competitive |
| ____ has me use my imagination | ____ has rigid guidelines |
| ____ has guaranteed regular hours | ____ may require overtime |
| ____ has me work with others | ____ allows me to work alone |
| ____ pays me an annual salary | ____ pays me an hourly rate |
| ____ is intellectually stimulating | ____ requires physical activity |
| ____ gives me a leadership role | ____ allows me to be managed |
| ____ has me work outside | ____ has an inside work setting |
| ____ influences/persuades others | ____ offers direct communication |
| ____ deals directly with the public | ____ is more private business |
| ____ is research-oriented | ____ is more creative in nature |
| ____ is very routine every day | ____ offers a diversity of duties |
| ____ is a full-time position | ____ is part-time, seasonal work |
| ____ involves little or no travel | ____ allows for frequent travel |
| ____ has me work for myself | ____ lets me work for a company |
| ____ is Monday to Friday | ____ is on weekends or at night |
| ____ is fast paced/high pressure | ____ is slow paced/low pressure |
| ____ is with a small company | ____ is with a large company |
| ____ offers benefits and perks | ____ has no employment contract |
| ____ is within a geographic area | ____ may involve relocation |
| ____ involves little machine work | ____ involves equipment work |

# Appendix E

Use strong action verbs to describe your accomplishments.

| | | | |
|---|---|---|---|
| Achieved | Designed | Installed | Repaired |
| Acquired | Determined | Introduced | Replaced |
| Adapted | Developed | Joined | Reported |
| Administered | Devised | Learned | Researched |
| Advised | Directed | Led | Resolved |
| Advocated | Displayed | Logged | Restored |
| Arranged | Documented | Maintained | Retrieved |
| Assembled | Drafted | Managed | Revised |
| Assisted | Earned | Measured | Scheduled |
| Authored | Educated | Mediated | Served |
| Built | Edited | Mentored | Set up |
| Calculated | Entertained | Motivated | Simplified |
| Cared for | Engaged | Negotiated | Sold |
| Coached | Equipped | Obtained | Solved |
| Coded | Established | Operated | Spearheaded |
| Collected | Evaluated | Orchestrated | Specialized |
| Communicated | Exceeded | Ordered | Strengthened |
| Completed | Executed | Organized | Submitted |
| Composed | Experienced | Outlined | Succeeded |
| Computed | Fabricated | Oversaw | Summarized |
| Condensed | Facilitated | Participated | Supervised |
| Constructed | Filed | Performed | Supplied |
| Contributed | Formed | Persuaded | Supported |
| Controlled | Formulated | Photographed | Surpassed |
| Contacted | Furnished | Planned | Taught |
| Converted | Generated | Presented | Trained |
| Conveyed | Guided | Printed | Transformed |
| Convinced | Handled | Processed | Translated |
| Coordinated | Headed | Produced | Transported |
| Corresponded | Helped | Programmed | Treated |
| Counselled | Illustrated | Promoted | Updated |
| Created | Implemented | Provided | Upgraded |
| Debugged | Improved | Recorded | Utilized |
| Decided | Incorporated | Recruited | Validated |
| Defined | Influenced | Reduced | Verified |
| Delivered | Initiated | Rehabilitated | Volunteered |
| Demonstrated | Insured | Remodeled | Won |
| Delegated | Interacted | Reorganized | Wrote |

# Appendix F

Complete this worksheet to help you prepare for your interview.

1. What products/services does the company you are interviewing with offer? How is the company organized?

   _____

   _____

2. Which type of interview should you expect?

   _____

3. If there is an awkward silence at the beginning of the interview, what will you talk about to make small talk?

   _____

   _____

4. How has your education prepared you for this job?

   _____

   _____

5. How has your work, school, or community experience prepared you for this job?

   _____

   _____

6. What skills do you have that you will use in this job?

   _____

   _____

7. What interests or hobbies of yours would you like this interviewer to know about?

   _____

   _____

8. How will you answer the following questions?

   a. Why are you leaving your present job?

      _____

      _____

      _____

     b.   Tell me about yourself.

_____

_____

_____

     c.   What is your biggest weakness?

_____

_____

_____

     d.   What is your biggest strength?

_____

_____

_____

     e.   Why is your GPA so low (if below 3.0)?

_____

_____

_____

9.   What questions will you be prepared to ask?

_____

_____

10.  How will you dress for this interview?

_____

_____

11.  Where exactly is the location of the interview?

_____

12.  What is the pay range you have in mind for this job?

_____

13.  If pay is not brought up before you accept an offer, how will you bring it up? _____

_____

14.  If next steps are not mentioned, how will you bring it up?

_____

_____

# Appendix G

Company: _____ Date: _____

Interviewer Name: _____

Evaluate your performance, 1 – 5 (lowest to highest):

Interview Preparation:     1     2     3     4     5
- ✓ Resume/Cover Letter
- ✓ Knowledge of company
- ✓ Knowledge of job     Comments:

Physical Presence     1     2     3     4     5
- ✓ Dress
- ✓ Punctuality
- ✓ First impression     Comments:

Oral Communication     1     2     3     4     5
- ✓ Articulate
- ✓ Use of Standard English
- ✓ Lack of Filler Words     Comments:

Presentation of Qualifications     1     2     3     4     5
- ✓ Educational background
- ✓ Work experience     Comments:

Presentation of Characteristics     1     2     3     4     5
- ✓ Motivation/Enthusiasm
- ✓ Initiative
- ✓ Independence
- ✓ Interests     Comments:

Quality of Questions Asked     1     2     3     4     5
Comments:

Overall Evaluation     1     2     3     4     5
Comments:

What improvements will you make for your next interview?

_____

_____

_____

_____

_____

What will you review or clarify with the employer during your follow-up?

_____

_____

_____

_____

_____

# Bibliography

"5 work skills students lack, according to employers." EAB, July 24, 2018. www.eab.com/daily-briefing/2018/07/24/5-work-skills-students-lack-according-to-employers.

Canon, Maria E., Marianna Kudlyak, and Yang Liu. "Youth Labor Force Participation Continues to Fall, but It Might Be for a Good Reason." Federal Reserve Bank of St. Louis, January 26, 2015. www.stlouisfed.org/publictions/regional-economist/january-2015/youth-labor-force.

DePillis, Lydia. "What's really going on with youth unemployment." CNN, August 17, 2018. www.cnn.com/2018/08/17/us/trump-youth-unemployment/index.html.

"Payscale and Future Workplace Release 2016 Workforce-Skills Preparedness Report." May 17, 2016. www.payscale.com/about/press-releases/pascale-and-future-workplace-release-2016-workforce-skills-preparedness-report.

"Teen labor force participation before and after the Great Recession and beyond." United States Department of Labor, Bureau of Labor Statistics, February 2016. www.bls.gov/opub/mlr/2017/article/teen-labor-force-participation-before-and-after-the-great-recession.htm.

"Why 50% of College Grads End Up Back Home." The Jayblock Companies. https://jayblock.com/85-of-grads-live-at-home-and-are-unemployed/.

Wyman, Nicholas. "Hiring Is on The Rise, But Are College Grads Prepared for The World of Work?" Forbes, August 3, 2018. www.forbes.com/sites/nicholaswyman/2018/08/03/hiring-is-on-the-rise-but-are-college-grads-prepared-for-the-world-of-work/#16febe254e7e

## CHAPTER 1

Cao, Steffi. "Warren Buffett's Net Worth as the Oracle of Omaha Turns 89." GoBankingRates, August 26, 2019. www.gobankingrates.com/net-worth/business-people/ warren-buffett-net-worth.

Economic New Release, Table 3. United States Department of Labor, Bureau of Labor Statistics, July 1, 2019. www.bls.gov/news.release/wkyeng.t03.htm.

Harding, Amanda. "What Is Oprah Winfrey's Net Worth?" Showbiz Cheat-Sheet, November 26, 2018. www.cheatsheet.com/entertainment/what-is-oprah-winfreys-net-worth.html/.

Hess, Abigail. "Students who work actually get better grades—but there's a catch." CNBC Make It, Oct 10, 2017. www.cnbc.com/2017/10/04/students-who-work-actually-get-better-grades-but-theres-a-catch.html.

Kapusta, Michelle. "Who Has the Higher Net Worth Now Tom Brady or Gisele Bundchen?" Showbiz CheatSheet, October 1, 2019. www.cheat-sheet.com/entertainment/what-is-oprah-winfreys-net-worth.html.

Kimbrell, G. and Ben S. Vineyard. (1970). Succeeding in the World of Work. Mission Hills: Glencoe Publishing Company.

Peterson, Hayley. "Everything You Need to Know About How Teens Are Spending Money, What They Like, And Where They Shop." Business Insider, October 8, 2014. www.businessinsider.com.au/how-teens-are-spending-money-2014-2014-10.

Rubenstone, Sally. "Do Colleges Verify Information in Applications?" College Confidential, June 20, 2007. https://insights.collegeconfidential.com/000323.

## CHAPTER 2

Fredman, Josh. "Expectancy of Job Growth for a Video Game Tester." Chron. https://work.chron.com/expectancy-job-growth-video-game-tester-5098.html.

Kimbrell, G. and Ben S. Vineyard. (1970). Succeeding in the World of Work, Student Activity Book. Mission Hills: Glencoe Publishing Company.

Skills Matcher, CareerOneStop. www.careeroestop.org/toolkit/Skills/skills-matcher-questions.aspx.

Weaver, Jane. "College Students are Avid Gamers." MSNBC.com, July 6, 2019. www.nbcnews.com/id/3078424/ns/technology_and_science-games/t/college-students-are-avid-gamers/#.XexZgVdKg2x.

## CHAPTER 3

Khaleghi, Karen, Ph.D. "Are You Empowering or Enabling?" Psychology Today, July 11, 2012. www.psychologytoday.com/us/blog/the-anatomy-ad-diction/201207/are-you-empowering-or-enabling.

Moro, Bernice, Ph.D. "Scaffolding Strategies for English Language Learners." Fordham University, December 18, 2014. www.fordham.edu/down-load/downloads/id/4912/scaffolding_strategies_for_ells-.pdf.

## CHAPTER 4

Bortz, Daniel. "5 big benefits of doing an internship." Monster. www.mon-ster.com/career-advice/article/students-benefits-internships.

Duffin, Erin. "U.S. unemployment rate by age 1990-2018." Statista, September 17, 2019. www.bls.gov/news.release/ wkyeng.t03.htm.

"Healthcare Occupations." United States Department of Labor, Bureau of Labor Statistics, Occupational Outlook Handbook. www.bls.gov/ooh/healthcare/home.htm.

"Jobs for Teenagers: 28 Great Ways to Make Money & Get Experience." Trade Schools, Colleges, and Universities. www.trade-schools.net/articles/jobs-for-teenagers.asp#online-jobs.

"Know the Rules." Youth Rules!www.youthrules.gov/know-the-limits/in-dex.htm.

"Labor Force Statistics from the Current Population." United States Department of Labor, Bureau of Labor Statistics, December 1, 2019. www.bls.gov/web/empsit/cpseea10.htm.

O*Net Online. www.onetonline.org/.

"Prohibited Occupations for Non-Agricultural Employees." United States Department of Labor. https://webapps.dol.gov/elaws/whd/flsa/docs/haznonag.asp.

"Selected State Child Labor Standards Affecting Minors Under 18 in Non-farm Employment." United States Department of Labor, Wage and Hour Division, January 1, 2019. www.dol.gov/agencies/whd/state/child-la-bor#Pennsylvania.

## CHAPTER 5

Gladstone, Jennifer. "60 Hiring Statistics You Need to Know." EBI, Inc., June 1,

2017. www.ebiinc.com/resources/blog/hiring-statistics.

Joyce, Susan P. "Finding Jobs Online Today." Job-Hunt.org. www.job-hunt.org/findingjobs.shtml.

"The Top 5 Sites for Employer Reviews & Ratings." https://blog.ongig.com/employer-branding/the-top-5-sites-for-employer-reviews-ratings.

## CHAPTER 6

"50 HR and Recruiting Stats that Make you Think." GlassDoor. https://b2b-assets.glassdoor.com/50-hr-and-recruiting-stats.pdf.

Anderson, Monica, Jingjing Jiang. "Teens, Social Media & Technology 2018." Pew Research Center, May 31, 2018. www.pewresearch.org/internet/2018/05/31/teens-social-media-technology-2018/.

Barreiro, Sachi. "State Laws on Social Media Password Requests by Employers." NOLO. www.nolo.com/legal-encyclopedia/state-laws-on-social-media-password-requests-by-employers.html.

Gaenzle, Anthony. "7 Job-Search Statistics You Should Know." Top Resume. www.topresume.com/career-advice/7-top-job-search-statistics.

Smith, Aaron, Monica Anderson. "Social Media Use in 2018." Pew Research Center, March 1, 2018. www.pewresearch.org/internet/2018/ 03/01/social-media-use-in-2018/.

"Social Media Fact Sheet." Pew Research Center, June 12, 2019. www.pewresearch.org/internet/fact-sheet/social-media/.

West, Chloe. "Social media demographics to drive your brand's online presence." Sprout Social. https://sproutsocial.com/insights/new-social-media-demographics/#LinkedIn.

Winterer, Seth. "Top 10 Social Media Sites for Business." Digital Logic. www.digitallogic.co/blog/social-media-sites-for-business/.

## CHAPTER 7

"Resume Power Words." Indeed.com. www.indeed.com/ career-advice/resumes-cover-letters/resume-power-words.

**CHAPTER 9**

Employment/Age Certificate. Department of Labor, Wage and Hour Division, January 1, 2019. www.dol.gov/agencies/whd/state/age-certificates.

How to Apply for a Social Security Number. Social Security Administration. www.ssa.gov.

How to Apply for Deferred Action of Childhood Arrivals (DACA). U.S. Citizenship and Immigration Services. www.uscis.gov.

**CHAPTER 15**

Heathfield, Susan M. "Are Your Job Interview Questions Illegal? What You Need to Know...." The Balance Careers, updated December 9, 2018. www.thebalancecareers.com/job-interview-questions-that-are-illegal-1918488.

**APPENDIX A**

Kimbrell, G. and Ben S. Vineyard. (1970). "Identifying Your Values." Succeeding in the World of Work, Student Activity Book. Mission Hills: Glencoe Publishing Company.

**APPENDIX B**

Kimbrell, G. and Ben S. Vineyard. (1970). "Interests and Activities." Succeeding in the World of Work, Student Activity Book. Mission Hills: Glencoe Publishing Company.

**APPENDIX C**

Kimbrell, G. and Ben S. Vineyard. (1970). "Marketable Skills." Succeeding in the World of Work, Student Activity Book. Mission Hills: Glencoe Publishing Company.

**APPENDIX D**

Kimbrell, G. and Ben S. Vineyard. (1970). "Working Environment." Succeeding in the World of Work, Student Activity Book. Mission Hills: Glencoe Publishing Company.

# About the Author

 **Tenaz Purdy** was a Management Consulting and Information Technology business professional for 15 years but found her calling when she, at the age of 35, changed careers and became a high school business teacher. Although she loves being a classroom teacher, nothing was more gratifying for her than the seven years she spent running her school's Co-op program, where students supplemented their academics with a part-time job.

She earned a B.S. in Business and Marketing and an M.Ed. in Curriculum and Instruction. Because she's not busy enough with a full-time job, raising a family, and writing a book, she's also the head coach of the Girls' Varsity Tennis Team. Her hobbies include traveling, binge watching great TV shows, and above all, spending as much time on the tennis court as possible. She lives in Bucks County, Pennsylvania with her loving and patient husband, Steve, her two bright and talented daughters, Marisa and Samantha, and her needy dog, Jack, who loves her unconditionally.

Made in the USA
Middletown, DE
02 February 2021